JN440514

Understanding on Social Welfare in Korea

By

Professor Ok, Pil-Hun

Understanding on Social Welfare in Korea
Ok, Pil-Hun

2022년 07월 11일 초판 인쇄
2022년 07월 14일 초판 발행

발행인 박 진 영
발행처 도서출판 진영사
인천광역시 부평구 주부토로 236번지 인천테크노밸리 U1 지식산업센터 B동 1507호
전화 : 032)505-4207
팩스 : 032)505-4206
E-mail : 0183734207@hanmail.net
신고번호 : 제2007-000001호

ISBN 978-89-6541-571-8 93330
값 22,000원

Preface

Social welfare can be defined as social efforts to achieve human mental enrichment and material happiness and organizational activities accordingly. Social workers are the ones who lead the future community that we need in the future society. It is clear that it should be a step-by-step position as a professional and improving the treatment of social workers who sympathize with our society. This is what I feel while giving lectures on social welfare every semester, but the constitution stipulates that a welfare state will be realized, so every time the regime changes, the ideology of welfare is realized, but the ideals and reality are very different. However, the public's awareness of welfare is increasing, and it is thought that the national welfare system is steadily progressing in response to this. Since overall efforts to protect the rights and interests of the people in various fields are eventually linked to the resolution of welfare problems, learners who take the introduction to social welfare as prospective social workers should read this book with a sense of problem.

This book was written in the middle of the question of how to help students who are new to social welfare understand the concept of social welfare, foreign cases, and social welfare fields in each field in Korea. While targeting the social welfare qualification test, it contains systematic and general contents on social welfare, and requires professional knowledge at the level of university education required by social welfare departments and related departments, so textbooks are needed. This book is largely divided into six parts: basic knowledge of social welfare, the second part deals with social welfare practice methodology, the third part with social welfare policies and systems, the fourth part with social security, the fifth part with individual social welfare prospects and tasks. Test takers and enrolled students who study with this book should note the following points. First, it was systematically analyzed and organized mainly based on domestic literature. Second, difficult contents and complex theoretical parts are briefly displayed in diagrams or pictures. Third, related English reading and multiple-choice problem solving were included for enrolled students who needed in-depth learning and confirmation learning. In the future, if there are parts to be supplemented and new theories or information to be supplemented during lectures, it will be supplemented later. First of all, I would like to thank God for allowing me to become a university professor and health until I publish this book. I would like to express my gratitude to the president of Vision College of Jeonju and many professors for opening academic opportunities for social welfare, and to the president of Jinyoung publishing company Park, Jin-Young, who willingly allowed this book, and editorial staff. Lastly, I would like to share my joy with my beloved wife Park, Sun-Hyun and my sons Ok, Sung-Kyun, Ok, Sung-Kuk, and Ok, Sung-Min. Thank you.

March 2022.

written by Pilhun Ok

Table of Contents

Part I What is Social Welfare?

Chapter 1 Concepts of Social Welfare

1. The Linguistic Concept of Social Welfare

Historically, it has been a principle that the provision of living services that people need has been resolved at the family level since the early days of mankind. As races were formed and the population increased, the problem of individuals who could not procure supplies and services by themselves emerged as a social problem and was solved by the spirit of mutual assistance centered on neighbors or races in the community. Mutual aid is distinguished from other types of social welfare, such as charity, philanthropy, public welfare, and social services, in that control over how help is provided can change positions, and has a long history, as shown in the case of mutual benefit.

In Western society, the origin of charity can be found representatively in Christian religion, and the origin of philanthropy can be found in Greece and Rome. Religiously, in Christianity and Judaism, charity to help the unfortunate has led to religious obligations, and as the church's power expanded in medieval Europe, the church has started to provide relief for the poor and run welfare facilities such as orphanages and nursing homes. Of course, at that time, it refers to the act of personally helping those in need or dependent on charity on a small scale, which is different from modern philanthropy or social contribution.

In the modern sense, social welfare emerged with industrialization in the 1960s and is widely used in various fields as modern social problems. However, the concept of social welfare varies from ideology, value, time and country to country, and it is difficult to conclude in a word because scholars have different opinions. This is because it is influenced by various factors such as social philosophy, ideology, economy, and social development policy corresponding to each era according to the historical development stage, and is made in various ways. As such, the practice of social welfare has been developed in various ways in the West according to the times and countries. Then, what can be defined as the concept of social welfare?

Not all scholars speak of such a definition as one, but they approach it roughly in the following points.

The term social welfare has been used as a synonym for the state of well-being or conditions of well-being from the end of the 19th century to the 20th century.

Etymologically, it translates the social welfare of English. 'Social' in English refers to the quality of life within society and the internal relationship between individuals, groups, and society as a whole. Here, '**in-social relationship**' refers to non-selfish interrelationships between individuals and individuals, individual-to-group, individual-to-total society, group-to-total society, and group-to-total society, except for external relations such as the individual's mental world or international relationship. Therefore, the meaning of '**social**' can be said to be non-profit rather than material or commercial elements, and to pay attention to the elements of community life of altruistic attributes.

When it comes to society, it means not only pursuing individual happiness, but also efforts to pursue the happiness of all members of society. From this point of view, the word social is related to means and methods for social welfare, and for those who do not enjoy welfare, it means that social motivation such as mutual aid or altruism is not economic motivation such as profit pursuit.

What is social welfare? Well-are, which means welfare, means "*a state of being satisfied*" by combining "**being satisfied**" or "**being appropriate**" with "**fare**," which means "**to live.**" So, according to Webster's dictionary, welfare is defined as a "*healthy, happy, and comfortable state.*" In other words, welfare can be said to be a concept representing the ideal state of a healthy and comfortable human being, that is, a state of well-being. Therefore, social welfare can be defined as a socially comfortable and satisfactory state based on the meaning that humans have the right and dignity to enjoy happiness. It can also be defined as an overall activity to enable humans to enjoy a happy life in a practical sense.

Above all, as capitalism develops, the gap between the rich and the poor widens and the socially vulnerable groups such as the poor, the disabled, and the elderly who cannot adapt properly to the economic growth process appear, so it is necessary to establish a national protection system.

Following these economic and political needs, European countries began to pay full attention to social welfare from the late 19th century. In particular, a social security system is needed to prepare in advance for livelihood and medical problems that occur in the event of accidents such as old age, illness, or injury.

In addition, the Chinese character "**社會福祉**" means material abundance in society, and "ji(祉)" means mental well-being in society, but this all means a lot of blessings, and blessings mean both material abundance and mental happiness.

As the old Korean word "**five blessings(五福)**," "**bok(福)**" means a state of abundance or discomfort at a material level such as "**wealth**," "**prosperity**," and "**goodbye**" because the concept is comprehensive, and even a state at a psychological, mental, and spiritual level such as happiness. However, today's welfare has a more comprehensive meaning than the material abundance or longevity implied in the Chinese word welfare, so it can be understood that there is a difference between today's welfare and ancient welfare. The meaning of welfare in the East is as follows in detail. Analyzing the formation of the term welfare, it means that it is materially abundant because it fills the mouths of many people with fields.

Social welfare(社會福祉), a Chinese character notation for social welfare, is a compound word of society and welfare. When analyzing the term "福" of welfare, many people are related to God in the form of "示" seen from the side as a statue on which offerings are placed on the god. The term "田" in the remaining part of the following "福" means a field where grain is harvested. The phrase above it stands for high, symbolizing the high accumulation of grains, and means material abundance. This is a gift from nature, that is, God, so it has a "示" on it. In addition, the term "祉" has the meaning of stopping the promotion of desire in a posture of praying for peace of mind to God. In other words, it implies that emptying the mind is the path to psychological stability. Therefore, it can be said that welfare implies material abundance and mental stability.

In this way, the linguistic meaning of social welfare can be said to be "*social efforts to pursue healthy, comfortable, and desirable lives throughout the lives of members based on social internal relationships in a community society.*"

2. Academic Concepts of Social Welfare

There is a limitation to grasp the concept of social welfare at the level of understanding the etymology of social welfare. It is more difficult to grasp the reality because social welfare is not fixed, but changes according to the times, the country, and society. Therefore, the term tends to be used differently, such as social services, social welfare, and social work. In some countries, the term "**social administration**" is commonly used, and the terms "**human services**" and "**social-service administration**" are also used.

3. Legal Concepts of Social Welfare

The concept of social welfare under the Constitution is as follows in Article 34 of the Korean Constitution.

Article 34 of the Constitution

1. Every citizen has the right to live a human life.
2. The state is obligated to make efforts to promote social security and social welfare.
3. The state shall endeavor to improve the welfare and rights of women.
4. The state is obligated to implement policies to improve the welfare of the

elderly and adolescents.

5. Persons with physical disabilities and citizens who do not have the ability to live due to illness, old age, or other reasons, as prescribed by law, should be protected by the state.
6. The state should make efforts to prevent disasters and protect the people from the dangers.

Social welfare referred to in the Constitution is used as a term distinct from social security, as shown in paragraph 2. Then, how do we accept the distinction between social security and social welfare? The relationship between the two can be interpreted as meaning social services other than social security. In other words, the meaning of paragraph 2 means that all policies attempted by the state can be largely divided into social security and social welfare so that people can live a "**human life**" in paragraph 1, and thus it is accepted as a collective concept of all social services except social security.

In addition, when looking at the "**Basic Social Security Act**," which is the parent law of all laws on social security in Korea, the definition of social security is stipulated in Article 3. Through this regulation, social security, social insurance, public assistance, social welfare services, and related welfare systems can be clearly classified and identified.

Article 3(Definition) of the Framework Act on Social Security

The definitions of terms used in this Act are as follows.

1. The term "**social security**" refers to social insurance, public assistance, social welfare services, and related welfare systems provided to protect all citizens from social risks such as disease, disability, old age, unemployment, and death, relieve poverty, and improve the quality of life of the people.

2. The term "**social insurance**" refers to a system that guarantees national health and income by coping with social risks arising from the public through insurance methods.

3. The term "**public assistance**" refers to a system that guarantees the minimum life of people who do not have the ability to maintain their lives or have a difficulty in living under the responsibility of the state and local governments and supports independence.

4. The term "**social service**" refers to a system that provides counseling, rehabilitation, job placement, guidance, and use of social welfare facilities to all citizens in need of help from the state, local governments and the private sector.

5. The term "**lifetime social safety net**" refers to a customized social security system that guarantees income and services in consideration of both basic needs that must be universally satisfied throughout the life cycle and special needs arising from specific social risks.

4. Functional Concepts

Traditionally, social welfare systems have a strong residual character, but institutional characteristics are emphasized along with the progress of industrialization. According to Wellensky & Lebeaux (1965), the residual concept in the cause of social problems emphasizes individual responsibility, while the institutional concept emphasizes social structural responsibility. Furthermore, they predict that social welfare will develop into a continuous and independent system that prevents and mitigates social problems, away from charity and relief derived from residual characteristics(Kim, Sang-Gyun et al., 2009).

1) Residual Social Welfare and Institutional Welfare

The perspective of social welfare, or social welfare, was first presented by Wilensky and Lebeaux in their book Industrial Society and Social Welfare in 1965, and is a residual and institutional perspective.

From a residual perspective, social welfare is primarily entrusted to the home or community when social problems arise, and is used to compensate for problems that occur when their functions are not smooth or to perform temporary functions. For example, it can be seen as a residual concept, that is, the concept of consultation, to receive services through public welfare policies socially when families with disabilities are no longer in charge of long-term rehabilitation treatment costs or care. Contrary to the residual concept, the concept of social welfare in the broad sense corresponds to social welfare from an institutional point of view in the sense that it is intended to satisfy the universal needs of the entire people. Wellensky & Lebeaux argued that the social welfare system must play an important role as a means of stabilizing the whole nation and family, as the nuclear family is inevitable and the welfare and educational functions of the family are weakened. Therefore, it is natural that social welfare performs essential functions to maintain society, and such functions are organized and institutionalized as a type of continuous social activity(Oh, Jung-Soo et al., 2010). According to Romanyshin, the concept of social welfare is changing from complementary to institutional. For example, the "**Cancer Management Act**" passed the National Assembly on October 2, 2002, and the Cancer Management Act(Act No. 6908) is a law that integrates sporadic cancer-related activities at the government level.

Therefore, social welfare is a systematic and organized effort by governments or private organizations to promote human happiness to prevent·and reduce social dysfunction through various programs, social services, or systems, and is a practical activity.

2) Selectiveism and Universalism

Social welfare based on selectivity is limited in scope as the eligibility of recipients is determined by the level of desire or personal assets, but social welfare based on universalism is provided as a right to anyone if it meets certain classes, categories, etc. In the former case, the basic living security system can be said to be a selective program, and the social insurance system can be said to be a representative program based on universalism.

Selectivism can reduce the cost of social welfare by limiting the subject of social welfare to the socially vulnerable and is in line with the conservative ideology that advocates minimal welfare. Stigma is stamped as an asset survey to select a person eligible for benefits, which is likely not to use the system even if they are eligible for benefits, and can lead to problems of avoiding applications and illegal supply and demand(Yoon, Chul-Soo et al., 2011).

The universalism program targets not only the poor but also all members of society, and is a policy that responds to the needs of members in a wide range of areas such as health, income, housing, education, and leisure activities. If a selective program is a follow-up measure, universalism can be said to be a proactive precaution(Bae, Ki-Hyo, 2009).

5. Concepts of Social Security

1) Definition of Social Security

There have been various discussions on the concept of social security, but there is still no consensus today. The reason seems to have been recognized as such in the idea that social welfare is social security. This is because there are subtle differences depending on how you understand the relationship between social welfare and social security. The first time the term social security was used in the world was the Social Security Act promulgated and enacted in the United States in 1935. After that, laws were enacted in New Zealand under the same name in 1938. The content was selective and limited, so the focus was on worker insurance for some workers and relief for the poor. It was after World War II that a universal social security system was established to cope with all citizens' living standards. In developed countries centered on the United States and Europe, it was necessary to impose the stability of people's lives and the protection of human rights on the responsibility of the state in establishing a peaceful welfare state based on World War II. Based on this necessity, the foundation of today's social security system has been reorganized.

A schematic view of the specific improvement process of the social security system is as follows. The Beveridge Report and the Universal Declaration of Human Rights adopted at the 1948 General Assembly of the United Nations and the Treaty No. 102 adopted by the International Labor Organization(ILO) in 1951(the Treaty on the Minimum Standards of Social Security). It is noteworthy that the state guarantees the basic human rights of the people and that all citizens have the right to social security. In that sense, social security can be defined as a system for guaranteeing life for all citizens of the country under the responsibility of the state.

In response, Furukawa and others in Japan said that there is a difference depending on whether social security is identified as an income security system for poverty problems, social security systems for other disabilities in life, or comprehensive understanding.

Therefore, social security can be defined as a national security system for all citizens of a country, but it is not internationally unified because it varies from country to country, varies from time to time, and varies from researcher to researcher. In the meantime, the International Labor Organization has healthcare, disease insurance, unemployment, old age, disaster, family, childbirth, and bereaved family insurance as the main contents of social security. Therefore, social security is a system for guaranteeing living for all citizens of the country at the responsibility of the state, but this definition is also related to the concept of social security purposes. Securing the minimum amount of life is a public aid to the poor since the Elizabeth poor Law. One of the representative examples is social insurance under the social security policy of the Bismarck era in Germany.

In addition, there is also a legal perspective based on the National Minimum of the State that "*Securing the minimum limit of life and its stability meet the basic needs of the people.*" This meaning can be seen as in the broadest sense in terms of the nature of social security, and as the term '**national**' implies, it can be said to be the meaning of the social security system.

2) Scope of Social Security

According to Friedlander, social security system is defined as a system that protects it by social legislation when it cannot be solved by itself due to illness, unemployment, death of the head of the household, old age or disability caused by accident. The reason why it is difficult to solve these difficulties alone is called social thinking, which means an accident that several people need to work together to solve socially. Therefore, when the ability to work guaranteed by the social security system is lost, cash or in-kind, that is, income, and when health is lost, medical expenses or medical services are guaranteed, that is guaranteed.

The social security system is divided into a social insurance system, a public assistance system, and social welfare services. The social insurance system refers to a system in which a certain amount of money is contributed in advance to cope with economic losses caused by constant accidents and risks during human life, and a certain amount of salary is paid from common property in the event of an accident. In other words, it is a system that guarantees income or medical care necessary in the event of various social accidents by imposing insurance premiums on people with ordinary income(including employees and employers).

(1) ① Social insurance has a similar nature to private insurance in that it distributes risks among subscribers through insurance methods, but differs in that it pays premiums according to its income and receives

salaries according to its contribution level. ② The public assistance system, also known as the public social system, is a system that guarantees necessary income or medical care for low-income people who do not have any income or are unable to pay insurance premiums due to various social accidents. In other words, it refers to a national protection system provided free of charge to people in need of living, such as low-income families.

(2) Social welfare service is a social security law system that provides professional services such as counseling, rehabilitation, job placement, social welfare facilities, etc. to individuals or groups in need of social accidents, etc. The terms social welfare service and social welfare service are commonly used in Korea and Japan. Social welfare services are mainly targeted at the elderly, disabled children such as orphans, and women in need of help such as widows. Article 2 Subparagraph 1 of the Social Welfare Services Act limits laws related to social welfare services as follows.

(3) In broad sense, the social safety net is an institutional device to protect all citizens from social risks such as unemployment, poverty, disaster, old age, and disease. As a complementary device for social insurance and public assistance, the state plays a role in ensuring basic life for the people in national crises such as mass unemployment, disasters, and wartime, allowing them to live a stable social life(Choi, Il-Seop, 2018).

6. The Academic Characteristics of Social Welfare Studies

The basic object of social welfare studies is humans. Social welfare studies are studies on humans that study human social survival, and become practical activities that systematically cope with social problems, social needs, or risks to ensure the human life of all citizens.

As an academic characteristic of social welfare studies, it is a value-oriented study, a social science centered on practice in society, and has a multidisciplinary character that combines various adjacent studies. In addition, in order to understand the behavior of helping humans, the use of knowledge provided by various fields of social science such as statistics is required.

Chapter 2 Ideas and Values of Social Welfare

1. Social Welfare Philosophy

In general, ideology can be said to be a belief system that members of an individual or group have in common. The meaning of social welfare(ideology) varies with the flow of the times, and has a comprehensive concept with changes in society due to its dynamic nature. Therefore, social welfare has different meanings depending on the country and the times. The social welfare ideology refers to an ideological belief system that connects the cognitive and evaluation form of the social situation with social welfare. The ideology of social welfare plays an important role in determining the subject, object, financial resources, etc. of social welfare by providing the standard of motivation or value of social welfare.

Ideology can be seen as a kind of value systematic collection and a basic framework. Therefore, according to the ideology, all values are interconnected and have a systematic position. And according to ideology, people's thoughts and actions develop consistently, and social welfare may vary in content and form depending on ideological characteristics.

It is common to understand the change in the national view of 19C and 20C as the concept of a passive state and an active state. In 19C, freedom from the state was the most important issue, and the role of the state should only be to ensure compliance with defense, security and contracts. Other activities are an infringement or interference in the political and economic freedom of citizens. At that time, the ideal state was a Night-Watchman State and a free country. As it reaches 20C, it can be understood that the problems created by 19C, in particular, the concept of a state that has accepted socialist factors to correct economic inequality, is an active state. Here, it is emphasized that the state should be responsible for guaranteeing the minimum living conditions of the people, and proper distribution of wealth becomes a major task. The New

Right, the anti-collectivist below, shows the strongest hostility to the strengthening of the state's role in welfare, because it is based on the judgment that the welfare state worsens the economy by imposing high taxation on businesses and individuals. In other words, the welfare state is in a position of social harm because it reduces the opportunity for human happiness and poverty reduction by worsening growth potential, promotes a culture of dependence, and weakens the power of punishment for success and failure. The Middle Way, a passive collectivism below, believes that the welfare state is a strong power for social problems and social stability. In other words, the welfare state alleviates the contradictions of the free market system and gives the feeling that the government is actively interested in the well-being of the people, thereby giving legitimacy to the authority of the state. In addition, the government's economic policy is considered essential to achieving full employment and economic growth. In addition, Fabian Socialism below is a gradual socialism adopted by the British Fabian Association, founded in 1884. In general, it is a way of thinking to realize a socialist society through parliamentary democracy. Fabian socialism is the same as state interventionism in that it believes that the state plays a very positive role in pursuing and achieving social good, but is different from state interventionism in that it ultimately considers capitalism as an object of overcoming rather than modifying. Although Marxism is said to be similar in this respect, it is divided in that it denies proletarian dictatorship and class revolution, and aims for pacifism in a peaceful(constitutional) and gradual way. He believes that the welfare state is an important power to reconcile the limits of the free market, which emphasizes only the political rights provided by democracy and the power of the market, thus reducing inequality and promoting a more equal society. Today, Fabian socialism has changed its appearance to 'the third way'. The third path is the Labor Party's new political line proposed by British Prime Minister Tony Blair, which was theoretically organized by Anthony Giddens. The third path, well known to us, is a new Labor Party project that guarantees citizens' socio-economic life and enhances market vitality by avoiding the social-democratic welfare state route(first path) and neoliberal market economy route. The third way is to pursue active welfare instead of passive welfare. Active welfare is summarized as a social investment country, welfare dualism, and conversion of consciousness. Below is a schematic diagram of the flow of social welfare ideology.

1) Laissez-Faire Type

Among social welfare ideologies, laissez-faire originated from economic ideas and policies to ensure the maximum freedom of individual economic activity and to exclude state interference as much as possible. The laissez-faire type is based on individualism, and its central values are freedom and inequality. Freedom is a passive concept that is free from the interference of others, meaning a state without coercion, and is recognized as the best value of action.

Libertarians oppose state intervention in social welfare because state intervention in welfare violates individual freedom. Income and wealth, education, health care, and all other forms of protection depend on the production system and depend on individual contracts and exchange power under minimal state intervention, whether it protects the weak or the strong.

2) Liberal Type

Historically, liberalism has emerged as a principle against medieval social principles. The medieval society was established based on the political, economic, and personal control of the lord's serfs. Therefore, the collapse of medieval society, on the one hand, developed a new style of production that replaced the permanent residence system, and that is liberalism. In other words, liberalism emerged in the process of increasingly gaining independence in economic activities, away from regulations by the power of the lord, which began to gain strength due to the improvement of productivity and the penetration of the monetary economy.

Among social welfare ideologies, the liberal type basically trusts the capitalist system, but recognizes the problems of capitalism such as poverty, inefficiency, waste, and market failure. It is believed that this problem can be solved through government intervention. However, the government is negative about playing an unlimited or all-around role, such as taking responsibility for the minimum living standards of the people. It is desirable to minimize state intervention because it recognizes that government intervention should be intervened only when it is inevitable and efficient.

3) Neoliberal Type

Neoliberalism criticizes government power's intervention in the market and values the function of the market and the free activities of the private sector. Since the 1970s, it has emerged in earnest, pointing out the failure of revised capitalism, which introduced Keynesian theory, and insisting on economic laissez-faire. Neoliberals' arguments were reflected in the Nixon administration's economic policy and became the basis of so-called Reaganomics and Thatcherism. As a market-oriented economic policy implemented in the United States, it became the basis of neoliberalism in the 1980s along with Thatcherism, advocating a 'small government theory' that minimizes government intervention in the market. Reaganomics refers to a market-oriented economic policy or similar policy implemented by U.S. President Ronald Reagan during his term from 1981 to 1989. It is a combination of Reagan and economics, which means his economics. The main contents of Reaganomics are: reduction of government spending, reduction of marginal income tax rates on labor and capital, abolition of regulations, and adjustment of money supply to reduce inflation. Reagan's economic policies differed greatly from his predecessors in that they lowered taxes and reduced domestic spending. Thatcherism is compressed as "*the market is good and the government is bad.*" Thatcher's reign means that the Conservative mainstream has shifted from traditional conservatism, which values paternalistic consideration for the socially disadvantaged, to market liberalism, which values free markets and competition. Prime Minister Thatcher, who won the 1979 general election with the Conservative Party's victory, abandoned the nationalization and welfare policies that the Labor Party government had adhered to and pushed for strong economic reforms based on monetarism. The reform included cuts in public expenditures for welfare and tax cuts, privatization of state-owned enterprises, regulation of trade unions' activities, suppression of inflation based on thorough monetary policy, guarantee of free activities between companies and the private sector. In addition, Thatcher promoted policies such as the realization of small governments, education policies centered on industry-academic cooperation, and opposition to European integration. In addition to promoting these social and economic reform policies, the sluggish and lethargic situation of British society at the time was diagnosed as "**British disease**," and it was said that social consciousness reform was necessary to overcome it. As a result, it has been successful in overcoming inflation and recovering the economy, but the growing unemployment problem has raised public dissatisfaction and raised criticism of copingism. In the UK, there is a term "**coupling generation**" or "coupling children" that reflects this social atmosphere as it is. They are teenagers who grew up with basic education under Prime Minister Thatcher, characterized by indifference to politics, dependence on smoking and alcohol, and irrational tendencies, including their uncertain future due to high unemployment, divorce of parents and family dissolution(Source: Doosan Encyclopedia).

Neoliberalism is an ideology that emerged after the late 1970s when global capitalism fell into a recession and a capital accumulation crisis came, criticizing the welfare state as the main cause of this crisis. In other words, the expansion of welfare states has been put on hold in the West due to the economic downturn since the late 1970s. Neoliberals of social welfare argue that intervention by government power does not completely deny it, but rather deteriorates economic efficiency and equity. Therefore, it is argued that expanding the public welfare system causes so-called "**welfare diseases**" by expanding the government's finances and reducing its willingness to work. However, I do not object to a limited and moderate form of social welfare designed to allow only minimal interference in the market.

4) Social Democratic Type

Democratic Socialism is an ideology that seeks to realize social reform by social(public) ownership and social(public) management of means of production through democratic methods. Social democracy is the strongest advocate of the welfare state, and it is believed that it can transit from a capitalist society to a socialist society through various policies of the welfare state. Capitalism is economic '**individualism**' originally operated by individual competition on private ownership for the purpose of personal profit. However, socialist thinkers in the 19th century thought that the cause of capitalist democracy's failure to realize freedom and equality was the individualism of capitalism. Therefore, in order to realize a democratic society of freedom and equality, it was believed that capitalism's '**individualism**' had to be changed to the opposite principle, that is, '**socialism**', and social democrats tried to realize its purpose through democratic methods, not violence.

The important values of social democracy are equality, freedom, and fraternity, and emphasize equality as a central value. In other words, equality means a reduction in excessive inequality, and recognizes opportunity and wealth equality and inequality in income to some extent.

Since the social democracy type cannot achieve the goals of socialism without economic growth, the government's responsibility to reduce the gap between the rich and the poor and to increase social capital is essential to ensure economic growth. In other words, the mitigation and redistribution of inequality in the unjust distribution process of the market economy is regarded as the responsibility of the government. Therefore, we are actively in favor of the welfare state, and through gradual and democratic methods, we will expand the national welfare and reform it into human capitalism to transition to socialism.

5) Marxist Type

Marxism regards the capitalist economy as class conflict and exploitation. The welfare state is also regarded as performing the functions of reproducing the labor force and accumulating capital in order to maintain capitalism, and is taking a critical position. Marxism was formed by critically inheriting, developing, and unifying socialist ideas from French socialists, especially Ricardo's economics, in 19th-century German classical philosophy such as Hegel and Feuerbach.

For Marxists, freedom, equality, and fraternity are the main values. As a value opposed to individualism, equality is emphasized by emphasizing friendship, guaranteeing the realization of minimum needs, and quantitatively equivalent distribution. Economic inequality causes conflict and cannot be expected to freedom, so it insists on complete government intervention of means of production.

According to Marxism, welfare refers to providing the maximum service "*to each person according to their own needs.*" For Marxists, the welfare state is nothing but social control to curb fundamental changes in the socioeconomic structure and maintain the authority of the ruling class. Therefore, since welfare states cannot solve poverty, income, housing, or political inequality, the collapse of capitalism through social revolution is said to be the solution to solve various social problems that arise in a capitalist society.

6) Neo-Marxist Type

Marxism maintains the position of traditional Marxism, which regards the state as a tool for class control of the capitalist class, but acknowledges that the state can have some degree of autonomy in the policy process. It is recognized that the state needs to maintain some degree of autonomy from the capitalist class in the process of pursuing welfare policies, etc. for continuous capital accumulation. The neo-Marxist type says that there is no fundamental change in Marx's historical development and modern function of social policy, the importance of capital accumulation, and the revolutionary role of the proletariat. And the neo-Marxists deny that Marx's analysis of capital accumulation and social change needs major revisions in relation to modern Western society.

7) Feminism

Feminism is a movement or ideology that describes the cause and state of oppression of women and aims to liberate women. It is a concept that includes theories that explain it, starting with the women's suffrage movement that began in the mid-19th century. Feminism originated from liberalism, and according to liberal feminism, custom and legal restrictions preventing women from entering and succeeding in society are the causes of women's subordination to men. Therefore, it is said that if women are given equal educational opportunities and citizenship as men, women's subordination disappears. Feminists argue that welfare states are male-dominated countries where men are policy makers and women remain policy beneficiaries, although they show strong support in providing services necessary to ensure equal status in the labor market, which greatly affects equality for all citizens.

2. Value of Social Welfare

In general, value can define the concept as a belief that a professional has regarding humans and appropriate ways to deal with humans(Lee, Young-Chul et al., 2007). Value is evaluated by people, and it has meaning only when it transcends time and space and appears realistically. Therefore, the values pursued by humans themselves must be objectively valid beyond each person's subjectivity(Cho, Chu-Yong et al., 2008). The value of social welfare is "*the value and dignity of all human beings.*" At the beginning of Korea's social worker code of ethics, it states, "*The social welfare ideology is based on the philosophy that the entire society is jointly responsible for self-realization while maintaining the human dignity of all social members based on the values of justice, equality, freedom, and democracy.*"

1) General Value of Social Welfare

(1) Justice

The concept of justice is used as procedural justice, practical justice, and justice as an active process. Procedural justice emphasizes legal procedures prescribed by law, practical justice emphasizes distributive justice as a result, and justice as an active process emphasizes the social process of preventing and treating unfair phenomena. In particular, social welfare emphasizes distributive justice, and strives to distribute better treatment, authority, and resources to the socially vulnerable or disadvantaged.

(2) Equality

The idea of equality is a dictionary concept that advocates the elimination of privileges and equal opportunities, and argues that all people are equal before the law. One of the most serious social problems in today's liberal capitalist society is a social problem based on the idea of human equality. It is a social problem that starts from the position that humans must acknowledge the desire to live as long as they are human, that is, the right to live. These social problems are arising from the contradictions of capitalist society based on individualistic liberalism. Of course, any society has its own contradictions, but the social problems caused by them have been solved by their own methods prescribed by their respective social systems or lifestyles. Likewise, the generalization of poverty in the era of state monopoly capitalism is a characteristic of the social problems of this era, and it is the idea of living rights based on the idea of equality that emerged as a new social measure. One of the most important values of social welfare is equality. Equality is the value of evenly improving the quality of life of members of society through redistribution of social resources. However, there is a lot of controversy over the specific concept of equality. The concepts of equality include quantitative equality, proportional equality, and equality of opportunity. Among the concepts of equality, equality was based on the formation and expansion of a welfare state, and the equality strategy of the welfare state tried to guarantee a certain level of basic life and reduce social inequality through social welfare benefits and services that are universally provided as universal rights.

(3) Freedom

One of the most controversial concepts in the value of social welfare is freedom. The concept of freedom has passive freedom and active freedom. This concept of freedom is used differently depending on differences in ideological positions. Anti-collectivists use passive freedom, while Fabianists and Marxists use active freedom. The former considers state intervention in welfare as an infringement of freedom by emphasizing freedom of exercise of private property rights or freedom of choice of benefits or services. On the other hand, the latter recognizes the freedom to enjoy welfare as a social right, and considers state intervention in welfare as an expansion of active freedom.

(4) Social Integration

Social integration refers to the process of integrating groups or individuals in a non-integrated state into a single assembly by applying them to each other. In the field of social welfare, the concept of social integration means the formation of a sense of solidarity or attachment between members within a certain social unit or members to society. Warren(1963) used the term social participation instead of the term social integration. This refers to allowing members to voluntarily participate in all activities provided by the community. Social welfare in modern society aims not to remove the guardians from society, but to make them economically independent or physically rehabilitated to become productive human beings to achieve social integration(Nam, Il-Jae et al., 2009). One of the most representative values of social welfare is solidarity. Durkheim divided the dates into mechanical and organic. Society before differentiation is mechanical solidarity, and society after differentiation is organic solidarity. Durkheim used the concept of '**solidarity**' in discussing social structure. Durkheim argued that cooperation inevitably had a moral character, and that differentiation made social integration difficult and produced only fragmented individuals. Social welfare redistributes social resources through the exchange of help between members. Therefore, such aid acts lead to emotional integration between members. On the other hand, this emotional solidarity and integration enable redistribution of social resources. In a traditional society, resource redistribution could be achieved and social integration could be achieved based on the interdependence of families or local communities. However, after the Industrial Revolution, with socioeconomic progress, families and local communities lost their functions, and new social devices for social integration were needed. The social welfare system in modern society achieves social integration by restoring the interdependence of community members as an institutional device.

(5) Altruism

Altruism is a concept contrary to selfishness and means performing actions that benefit others without expecting any reward from the outside. Altruism is different from mutual aid, which helps each other and receives help because of the nature of not expecting any reward from the outside world. Titmus explained altruism from the rich to the poor as a unified transfer as before, and a dual transfer in which both sides exchange help with each other. Social welfare is based on altruism that does not require a price from the other party, and is largely distinguished from economic activities that seek maximum personal profits and efficiency based on equivalent exchanges made through the market system.

2) practical value of social welfare professionals

(1) The dignity of Man

The goal pursued by social welfare is the realization of human dignity, so social welfare can be a value concept. In this sense, the idea of human respect forms the essential value of social welfare. The idea of human respect is the value that humans are born with, and should be respected regardless of what humans are actually doing, what they can do, or in what state or situation they are in. In other words, they should not be ignored or discriminated against due to the attributes of race, sex, economy, politics, society, status, religion, nationality, intelligence, and physical conditions. The value of human respect can be found in the Universal Declaration of Human Rights, and in the case of Korea, Article 10 of the Constitution declares that "*all citizens have the right to dignity, value, and happiness as humans.*" The value of human respect is not limited to these institutional regulations, but is also included in 'acceptance', one of the practical principles of social welfare.

In this regard, scholars like Watson from abroad said that the idea that humans should be respected as individuals applies to all humans. It was said that human beings, regardless of their achievements, should be respected, even if they were defective. Therefore, respecting humans is the most basic value in social welfare. This is because social welfare lengthens and develops a person's ability to live satisfactorily without anxiety in a relationship that is emotionally stable, loved by people, and friendly. Human dignity begins with the perception that "**any human being is human.**" Therefore, all human beings have dignity, so they must be guaranteed with dignity. All human differences and similarities should be recognized, and opportunities should be given to grow in the direction in which one's potential is achieved for oneself. Individuals should not be treated discriminated against due to attributes such as race, economic, political, and social status, religion, nationality, intelligence, and physical conditions, and should be guaranteed equal dignity and opportunity as humans. In other words, they should be treated fairly and equally as human beings.

(2) Right to Self-Determination

Self-determination is a very important professional practical value along with human dignity as a right for humans to make their own decisions in a given selective situation. Self-determination means that humans have the free choice to make their own decisions. Recently, the right of self-determination in the field of social welfare is one of the most important issues. The most basic interest in the right to self-determination is that it emphasizes the needs and preferences of the subject over the adjustment of the service to the needs of the subject and the service provider. This means that the right to self-determination and freedom of choice in pursuit of individualization of services will develop into an increasingly important issue in social welfare.

It is also an important personal right to make a wrong choice in the subject's self-determination. However, many clients are often unable to make qualified choices and self-determination for services on their own. In some cases, the lack of social environment to obtain appropriate information and knowledge so that they can make qualified choices, the lack of social environment to obtain appropriate information and knowledge so that they can make qualified choices, and their physical and mental abilities are problematic. Therefore, social workers may be in a dilemma about the balance between acceptable and unacceptable choices.

(3) Equal Opportunity

The principle that all humans are equal and have equal rights of opportunity is a value that must be accompanied in the professional practice process of social welfare. Individuals, families, groups, communities, and countries have the potential to grow and develop. Therefore, social welfare should provide equal opportunities for humans to grow and develop according to their respective potentials in the process of preventing and solving human problems. Equal opportunities given to subjects in the professional practice process of social welfare provide some realistic opportunities to define their own needs and the types of services to meet their needs. In addition, this can take effect only when specified in laws or official guides.

3. Practical Ethics of Social Welfare

Ethics means occupational ethics and refers to the criteria for judging 'what is right and what is not to be done'. Ethics is a concept that includes standards or principles that control or regulate human behavior, and generally refers to expectations for humans from a sense of responsibility for others(Bae, Gi-Hyo, 2009). Social welfare values and ethics provide standards for social welfare practitioners to work as experts. In addition, it has been an important factor influencing the role and concept formation of social workers.

1) Necessity of Social Welfare Ethics

Reamer suggests the need for ethics in social welfare practice as follows(Kim, Sang-Gyun et al., 2009).

① The ethics of social welfare practice are necessary to systematically identify the commonalities and differences between experts' own values and the values of others such as clients, local residents, colleagues, and supervisors.

② Social welfare practice ethics is necessary for social workers to understand ethical dilemmas and to have the ability to cope with them. Experts should be able to make desirable ethical judgments in a dilemma situation.

③ Social welfare practice ethics is necessary to determine the ranking of relationships among various values. Since there are many values that support ethics, it is possible to establish guidelines for practitioners to make ethical judgments by deciding which values to prioritize in the event of conflicting values.

④ Social welfare practice ethics is necessary to develop social welfare expertise and develop practice methods. Social welfare studies is a discipline that is practiced for humans based on expertise, so it is necessary to continuously develop and train practical skills. By understanding social welfare ethics, you acquire social welfare knowledge and skills.

2) Code of Ethics

During the beginning of social welfare, basic livelihood maintenance, such as solving the hunger of clients, was the main purpose of the service, and specific services were provided. In order to solve various social problems that occurred during the transition from an agricultural society to an industrial society, values such as human dignity, love, and philanthropy suggested and led the direction of social welfare services. With industrialization, society has developed and changed rapidly. Ethics and morality, which supported traditional society, disappeared, and the form of the family, which is the basic unit of society, has changed in various ways. Each person boasted their own unique personality, and their needs erupted in different ways.

Since the 1960s, American society has begun to pay significant attention to various value systems of clients as their desire for welfare rights, equality, human rights, and social justice has increased. In addition, during this period, various professionals, including doctors and lawyers in other fields, began to be interested in ethical behavior and code of ethics. In the United States, the first code of social welfare ethics was adopted in 1947, and the current code was revised in 1996 and continues to this day. Social welfare is a more ethical and value-oriented profession than any other profession in other fields, so more specific and clear guidelines are needed to fulfill responsibility. The value of social welfare professionals is the basic premise of the social worker's code of ethics. In other words, the ethics of social welfare experts are intended to help social workers recognize that the practice of services should be ethically correct. In social welfare practice, ethics is an action guideline to be taken as an expert in all relationships with clients. This leads social workers to be faithful to social welfare professions and fulfills their ethical responsibilities to themselves, clients, affiliated organizations, colleagues, social welfare professions, and society.

The ethical behavior of social workers can be said to meet the ethical standards required by the code of ethics in the social welfare practice process. The American Society of Social Workers(NASW) enacted the Code of Social Welfare Ethics in 1960 and promulgated the current Code of Ethics in 1999 after several revisions. The composition of the code of ethics is service, social justice, human dignity and values, the importance of human relations, integration, and ability. Specific ethical principles are described, and ethical standards for the behavior of social welfare experts are specifically listed, suggesting the principles so that social workers can use them in the field of practice.

Korea enacted a draft code of ethics in 1973 by the Korean Social Welfare Association, and enacted and promulgated the code of ethics in 1988. The first revision was implemented in 1992, and it was supplemented and revised through the second revision in 2001. The code of ethics consists of six items: basic ethical standards for social workers, ethical standards for clients, ethical standards for society, ethical standards for institutions, and composition and operation of the ethics committee. Each ethical standard consists of 46 guidelines for behavior, and presents the formation of professional values of social workers and the basis for correct ethical judgment. The Korean Society of Social Workers revised the code of ethics and enacted the '**Oath of Social Workers**' as follows.

I want to show human dignity so that everyone can enjoy a human-like life. By Based on the belief in social justice, together with individuals, families, groups, organizations, communities, and the entire society, I am always on the side of the marginalized and suffering, and their human rights, the public interest rather than the individual interest, defending the rights and interests of society and rejecting injustice put before morality and accountability by adhering to social workers' code of ethics devote oneself to a social worker equipped with I swear on my free will, and I swear on my honor. I solemnly swear this.

3) Ethical Dilemma of Social Workers

Values and ethics are often mixed, but their meanings are different. Ethics is derived from value and must be in harmony with value. While values are concerned with what is good and desirable, ethics is concerned with what is right. For example, protection of individual privacy is a primary value in modern society. Among the ethical rules of social welfare, '**informed consent**' is an ethical principle in which social workers record the client's actions and explain them in advance and seek consent before allowing third-party observation. This comes from the value of privacy protection(Bae, Ki-Hyo et al. 2009). However, there is a problem of having to notify a certain part of the service. If providing information about services poses serious risks to clients(serious diseases, etc.), it should be able to be defined and restricted as exceptional situations. In this way, limiting information and the client's right to self-determination may conflict(Won, Suk-Zo, 2009).

Social workers can sometimes be confused about what to decide because two or more values or obligations conflict with each other when performing their duties in the field of practice. This is called an '**ethical dilemma**', and it is very important to come up with appropriate countermeasures. Ethical dilemmas can arise in the relationship between social workers and clients, and can also arise in the relationship with fellow social workers or with bosses or affiliated organizations.

Ethical dilemmas in relationships with clients can be confidentiality, self-determination, and respect for life. For example, let's say a young man with AIDS who is taking a prospective marriage program at our welfare center finds out that he has a premarital relationship without telling his girlfriend about his medical history. In this situation, social workers face an ethical dilemma between the confidentiality of the client and the value of respect for the life of the other girlfriend. At this time, social workers must determine their attitudes and directions based on the code of ethics. The most important ethical principle prioritized in the professional value of social welfare practice is the principle of respect for life. This is because there is no value in the world that is more important and prioritized than human life.

Chapter 3 History of Social Welfare

Social welfare is a method and institution for solving various problems derived from human life, so considering this from a historical perspective, it is necessary to examine how mankind has dealt with these social problems. The beginning of social welfare activities in Korea originated from mutual support and community activities, and in the West, it was developed by charity of religious organizations. Korea has lived to help each other when difficulties arise from an early age, which can be found in our own beauty and customs such as Pu-Mma-Ssi, Du-Rae, and Hyang-Yak.

In the case of the West, the first place to start social welfare activities was the UK, and Christian charity was premised and became the central area of social welfare activities.

Influenced by social welfare projects in the UK, social welfare activities in the United States were also actively carried out, and in this chapter, we will examine the significance of social welfare development processes in the United Kingdom, the United States, Japan, and Korea.

1. United Kingdom

The UK was the first to experience industrialization in the world, enacted the Poor Law, and played a leading role as a welfare state by creating a social welfare system based on the Beveridge report.

1) Transfer of the Poor Law

In the Middle Ages, poor activities were mainly mutual aid activities between believers at the religious level, and the degree of protection for orphans was all. The beginning of the Middle Ages' full-fledged poverty law was reduced by the disaster of 1348(Black Death), and wages began to rise gradually as a large labor force became scarce. As a result, the number of beggars and vagrants began to increase in the streets, and Christian indiscriminate charity activities led to an increase in professional beggars and vagrants. Therefore, Edward III's Labor Decree was enacted in 1349, and the main content of this ordinance was that the Henry III Act of 1531 prohibited indiscriminate Christian benefits against the poor and sentenced the vagrants to death if they were branded as slaves and re-offended in 1547.

2) Elizabeth Poor Law

Elizabethan Poor Law of 1961 compiled various laws of the Middle Ages. This law is meaningful in that the responsibility for poor activities, which have been implemented without a plan by the private sector, is recognized as a national responsibility and legally institutionalized. Britain's poor law can trace its origins back to the 1349 Labor Ordinance by Edward III, who came out as a policy to secure labor following the epidemic of the Black Death. Under the ordinance of 1513 by Henry VIII, the measure was intended to focus on the subject of the poor with labor capacity. It is based on the prohibition of begging, vagrancy, and compulsion of work based on strict punishment, and even the death penalty was executed for excessive vagrancy.

Thus, as the stout beggars, they were forced to prepare materials and work, and the workers were sent to correctional facilities or prisons. Ordinary citizens were prohibited from receiving benefits. It is protected in the Poor House for the sick, the elderly, the mentally and physically disabled, and wives with infants, but it is also protected in housing only if it is particularly recognized by the poor supervisor. Among the orphans and those suffering from hunger, children over the age of 8 with labor capacity were forced to apprentice until the age of 24 for men and 21 for women.

(1) The Settlement Act(1662)

In order to secure the labor force, each parish tried to have the legal right of residence of the born, which led to the enactment of laws prohibiting the free movement of the poor.

(2) Workhouse Fest Act, 1722

Several dioceseses formed a coalition to create a joint workshop and provide jobs to the poor, which has the nature of today's job report.

(3) Gilbert Act(1782)

The bill proposed and passed by Congressman Gilbert recognized an outdoor relief that allows workers to work in their own homes or nearby suitable jobs instead of sending poor people who are capable of labor to work for the purpose of improving the miserable life and exploitation of the poor.

(4) Speenhamland Act, 1795

It is a law enacted by the Magistrate's Council in Speenhamland, Berkshire, that stipulates a wage subsidy system for the poor, and aims to subsidize the shortage of wages that fall short of the minimum living residence. This can be seen as a law that forms the basis for today's family allowance or minimum living security. However, this law has also been criticized for its many problems by increasing the burden of poor taxes on citizens.

3) Old and New Poverty Method

In the early 19th century, the social welfare system in Britain was heavily burdened by high taxes on the poor, and capitalists were dissatisfied with the existing system. In addition, the number of people seeking relief exploded as hunger surged due to the rise in unemployment following Napoleon's defeat and the collapse of many small farmers due to the plunge in food costs. Accordingly, the Royal Commission, which was established in 1832, submitted a report based on the investigation and suggested the following six things.

The Speenhamland Act abolishes partial relief, secondly, the relief of the working poor, thirdly, the homeless(e.g., elderly, lung disease, young women) should be protected, fourthly, fifthly, under the control of state-appointed committees. In addition, this law served as an opportunity to prepare the following principles of the poor administrative system. First, the Principle of National Unification means centralization of the poor administration by reforming the administrative body at the national administrative level; second, the Principle of Less Eligibility; and third, the Principle of Workhouse System. The principle of eliminating the poor system that protects such wages, rejecting the protection of the homes of the poor with labor capacity, and turning a blind eye to the poor and reducing the eligible was applied.

The New and Old Poor Act was returned as a remedy that had been implemented until the first half of the 18th century. The first revision of the Election Act in 1832 gave the emerging commercial and industrial classes wide voting rights, but this meant the victory of the bourgeoisie along with the New Poor Act. Workers were widely neglected in society as working poor, but unity and struggle have become common enough to make certain modifications. In particular, the Chartist movement from 1838 to 1848 was an intensive expression. It was a British popular movement led by the working class from 1838 to 1848, and even in the revision of the election law in 1832, workers began with economic and social complaints and demands to acquire voting rights. Although they have fought hard for 10 years, they are defeated by force. The Chartist Movement was the first nationwide labor-class movement to take place against social injustice, a product of Britain's new industrial order in terms of its nature and scale, and it has the character of a transformation movement calling for the promotion of civil rights.

This movement originated from local riots caused by unemployment and living insecurity, and gradually developed into a nationwide human rights struggle. In 1838, the People's Charter(People's Charter) was established, but its main focus was on the demands of adult men's common election(right to vote) and full parliamentary democracy. It is a document that embodies the demands of the 1938 British Chartist Movement, consisting of six items: adult men's right to vote, anonymous voting, annual improvement of equal constituencies and parliament, abolition of property qualifications, and payment of taxes to lawmakers. Since May 1837, basic preparations have been promoted by members of the radical Parliament and members of the London Workers' Association, and were published on May 8, 1838. The content itself did not go far beyond the claims of the previous radical movement, but it served as an opportunity for the Chartist movement to be unified nationwide. The true power behind the charter was an urgent call for relief of the economic poverty of the working class. These included the abolition of the New Poor Act, an increase in wages and improvement of working conditions, and the establishment of a better Factory Act.

4) Private Social Welfare Activities

In the 19th century, social philosophy and poverty in England were influenced by social improvement movements, charity organization movements, and social surveys.

(1) Charitable Organization Movement

During the period of economic panic and unemployment, many private charity organizations were organized to promote poor activities, which were criticized for wasting resources and making people beggars, and needed to form a coalition for efficient charity work. The first Charity Organization Society was established in London in 1869 at the suggestion of Father Henry Solly to set up a committee to coordinate private and public charity activities as the social need for such a coalition increased. The association has guidelines that individuals are responsible for their own poverty, public relief benefits destroy the self-esteem of the poor, and that the poor should exercise all their abilities for their survival. The activities of this charity association became the basis for case studies and community organization projects, which are methodologies for social work. The COS movement is a liberal social weighing movement that has an individualistic view of poverty that places the responsibility for poverty on individuals. The first British charity society was founded in London in 1869, and the first American charity society was established in Buffalo, New York, in 1877.

After studying the charity movement in London, England in 1877, Pastor Gurteen returned to the United States to create a COS model. COS was invited by experts, female members of the association, and well-educated local governments to discuss cases and present formal alternatives, and while maintaining the COS spirit of "**not alms, but a friend**," the committee appointed friends to the family.

Friendship visitors are volunteers mainly composed of middle-class women who visited poor families and gave advice on family life, education for children, and household economy. The poor learned diligence, moderation, and saving based on independence, and the rich provided friendship to the vulnerable while maintaining the moral superiority of the middle class.

The main content of the COS was to investigate the poor, connect work arrangements for those with labor, and public assistance· for those without labor, and develop individual aid technologies for the first time, creating case workers and enhancing the science of social welfare. Since COS was formed for the purpose of controlling the activities of private social welfare institutions, institutions cooperatively coordinated with each other through institutional registration to prevent duplicate relief and increase the efficiency of social welfare relief. The implications of the COS movement include the creation of casework and community organization projects(CO) as an opportunity to develop professional social projects, enhancing volunteer activities, developing case conferences, and coordinating institutions(Lee, Jong-bok, 2008).

(2) Settlement House Movement

The Social Reform Movement caused by the rapid industrialization of the UK was centered on the trade union movement. Therefore, in 1844, the first joint purchase store for workers was opened. In addition, a mutual deduction system was implemented in which labor unions supported union members' diseases, accidents, unemployment, and old age, and a labor union council was formed as a national union, and in 1867, workers' right to vote was recognized. Christian socialists tried to improve their social conditions by opening night schools for adult education to educate workers. The group that had the greatest influence on social improvement among British socialists was the Fabian Association, which was more interested in practical improvements such as legislation on women's participation and working hours, and housing business education than a revolution to achieve a classless society.

Among them, Pastor Barnett held a debate with college students on social issues facing them, studied the lives of the poor, helped education, and developed programs to help personal problems. To commemorate Toynbee, a college student who died early at the age of 29, a settlement house was established in London in 1884 under the name of Toynbee Hall and a social reform movement was carried out around it(Kwon, Oh-Gyun et al., 86).

The basic premise of the human resource center(current social welfare center) was to live with people in need of assistance, so that educated people and the poor could form interrelationships and exercise cultural influence through collaboration and research. A representative human resource was Toynbee Hall. It had activity goals such as the development of education and culture for the poor, the provision of information on the condition of the poor and the necessity of social improvement, and causing public interest in social problems, health problems, and social methods.

(3) Social Research

There have been numerous social surveys to solve the problem by revealing the reality of social problems. The most important social survey was conducted by Charles Booth(1840-1916) in 1886. He found that one-third of Londoners live below the poverty line by examining the living conditions, working hours, wages, and unemployment of the poor and argued that poverty could be caused by insufficient wages, inappropriate environments and housing, and unclean sanitation. And in 1899, a social survey was conducted by Rowntree(1871-1954), which proved that poverty was caused not by personal causes but by factors of social structure, and served as an opportunity to recognize that existing poor laws and private charity activities were not suitable. The result that the cause of poverty is due to the social structure is that it is directly opposed to the existence of the new and old poor law, and to find a solution to this, the Royal Poor Law Committee was established and the overall review of the poor law began. As a result, two reports, the Majority and Minority Reports, were submitted in 1909, mainly under the influence of the Charity Organization Association, emphasizing the autonomy of providing services to the Charity Fund, and the Minority Report proposed state-led insurance, medical services, and job security policies.

5) Transformation into a Welfare State

In the 20th century, Britain introduced a modern social security system later than Germany. The Liberal Party government, which took power in 1906, decided that the existing poor relief policy based on the principle of personal responsibility was insufficient and promoted social welfare legislation for the entire nation as it faced serious social issues such as strikes and closures. At that time, the finance minister, Lloyd George, was deeply interested in the health insurance system and visited Germany, where he had already implemented the health insurance system, and Churchill, a trader, promoted the introduction of the unemployment insurance system with the help of William Beveridge(1879-1963). As one of the pioneers of the British welfare state, he published a report called Social Insurance and Related Projects during World War II and served as a blueprint for social policy in peace. For the next 40 years, discussions on the advantages and disadvantages of the British social security system have been taking place under the principles announced by Beveridge. The basis for Beveridge to be regarded as one of the pioneers of the British welfare state is his original and fundamental contribution to social policy, which can be found in the causes and solutions of unemployment in the early 20th century. He argued that unemployment in the UK should be prevented, not solved. The main content of the Beveridge report stipulates five types of social evils(poverty, disease, ignorance, uncleanness, and laziness), among which 'poverty' is regarded as the top priority and the standard of the social security system to ensure income for 'poor' people from economic poverty. Under the leadership of these two, the National Insurance Act was enacted in 1911, and medical insurance and unemployment insurance are provided by contributing to insurance premiums. With the enforcement of this law, it can be said that the core issues of the British social security system have been converted from conventional public assistance to social insurance. With the enactment of the Old Age Pensions Act in 1908, the pension system was implemented as a public assistance method in which pensions were paid to low-income seniors aged 70 or older by state finances. However, the full-fledged pension system based on the method of contributing insurance premiums was implemented only when the Widow's Orphans and Old Age Property Pensions were enacted in 1925, and the introduction of the pension system was delayed compared to Germany and Sweden.

2. The United States

The poor policy of the United States was greatly influenced by the British poor law, and especially during the early colonial period, the Elizabeth poor law was applied as it was. It was only after industrialization and the Great Depression that the United States began its own poor business.

1) Colonial Era and Poverty Policy

The social welfare of the American colonial era established a poor house by applying the poor administration of the British poor law, and the subjects were mainly poor people without labor capacity except black people, and the level of protection was inferior treatment. Initially, the United States saw poverty as a result of personal laziness, and implemented inhumane poverty policies such as treating the poor and the vagrants as criminals, torture, and imprisonment. Therefore, during this period, he played a leading role in charity activities mainly in private organizations, and in 1877, the first American charity association was established. In addition to the Charity Organization Society, Jane Adams visited Toynbee Hall in London in 1889 in the United States and returned to the United States to establish the Hull House and carry out systematic settlement house projects.

As social welfare facilities and institutions in the public or private sector increased at the end of the 19th century, paid social entrepreneurs increased and professional educational institutions also appeared. Around the 20th century, the New York Charity Society's Social Work Training Summer Lecture was held for the first time, at Chicago.

Citizens' Philanthropy School(now Chicago University) in 1903, and New York Philanthropy School(now Columbia University) in 1904. In 1918, the American Medical Social Entrepreneurs Association and the American Psychiatric Social Entrepreneurs Association were established as professional organizations in 1926, and professional social enterprises in the United States were established.

2) The Great Depression and Social Security Policy

As the overall economic recession continued after World War I, the United States finally faced the Great Depression in 1929. In the U.S. society, which faced the Great Depression, the number of unemployed gradually increased, and most of the companies went bankrupt, and urban poverty poured in countless numbers. As a result, the United States became an important opportunity to recognize the national responsibility of unemployment and poverty, and established an active social security system under the epitome of expanding the social safety net.

As a representative example, in 1933, U.S. President Roosevelt implemented the New Deal for the main purpose of relief, reconstruction, and reform. Through this policy, the United States has deviated from the policy for relief workers and developed a universal welfare policy. The Social Security Act of 1935 was first implemented in social insurance, public assistance, health and disability insurance, second in public assistance, providing benefits to blind families, severely disabled people aged 65 or older, and third in health and health services.

After the Great Depression in the 1930s, when President Kennedy (1917.5.29-1963.11.22) and President Johnson(1908.8.27-1973.1.22) took power in the 1960s, the United States enjoyed an economic boom, especially, President Kennedy(1961-63) revised the Social Security Act in 1962 and emphasized poverty as a social responsibility. Since then, President Johnson(1963~69) has declared a war on poverty and developed various social welfare programs. The main social welfare programs of this period were Medicare, a kind of social insurance for the elderly aged 65 or older, and Medicaid, a form of government payment(public assistance), to the poor below a certain level.

3) Modern Social Welfare

In the 1970s, Nixon(1969-1974) took office and introduced a linkage system to change the level of benefits paid to beneficiaries according to fluctuations in prices, and in the 1980s, President Reagan(1981-89) took power to reduce and curb welfare budgets. President Reagan developed a policy to reduce and curb welfare budgets, arguing that "*Those who do not work have no welfare.*" He said, "The welfare policy has not been easy to pursue universalism due to the resistance of conservative lawmakers who pay workers, and the Bush administration(2001-2009) is also expected to change its conservative tendency and election strategy.

3. Japan

It can be said that the history of social welfare in Japan originated from the Meiji Restoration in 1868. The historical development process of Japanese social welfare can be viewed in four stages, and the classification is as follows.

1) The beginning of Social Welfare(after World War Ⅰ to before World War Ⅱ)

Since the mid-1920s, Japanese social welfare has increased interest in institutional-centered social welfare as a result of skepticism about contradictions in Japanese capitalism and workers' struggles. A social science system was established, and attempts to clarify the nature of social work began. Since 1920, the Impression Act was introduced to realize the purpose of social defense and the protection of bad adolescents, and the Employment Introduction Act was enacted in 1921 due to serious youth problems. In addition, in the late 1920s, in the wake of the financial panic, the Relief Act was enacted in earnest in 1929. However, the targets of relief were limited to those aged 65 or older, children under the age of 13, pregnant women, lung disease, injuries, and people with mental and physical disabilities who were unable to work. These social projects were transformed into wartime welfare projects aimed at protecting human resources, such as the Manchurian Incident(1931) and the Sino-Japanese War(1937), and the Maternal and Child Health Act and the Military Relief Act were enacted in 1941.

2) Social Welfare Expansion Unit(after World War Ⅱ to early 1970s)

(1) Social Welfare Services during the U.S. Military Government Era

Japan, devastated by the defeat of World War Ⅱ(1939.9.1-1945.9.2), has emerged as an urgent task to solve social problems due to the widespread life problems and crimes of people in need such as orphans, hunger, Jeon Jae-min, prostitutes, returnees, vagrants, injuries, and the disabled. Therefore, social work has focused on the protection of the needy and the relief of war orphans and the disabled. However, due to a lack of financial resources, social welfare service was extremely limited only to those who were unable to lead basic lives on their own. Immediately after World War II, the reforms were carried out by the General Command of the Allied Forces(GHQ), which occupied Japan. Accordingly, the Allied Forces Command planned to enact the Living Protection Act with the aim of demilitarizing and democratizing social work in Japan, including the principle of equality, public responsibility, and the principle of non-limiting relief costs. Under these principles, the so-called Welfare Three Laws were established in 1946 with the enactment of the Child Welfare Act for the Protection and Raising of Children, including War orphans, in 1947, and the Welfare Act for the Disabled in 1949. Each of these three laws has roles and characteristics, but it can be said that a government-led social welfare delivery system has been established in that all of them were implemented under the leadership of the government. In the private sector, a social welfare council was established in 1956 to strengthen private cooperation and resident participation in welfare administration.

(2) Social Welfare Services during the Economic Growth Period

In the 1960s, Ikeda(1899-1965) cabinet's economic plan "*National Income Redistribution Plan*" achieved rapid economic growth for more than a decade, but social problems such as rural life collapse, population concentration, changes in living conditions, and family growth of mentally disabled people increased. In addition to the previous three welfare laws, the Mental Weak Welfare Act was enacted in 1960, the Elderly Welfare Act in 1963, and the Maternal and Child Welfare Act in 1946 were expanded from the three welfare laws to the six welfare laws. This was to cope with economic and social fluctuations caused by rapid economic growth and the resulting increase in anxiety in people's lives. However, problems such as pollution, overcrowding, underpopulated areas, and family dissolution occurred as another social problem, resulting in various social reform movements and civic movements. In 1962, the National Insurance and Pension System was recommended in the Social Security System Council's Recommendation on the Policy on the Adjustment of the Total Social Security System and the Promotion of Social Security. From the late 1960s to the early 1970s, interest in social welfare tasks in response to new social changes increased, and the relationship between 'community and social welfare' began to be discussed. In other words, since the new social problems appear differently depending on the region, the local autonomy system independently promoted policies, resulting in the creation of innovative local governments. Against this background, the concept of community care has been established based on reflection on social welfare services in a number of provinces, including Tokyo, Kyoto, and Osaka.

3) Social Welfare Coordination Period(from Mid-1970s to Early 1980s)

In 1973, Japan tried to make welfare services free by growing so high that it was called the Welfare Year, but the first oil crisis and the dollar shock in 1974 required Japan to transform its social welfare system based on high economic growth. In addition, the demand for the focus and efficiency of social welfare administration has increased due to the re-evaluation of the pension and medical security systems according to the progress of aging. If Japan's existing social welfare services were centered on responding to monetary demand, social welfare during this period expanded response welfare services to respond to non-monetary demand. In the local welfare sector, the Social Welfare Council actively promoted home welfare, and some local governments also pioneered home welfare service projects. In response, in 1973, the state made it possible to provide meal services to the elderly at home as part of the Home Helper Project for the Elderly. In 1973, short-term protection projects for the elderly and daytime protection projects were implemented in 1974, and home welfare projects began to spread. In order to implement this, it was converted into a policy of social welfare services that emphasized the small government and emphasized the role of community cities, governments, and villages with local residents.

4) Social Welfare Reform Period(1980s-Modern)

The biggest change in social welfare during this period was the reduction of welfare finances. In addition, the core of Japan's social welfare reform is to prepare for a future aging society and realize the paradigm structure. It attempted to convert part of the authority on social welfare implementation from the state to local governments, and partially delegated the authority on social welfare implementation to the city, province, and village, which are local governments close to residents. In addition, it consists of easing standards for social welfare measures or the installation of social welfare facilities. In 1990, the main content was to further develop this decentralization and localization, which symbolizes the transition of the Japanese social welfare paradigm, from supplier-centered social welfare to user-centered social welfare, that is, normalization. The ideology of normalization allowed social welfare to change from facility-centered to home welfare.

At a meeting on the direction of social welfare in March 1989, the relevant authority of the city, government, and village was further transferred, emphasizing home welfare, strengthening solidarity in welfare, health and medical care, and improving welfare workers. In addition, a 10-year strategy(so-called 'Gold Plan') for promoting welfare for the elderly was created, quantitatively representing the future vision of the elderly welfare sector, forming the core of home welfare such as home helper, short-term protection, and data service. In June 1990, a law was enacted to partially amend the Elderly Welfare Act, the Physical Disability Welfare Act, the Mental Weak Welfare Act, the Child Welfare Act, the Mother and Widow Welfare Act, and the Social Welfare and Medical Service Act. The revision of the law was implemented to realize the 10-year strategy for promoting health and welfare for the elderly, which was expanded in December 1989. In particular, the

Senior Welfare Gold Plan provides health and welfare for the elderly in preparation for the full-fledged elderly society in the 21st century, including zero strategy for the elderly, establishment of a longevity welfare fund, 10-year plan for the elderly, and comprehensive facility maintenance. In addition, these projects are being promoted mainly in cities, governments, and villages.

Japan revised the social security ideology to ensure a healthy and safe life for all citizens as the subject of the social security system became common to all citizens. It presents universality, comprehensiveness, rights, and effectiveness as principles for promoting social security.

4. Korea

1) Traditional Social Welfare before the Establishment of the Republic of Korea

In order to understand Korea's social welfare today, it is necessary to understand the minimum historical background that is essential. Among the historical facts, in order to describe the influence on modern social welfare, it is inevitable to emphasize relatively over the past 100 years, which has the most influence among the 5,000-year history.

(1) before the Chosun Dynasty

Our history is 5,000 years old, dating back to Gojoseon. It is difficult to describe the social welfare history of Gojoseon, the Three Kingdoms, Goryeo, and Chosun periods, which account for most of them, in a narrow page. In the past, social welfare was not clearly distinguished from other social systems, so many social systems are related to social welfare in that they "**benefit the people,**" but at the same time, it is somewhat unreasonable to call a specific system a "**social welfare system.**"

The following were the poor projects carried out during the Three Kingdoms Period. ① The government is to distribute the rice to the people who have become poor due to various disasters. ② Sagung Relief: To provide clothing, grain, and government goods to the indifferent poor of suffering and loneliness(widower, widows, orphans, elderly children, etc.). ③ Tax reduction: Tax reduction or exemption is provided to the people who suffered severe damage in the disaster. ④ Daegok Jamo-Gu-Myeon: The original and interest are reduced or exempted for the Gwangok rented during the famine. ⑤ Jin-Dae-Beop: Rent grain to the people during the Spring Palace period and pay it during the harvest season.

According to Jeong In-ji's Goryeo history, the Goryeo Dynasty had the following relief system. ① Eun-Myeon-Ji-Je: After the founding of the country, the throne, the celebration, and the war, the king gives tax relief or various silver coins to the people. ② Jae-Myeon-Ji-Je : Tax, labor, and punishment are reduced or exempted for victims of natural disasters, wars, and diseases. ③ Hwan-Gwa-Ko-Dok-Jindae: widows, widows, orphans, and elderly children are designated as priority protection targets. ④ Su-Han-Jil-Rye-Jindae: It is a project to provide various items such as grain and clothing, as well as medical and housing.

The history of social welfare before the Joseon Dynasty can be largely divided into public and private systems. The public system includes an institutional system to prevent people from being in need due to spring and natural disasters, an old emperor system to save people suffering from natural disasters, a tax reduction system to help people in need, and a relief system to treat infectious diseases or poor people. The private welfare system mainly includes welfare activities through temples, activities through private organizations such as gye and Hyangyak, and volunteer work by philanthropists.

(2) Chosun Dynasty

The relief work of the Chosun Dynasty was based on Confucianism, and the ideology of Wangdo politics dominated by which the king was responsible for the misfortune of the people, and emphasized the sense of responsibility of the state.

(3) Japanese Colonial Era and Foreign-Dependent Era

After becoming a colony of Japan, the relief project by the Japanese Government-General of Korea emphasized the recognition of the emperor and aimed to dilute the dissatisfaction of the colonial people. In addition, social welfare projects during the U.S. military government era were to provide food, housing, and medical relief for victims, refugees, and unemployed people with the Health and Welfare Bureau in accordance with U.S. Military Government Act No. 18 in 1945.

2) Welfare Administration after the Establishment of the Government

(1) Attempts to Institutionalize Facility Protection and Provide Public Assistance

The history of modern and contemporary social welfare in Korea begins with facility protection. Among the patients and solitude that needed the most help in traditional society, protecting the orphan without parents and the elderly living alone without children in facilities began under the name of social work. This facility protection was attempted from the end of the Chosun Dynasty and was implemented on a small scale under Japanese colonial rule, but it exploded through the liberation of August 15 in 1945 and the Korean War in 1950. From 8.15 liberation to the end of March 1948, the total number of facilities such as childcare facilities for orphans and hunger, and the number of facilities increased more than tripled from 2,228 to 7,832. As the number of refugees increased rapidly due to the Korean War, the government's welfare policy was to set up camps or cafeteria for refugees. Between 1950 and 1951, the number of victims at once reached 10 million. In 1951, when refugees moving south due to the 1.4 retreat were concentrated in Busan, the government installed and accommodated refugee camps in various parts of Busan for them, while some of the refugees were transferred to Geoje Island to collectively accommodate them. In order to rescue them, the Ministry of

Health and Social Affairs established the loss of the Ministry of Health and Social Affairs in Geoje Island to supervise local officials. At that time, Geoje Island had 60,000 natives, but up to 200,000 refugees were collectively accommodated, making it a land of refugees. Although the number of requests reached a huge number, the government had no choice but to focus on emergency relief due to disasters because the funds and supplies required for relief were greatly insufficient. In particular, priority was given to children, the elderly, pregnant women, and women with infants. However, after the war situation improved and the ceasefire agreement was established, the existing relief policy was changed to focus on refugee settlement projects, housing projects, public assistance projects under the Joseon Relief Decree, and temporary emergency relief projects for natural disasters. During this period, facility protection and public assistance projects were almost entirely provided by the UN Relief Program, donations from various countries around the world, and foreign private relief supplies. In particular, grains, food, clothing, medicines, fuel, and building materials introduced by foreign private aid organizations that worked to rescue refugees contributed greatly to the settlement of refugees. As a result of the Korean War, foreign private aid organizations that entered Korea gathered in March 1952 to exchange information with each other, unify business plans, and smoothly promote projects through a cooperative system and launch the KAVA(Council of Private Aid Organizations). The number of member agencies of this council increased to 33 in 1954, and played a key role in postwar relief projects. The social work practices they carried out had a great influence on professional social welfare projects afterward. The history of social welfare during this period, which relied on foreign aid to provide emergency relief for war orphans, was also the beginning of limiting Korea's social welfare to facility protection and public assistance in the future. During this period, the government's administrative department in charge of welfare administration was systematized to relieve refugees, and professional social projects were introduced as university education from 1947, but the state's welfare policy did not deviate significantly from emergency relief projects and facility protection.

(2) Systematization of Public Assistance and Attempts to Provide Social Insurance

In the history of Korean social welfare, public assistance was systematized and at a rudimentary level in the 1960s and 1970s, but it can be found in that social insurance was attempted. In particular, through the April 19 Revolution, the people's sense of rights was greatly improved, and new political forces who took power through the May 16 military coup tried to win public sentiment by eradicating absolute poverty called "**barley hump**" and solving postwar social problems. The government enacted various laws on public assistance, including the Act on the Protection of Living(1961), the Act on the Compensation for Military Help, the Act on Special Protection for Veterans of Vietnam(1961), the Act on Disaster Relief(1962), and the Act on Temporary Measures for Self-Support Projects(1968). Among them, the Living Protection Act was the basis for public assistance as it inherited the Joseon Relief Decree(1944) under the Japanese colonial rule and the Welfare Bureau System(1946) under the U.S. military government. The Joseon Relief Decree was created at the end of World War II to mobilize all colonists and was rarely enforced, but it is significant in that it became the basis of the Life Protection Act. The Living Protection Act thoroughly turned a blind eye to the protection of livelihoods for the working age group aged 18 to 65 like the Western Poor Act until temporary living protection was implemented due to the economic crisis in 1987. Until the National Basic Livelihood Security Act(1999) was enacted and living benefits were expanded to the entire population, the Living Protection Act became the basis of public assistance in Korea for more than 40 years.

In addition, industrial and social problems such as industrial accidents, unemployment, disease, and post-retirement poverty increased as industrialization and urbanization progressed in earnest with the implementation of the five-year economic development plan from 1962. As a countermeasure, the government enacted social insurance laws such as the Public Officials Pension Act(1960), the Seafarers Insurance Act(1962), the Military Pension Act(1963), the

Industrial Accident Compensation Insurance Act(1963), and the Medical Insurance Act(1963). Among the laws that took effect immediately after enactment, the Public Officials Pension Act and the Military Pension Act are the state's payment of severance pay to public officials and soldiers, and in a true sense, social insurance is the implementation of industrial accident compensation insurance and expansion of applicants.

Although the Social Security Act(1963), which is the basis of social security, was enacted during this period, it is significant that the Medical Insurance Act(1963) and the National Welfare Pension Act(1973) were enacted to open the era of social insurance. The role of the Social Security Review Committee, established in 1962 as an advisory body to the Minister of Health and Welfare, was largely due to the enactment of social security legislation in the early 1960s before the social problems of industrial society emerged in earnest. The committee commissioned eight researchers as a joint public-private committee to systematically study social security systems in developed countries, review suitability for existing systems, and suggestions for the introduction of new systems for the first time in our history.

One of the indispensable things during this period was the Child Welfare Act(1961), which later became a model for social welfare-related laws, and the Act on the Prevention of indulgence Act(1961), which was enacted to protect women who rapidly increased during the Korean War, became a core law for women's welfare for more than 30 years. In addition, the enactment of the Social Welfare Services Act(1970) laid the foundation for social welfare services by defining the scope of social welfare services, defining the qualifications of social welfare workers, and changing a foundation to a social welfare corporation.

(3) Universalization of Social Insurance and the Establishment of Home Welfare

In the late 1970s, the center of Korean social welfare changed from public assistance to social insurance. Often, the era is divided into after the 5th Republic, which emerged in 1979 and the 4th Republic, but the era of social insurance began in July 1977 when medical insurance was naturally applied to workplaces with more than 500 workers. Initially, the Medical Insurance Act was enacted in 1963, but it was not implemented in earnest due to a voluntary application method, but it was fully revised and implemented in December 1976.

Over the years, medical insurance expanded to workplaces with more than 300, 100, 16 or more, and gradually expanded to rural residents and urban self-employed people, opening the era of national health insurance in July 1989 after 12 years of natural application Health insurance was managed and operated by a medical insurance association consisting of workplace and region, and the debate between those advocating integrationism and unionism had a great influence on the development of a model of Korean social insurance.

In this debate, the National Pension Service, introduced in 1988, designated all citizens aged 18 or older as insured except public officials, soldiers, and private school faculty members who are already subscribed to the public pension. The National Pension Service was enacted in 1973 and implemented under the National Pension Act(1986), which was completely amended by the National Welfare Pension Act, which was delayed due to the oil crisis. Unlike industrial accident insurance or medical insurance, which provides benefits by identifying income and expenditure on a yearly basis and receiving premiums from the insured, the National Pension Service is even more meaningful in that it is a long-term social insurance that requires retirement and death. The National Pension Service was initially applied to workers at workplaces with 10 or more employees, but gradually applied to five or more employees, rural residents, and urban self-employed people in April 2000, opening the era of national pensions except for full-time housewives.

In addition, with the enforcement of the Employment Insurance Act (established in 1993) in 1995, all four of the most representative insurances in the industrial society were implemented. Employment insurance began to gradually expand the number of people covered by the 1997 financial crisis from workplaces with 30 or more employees, and is currently applied to all workplaces with one or more employees. Since July 2000, the coverage of industrial accident compensation insurance has been expanded to workplaces with more than one person, and from July 2001, health insurance has also been reborn as a universal system by paying insurance premiums at work. This period can be found in that home welfare began to be established with the universalization of social insurance. Home welfare received social attention as the social welfare center project, which was piloted mainly by foreign institutions and social welfare centers established by universities, began to receive government support in the early 1980s. In particular, in the late 1980s, permanent rental apartments for the urban poor were built due to soaring housing prices, and social welfare centers were built as essential facilities, laying the foundation for practicing home welfare. Since then, the government has designated a social welfare center as a home welfare service center and has been continuously promoting policies to revitalize home welfare through senior welfare centers and welfare centers for the disabled.

On the other hand, the National Basic Livelihood Security Act(1999), which aims to provide livelihood benefits to those aged 18 to 65 who have not paid livelihood protection because they are judged to be capable of working, came into effect in October 2000. During this period, the Social Welfare Service Act(1981) and the Welfare of Persons with Mental Disabilities Act(1981) were newly enacted, and laws enacted during the previous period were fully enacted to promote more universal service. In particular, the Infant Care Act, enacted in 1991, proposed a model that aims for universal services according to needs, not selective services by asset surveys, by the government to solve the childcare problem of infants under the age of six.

During this period, social insurance was applied to the entire nation and social welfare services became a universal service, which was greatly contributed by the continuous legislative petition movement of labor unions, women's movement groups, and civil society organizations. In particular, the June uprising in 1987, in which students, workers, and citizens united and surrendered to the authoritarian government, exerted influence on the implementation of the national health insurance, national pension, and minimum wage system. After pre-economic development, the logic of social welfare could no longer be convincing to the people, and welfare rights became the main concern of the people. During this period, breakthroughs were also made in welfare administration. In 1987, social welfare specialists in charge of life protection administration were appointed on a trial basis, and then gradually expanded. In 2005, the number of social welfare officials working in Eup-Myeon-Dong offices and Si-Gun-Gu offices nationwide reached 7,200, and in 2006, 1,800 were increased. Accordingly, they are raising the level of welfare administration to the next level.

Social welfare is very closely related to the historical background of society because it satisfies basic human needs and takes countermeasures against social problems. For example, advanced Western countries also enacted the Poor Law to settle the vagrants increased by industrialization, and from the end of the 19th century, social insurance began to be institutionalized to solve industrial and social problems such as industrial accidents, diseases, and old age.

The social welfare system in developed countries, which was created in the process of experiencing industrialization, had a profound impact on social welfare in Korea as the U.S. military government was implemented along with liberation and foreign civil aid organizations directly carried out social welfare during the Korean War.

(4) Expansion of Social Welfare

The Kim, Dae-Jung government(1998-2003) advocated "productive welfare" to establish a social safety net, establish a basic health and welfare system, introduce a national basic living security system, expand the national pension, and integrate national health insurance as key policies. The Roh, Moo-Hyun government(2003-2008) emphasized the necessity of easing the gap between the rich and the poor and social integration through participatory welfare, enhancing the role of the private sector in achieving universal welfare and system, and establishing welfare and health infrastructure. The Lee, Myung-Bak government(2008-2013) has set the tone of "active welfare," which is said to provide jobs to those who are capable of working and warm hands to those in need.

Chapter 4 Composition and System of Social Welfare

1. Construction of Social Welfare

1) Subject of Social Welfare

Social welfare consists of subjects(institution), objects(objects), and functions (methods) in the construction of social welfare of the entire nation, as well as the disabled, the elderly, and children, who are socially vulnerable. These constituent factors are closely related to each other. This is to analyze the understanding of social welfare phenomena and social welfare activities with a close relationship between the constituent systems of social welfare. This is because it emphasizes the practical aspect of promoting effective and efficient service provision in the practice of social welfare. Historically, the subject and field of social welfare differed in emphasis depending on the period. In the case of the United States, when social welfare spread to one of the '**volunteer activities**' at the end of the 19th century, sites such as the Charitable Organization Association and the settlement house were emphasized. However, in the early 20th century, when universities produced social workers, activities by professional social workers were emphasized.

In Korea, there were social welfare programs during the Joseon Dynasty and under Japanese colonial rule. At that time, the subject of social welfare was not important because protecting so-called "**pain and solitude**" such as orphans, elderly people living alone, widows or widowers was done at the level of relief.

However, after liberation, social welfare studies began to be taught at universities, and social workers were produced in earnest after the 1970s, emphasizing professional activities by social workers.

Currently, few people deny that social welfare is the subject of social welfare in Korean society, but in reality, it cannot be concluded that social welfare is practiced because not only social welfare workers practice social welfare, but all social welfare workers are active in various fields.

Therefore, understanding the subject of social welfare is very important because it is to grasp the context of the interaction between the service provider and the recipient in the process of providing social welfare services.

In this sense, among the subjects of social welfare, the government, such as professional social workers, state and local governments that legally and systematically provide social welfare services, social welfare corporations that are entrusted by the government, and other related organizations are as follows.

(1) Social Worker

A. Role of Social Workers

Social workers were also called "**social workers**" in the past, and in Korean society, social workers refer to those who acquire legally recognized "**social workers**" from the Minister of Health and Welfare under the Social Welfare Act and practice social welfare. Social workers serve as major experts in satisfying the welfare needs of individuals, groups, families, and communities and solving social problems. In particular, unlike the United States, social workers rarely open and work personally in Korean society, and they work as government officials in social welfare positions, social welfare corporations, and employees of various welfare facilities.

The qualifications of social workers are specified by the Social Welfare Service Act enacted in 1970, and before the enforcement of this law, a qualification system called "**social welfare service workers**" was established. After that, when the law was revised in 1993, the qualifications of social workers were subdivided into three grades to strengthen the qualification standards, and in the 1997 revised law, the first level of social workers was further strengthened to those who passed the national qualification examination. The test subjects applied to the national examination of social worker level 1 are as follows.

As of 2009, the Korea Industrial Human Resources Development Corporation is entrusted with the test management work. In addition to legal and accredited qualifications, the Korea Social Welfare Association has been conducting civil qualification tests only for those with more than three years of clinical experience as social workers since 1996, and has been awarded "**professional social workers**" certificates. In addition, social workers mainly provide various social welfare services stipulated in the Social Welfare Service Act, and the role of social workers varies greatly depending on the specialized field and the characteristics of social welfare institutions and facilities to which they belong. In general, there are differences in emphasis depending on scholars, but they have something in common in that "*social workers are people who create a happy world.*" With the maturity of capitalism, the protection function of protective citizens in the traditional society has weakened, and social problems caused by weakening community functions are to be solved through the establishment of a "**welfare community.**"

B. Expertise of Social Workers

Is a social worker a professional? When it comes to social workers, they think of "**social workers**" or "**social welfare workers.**" With the revision of the Social Welfare Service Act in 1983, it was converted to a social worker. Social workers are often referred to as "*social workers are people who create a happy world.*" Friedlander and Apte are said to have a broader meaning than experts, while viewing social workers as experts. It is a service expert who helps individuals, groups, and communities based on scientific knowledge and technology in human relations. When trying to solve the maturity of capitalism and various welfare needs and social problems of citizens through the establishment of a '**welfare community**', it is necessary to discuss the professionalism of social workers. Currently, social worker certificates in Korea are pointed out as the cause of the rapid increase in the number of social workers every year since 2000, as only taking legal courses can be obtained without a national test. Korean social workers mainly work as government social welfare officials, social welfare corporations, and employees of various welfare facilities. The government is said to recruit 7,000 social welfare officials by 2014.

It is known that the first debate over whether social work is professional in the United States began in earnest in 1915 after Flexner, a doctor, published a paper titled "Is social work professional?" Currently, in the United States, evaluation and certification of educational institutions are conducted mainly by CSWE, a private organization, so if you graduate from an uncertified educational institution, you will not be recognized as a social worker. Although it has a different background from the United States, it is natural to discuss the specific expertise of Korean social workers directly affected by the United States.

Here, I would like to add policy suggestions for social welfare professionals by dividing them into several perspectives.

First, it is a question of the identity of a social worker's professional job. In the Korean Code of Ethics for Social Workers, the attitude as an expert is expressed as '**social workers maintain their dignity and qualities as experts...**'. In the code of ethics for social workers in Korea, social workers are definitely experts. Lawyers, doctors, and pastors have long established themselves in their professional fields, and it can be said that no one does not recognize them as experts, but not many people in our society recognize social workers as experts. However, it is true that not only the previous "**social welfare service workers**" were upgraded to "**social workers**" and their qualifications were strengthened, but the level of social workers was further strengthened by allowing them to go through the national examination.

Second, it is about the current social worker certification system. The social worker system, which is currently divided into grades 1, 2, and 3, is voicing its voice as it is related to qualitative services of social welfare. In the actual social worker labor market, there is little discrimination as well as differences in job or treatment. Therefore, it seems desirable to review the "*single social worker certification system*" through the national examination in the future.

Third, it is about the specialty of social workers. As a public sector, the name of a social welfare specialist, which began in 1987, has been changed to the name of a social welfare official since 2000, but the number is not large. On the other hand, in the private sector, many social workers are recognized as specialized areas in the health care sector, such as medical social workers and mental health social workers, and are building their positions. In the future, however, the activities and horizons of social workers such as school social workers, industrial social workers, volunteer experts, correctional social workers, and military social workers are expanding.

In conclusion, it is true that Korea's social work has been created through the Korean War with the colonial era, so the certification system and social treatment show a dual attitude of being passive in empowering social workers while acknowledging their expertise. Nevertheless, it seems to agree with the justification that social projects should secure a position as professionals in Korea. However, it would not be an exaggeration to say that the specific efforts of social welfare academia and social workers, not only time, will determine the status and position of professionalism, but also depend on the specific efforts of social welfare professionals.

C. Qualifications of Social Workers

In order for social workers to perform their duties as professionals, they must have their own qualifications as professionals. It can be said that the most important factor in social workers' professions is value, knowledge, and skills. First, social workers must be committed to the value of social work professionals. Social workers must first realize that clearly recognizing their personal values or beliefs is critical to helping clients professionally. Social work professionals are responsible for helping people and realizing their individuality and potential, and are obligated to practice social work based on democratic ideologies that respect the rights and opinions of the other party. Second, the knowledge used by social workers is broad, diverse, and comprehensive. Basic knowledge of a wide range of liberal arts subjects, human-to-human interactions, sufficient basic knowledge of the social situation in which humans function, interactions in helping relationships, processes, and intervention strategies suitable for various situations and systems. Third, skill of social work is a practical component that harmonizes the value and knowledge of social work well and turns it into action with the aim of improving the social function of the client in response to the needs of the client(Cho, Chu-Yong, 2008).

(2) National and Local Governments

The state and local governments encourage their public officials to practice social welfare, subsidize national or local expenses to social welfare corporations, or entrust government welfare institutions to the private sector to implement welfare. In the central government, the Ministry of Health and Welfare and the Ministry of Gender Equality and Family are the Ministry of Public Administration and Security, the Ministry of Culture, Sports and Tourism, the Ministry of Employment and Labor, the Ministry of Education and Human Resources. These administrative ministries implement social welfare directly or through affiliated organizations, and realize welfare mainly through local governments under the direction and supervision of the Ministry of Public Administration and Security. Therefore, most citizens often receive welfare services by public officials belonging to metropolitan governments(city/province) and basic governments(city/county/gu) rather than by the direct administrative system of the central government. Therefore, it is being promoted in the direction of establishing a community life support system and practicing community welfare.

In addition, social welfare by public officials may be carried out by public officials engaged in general administrative affairs rather than by public officials qualified as social workers. Therefore, there will be certain limitations in speaking of the state and local governments as subjects of social welfare practice. In this way, despite the limitations in professionalism, public officials in charge of welfare administration provide financial support to social welfare corporations with considerable expertise and perform guidance and supervision, emphasizing criticism and system improvement.

(3) Social Welfare Corporation

A social welfare corporation is a corporation created under the Social Welfare Services Act to perform social welfare. Legally, corporations with personality are largely divided into corporations, which are human groups, and foundations, which are property groups, and social welfare corporations are close to foundations, and are non-profit corporations among for-profit and non-profit corporations. In other words, a social welfare corporation can be seen as a non-profit foundation pursuing non-profit while a group of people and property created to perform social welfare. In many cases, Korean social welfare corporations initially acquired the status of "**social welfare corporations**" by individuals or voluntary organizations that intended social welfare. In addition, social welfare corporations are carrying out purpose projects stipulated in the articles of incorporation. In general, living facilities are operated or practiced through home welfare projects for tasks such as child welfare, elderly welfare, disabled welfare, and women's welfare.

However, according to the Social Welfare Service Act enacted in 1970, individuals or voluntary organizations intended for social welfare were initially approved as "**social welfare corporations**," and since the chairman of the board often formed a board of directors.

(4) Other Related Organizations

In addition to the individuals or organizations mentioned above, social welfare can be found in corporate welfare foundations, social welfare managers of religious institutions, and civil society organizations pursuing the public interest. In general, they often practice social welfare as one of the institution's target projects. In other words, religious institutions conduct social welfare as an extension of missionary or missionary activities, companies conduct it to enhance their image and return profits to society, and civic groups raise social welfare as important issues to form public opinion or conduct social welfare campaigns in specific fields.

Representative corporate welfare foundations in Korea include foundations belonging to large companies such as the Asan Social Welfare Foundation, the Samsung Welfare Foundation, and the LG Welfare Foundation, and they are carrying out scholarship projects and support projects for social welfare programs.

The Korean Corporate Welfare Foundation mainly belongs to large corporations, so it has a smooth aspect to carry out scholarship projects, social welfare program support, and facility operation support projects. In addition, Christianity, Buddhism, and Won Buddhism often have social welfare committees at the religious level, or organizations or monasteries dedicated only to social welfare projects. In particular, the social welfare activities of the Catholic Monastery are very systematic, and in the case of other religions, they are conducted in individual churches(temples, churches) apart from the welfare activities at the religious level. In this case, there are not a few cases where priests or monks practice social welfare themselves, or they study social welfare and acquire social welfare qualifications. Recently, the termination itself established a social welfare-related university or established a social welfare department at a university affiliated with the foundation.

Social welfare activities suitable for the purpose of school establishment are being carried out.

2) Social Welfare Object

The object of social welfare refers to those who need social welfare, and in the past, social welfare targets were mainly limited to guardians who needed social needs, but now anyone who needs social welfare from a universalist perspective is eligible. This has brought about many historical changes. In the early stages of social welfare, social welfare services were provided by limiting the few socially disadvantaged. Therefore, when it comes to social welfare or social work, orphans, widows, the disabled, and the poor were thought to be the main targets of social welfare. However, in modern society, social welfare is the primary object, but more attention is being paid to the social needs and social problems of the people.

Social needs and social problems, which are the main objects of social welfare, are as follows.

First, social needs can be divided into material needs and emotional needs.

Material needs include income, health, education, and housing as primary needs, and secondary needs include cultural needs such as sports and arts and social needs such as social participation. These first and second social needs are subject to social welfare. Second, social problems can be largely divided into social inequality and social dissolution in addition to antisocial behaviors such as deviation(delay). Here, derailing refers to crime, delinquency, suicide, alcoholism, and drug addiction, and inequality refers to poverty, unemployment, alienation, regional gap, class conflict, deprivation, and distribution problems. Social dissolution can point out the dissolution of families such as poor families, and the dissolution of local communities such as red light districts, pleasure districts, and slums, and national dissolution.

However, today, the subject of social welfare is expanding to all members of society. Modern people living in industrial society are expected to increase their welfare equity in modern society, as well as the risk of destruction of labor reproduction due to poverty, disease, overcrowding, traffic accidents, and other new pollution.

In particular, since countries aiming for a modern welfare state have higher public expectations for social welfare, it is expected that the improvement of equity to improve welfare will increase.

2. Approach to Social Welfare

Social welfare can be divided into a policy approach, a professional approach, and an integrated approach as an approach to achieving its purpose.

1) Policy Approach

The policy approach to social welfare is a view shown as a social policy that solves social problems caused by structural contradictions in capitalist society and economic system. This view is that social welfare should be developed by national policy as the responsibility of the state or society rather than the individual responsibility of social problems. This method emerged mainly when modern capitalist countries adopted the welfare state model, and is based on the basic right to live or to guarantee human life by improving the overall living and welfare level of all citizens.

In addition, this method is generally recognized as "**social welfare policy**", "**social security system**", or "**social security**" and emphasizes totality in terms of guaranteeing the human life of all citizens subject to social welfare. Therefore, it can be said that fixation is very strong rather than flexibility. As this policy approach, social welfare policies can generally be classified into social insurance, public assistance, and social welfare services.

2) Professional Approach

The professional approach is a view shown as a technique for adjusting human relationships to individual personality defects. This defines human needs as a crisis or a problematic situation, and believes that the subject of the problem arises from maladjustment or dissatisfaction with desire. The characteristics of this method emphasize human dignity and understanding of human behavior, and have been formed on the premise of the absolute conviction of American capitalism and the maintenance of a liberal economic system.

As a professional approach to social welfare, it is generally recognized as a "**social welfare method**" and is characterized by flexibility because it emphasizes the individuality of social welfare targets. As this professional approach, social welfare methods are classified into individual social projects, collective social projects, community welfare, social welfare administration, social welfare policy, and social welfare surveys. However, as the current social welfare trend, there is a tendency to recognize the limitations of individual social welfare service methods and ignore individual social work itself.

(1) Integrated Approach

Stump(1970) argued that "*the traditional approach has taken the form of partially cutting off and assisting only the problems that can be adequately handled from the social worker's perspective rather than intervening overall in the client's life.*"

In order to improve problem-solving skills, all possible approaches of policy(micro) and professional(microscopic) must be mobilized. This is because the policy approach and professional approach have their own ability to solve social problems. Therefore, both policy and professional approaches have affinity in terms of problem-solving, and the integrated method is to improve problem-solving ability by comprehensively accepting them in social welfare. Therefore, either a professional or policy approach to social welfare cannot work with one approach, so there may be two preferential applications and either approach may be more emphasized, but it should not depend on one approach. In other words, social welfare targets today carry out various business activities according to age, gender, region, nature of the problem, and type of service function, and the area of activity that classifies and organizes these business activities according to certain criteria is regarded as a field of social welfare. In summary, it can be said that integrating the professional approach to social welfare and the policy approach is the social welfare field.

The main perspective of the integrated method is: Individuals in the environment(social welfare practice is concerned with the interaction between humans and the social environment that affects people's ability to achieve life tasks, relieve pain, and realize wishes and values); General System Theory.

Part

II

Methodology for Social Welfare Practice

Chapter 5 Social Welfare Practice

In this chapter, we will look at the social welfare practice model in the concept and practice process of social welfare as an aid activity to solve countless social problems that appear in humans and the environment and improve the functions of individuals, families and communities.

In general, social welfare practice takes place at three levels. ① It is a one-to-one basis practice for individuals as a micro level. ② It is a practice for families and groups as a mezzo level. ③ As a macro level, it is a practice aimed at organizations and communities and a practice pursuing changes in social welfare-related laws and social welfare policies. It also includes micro-mezzo-level practice between micro-level practice and meso-level practice (Won, Suk-Jo, 2009).

1. Concepts of Social Welfare Practice

In order to understand social work practices, first of all, understanding the relationship between social welfare and social welfare practice precedes. If so, it is necessary to understand what social welfare is and what social welfare practice is. Social welfare is a systematic and organized activity to improve people's quality of life in its content. It is an organized system of social services and institutions that help members of society solve psychological, social, and economic problems and improve their potential and social functions to lead a happy and satisfactory life.

Therefore, if social welfare means ideology, social institution, and policy, social welfare practice can be seen as meaning services, practical skills, and professional practical activities to embody social welfare ideology. The purpose of social welfare practice is to promote or restore interactions between individuals and society that are beneficial to each other in order to improve the quality of life of everyone.

In this sense, Pincus and Minahan defined it as improving individual problem-solving skills and connecting social resources, services, and systems that provide opportunities. The Council of Social Work Education(CSWE) aims to promote, restore, and maintain the social functions of individuals, families, small groups, organizations, communities, plan and implement social policies, services, resources, and programs to develop human potential. In other words, social welfare practice is a professional aid activity that includes policies, administration, institutions, and services to solve needs and problems caused by human-environmental interactions, and can be said to be a practical activity to strengthen problem-solving functions.

2. Integrated Methods and Perspectives of Social Welfare Practice

1) Integrated Method

The perspective of Person in Environment, one of the basic principles of social welfare practice, emphasizes the need for a multifaceted and integrated approach, and critics have begun to criticize that it is not effective in solving complex problems caused by human-environmental interactions. An integrated approach means integration of methods by providing common principles or concepts that all social workers can use to cope with social problems raised in individuals, groups, and communities. In other words, it means educating traditional methods in whole or in part, or in combination of at least two, so that one social worker can intervene in clients using two or more methods integrally.

The main systems of social welfare practice are change agent system, social worker and employees of his facility, institution, and employment organization, client system, target system, people in need of impact or change, local resident leaders, neighborhood experts, etc. Goldstein combines a social system model, a social learning or problem-solving model, and especially a course model. The problem-solving model has been developed by Perlman in the 1950s and has been further refined by Compton and Galaway, which introduced an ecological perspective in 1975. Pearlman expressed the active components of the problem-solving model in 4P. In other words, it utilizes a series of processes that provide resources necessary for problem solving when a person with a problem comes to a place to get help. The life model was developed in the early 1970s by Germain and Gitterman by introducing an ecological perspective as a theoretical framework, focusing on human- environmental interactions and integrating practice principles and technologies that can intervene in various systems such as individuals, groups, and communities.

2) Main point of view

(1) Ecological Perspective

Emphasis is placed on the view of humans in the environment by emphasizing interactions occurring between various parts and in the shared domain of organisms and the environment. This is recognized as a perspective that helps to systematically assess and evaluate social phenomena rather than presenting specific intervention methods or techniques to social workers.

(2) Strength Perspective

It focuses on enabling more social adaptation by strengthening the potential, talent, and qualities of clients. The most important characteristic of the strength perspective is that social workers see their abilities and strengths rather than their clients' flaws.

(3) Empowerment Perspective

The integrated approach of social welfare practice values the ability and potential of clients, focuses on the relationship of the environment, and emphasizes participation and individualization. In particular, it emphasizes empowerment that clients can cope with on their own. The term empowerment is interpreted as the ability to get what one wants, the ability to influence the thoughts, feelings, and actions of others. The dictionary meaning of empowerment is defined as empowerment, ability development, possibilities, grants, and permits. The empowerment perspective appears to be applicable to various target groups, and it is confirmed to be effective, especially for youth groups and residents of accommodation facilities.

3. Role of Social Workers

In the field of social welfare practice, social workers must acquire not only professional knowledge but also theory that increases the possibility of problem solving, but also psychological and mental health knowledge is required because it is a comprehensive study of social welfare. It is important to have such practical knowledge, but it is even more important to play a professional role in the client's aid process. Therefore, from this point of view, social workers should be able to play the following roles to help social welfare recipients. It can be explained by dividing into assistants, arbitrators, integrators, managers, educators, analysts, arbitrators, facilitators, negotiators, and advocates.

4. Principles of Social Welfare Practice(Relational Theory of Social Welfare Practice)

In order for social workers to help social welfare recipients, the following seven professional principles must be observed. This is emphasized by Felix Biestek and is also called the relational theory of social welfare practice. In social welfare practice, Biestek describes the relationship as "*a link between clients and social workers or social resources that helps them properly mobilize and utilize individual capabilities and community resources to better adapt themselves to the environment surrounding them*"(Biestek, 1957).

1) Individualization

Individualization is the recognition and understanding of the unique qualities of a client, and uses different principles or methods to help each individual. In other words, it is based on the principle that humans are individual and should be treated as specific humans with their own differences, not as identical humans.

2) Intentional Expression of Emotion

Intentional expression of feeling refers to the need to help clients freely express not only positive emotions but also negative emotions. Therefore, social workers should deliberately listen to these emotional expressions and should not interfere or criticize them. Sometimes, if necessary, it stimulates, but it should encourage more.

3) Controlled Emotional Involvement

Controlled emotional involvement means that social workers must be sensitive to client emotions, understand the meaning of those emotions, and respond appropriately with the purpose of client emotions. Social workers are emotionally involved in responding to the client's emotions, and should be directed according to the overall purpose of the case, the client's desire for change, and active thinking and properly controlled emotional involvement.

4) Acceptance

Acceptance refers to a principle of behavior in which a social worker understands and accepts a client's strengths and weaknesses, desirable and negative characteristics, positive and negative emotions, constructive and destructive behaviors and attitudes without criticism. At this time, it is necessary to maintain the concept of the dignity of the client and the value of its personality. However, acceptance does not mean acknowledging an attitude or behavior that deviates from the normal path. The object of acceptance is not a choice, but a true one as it is. Therefore, criticism and moral judgment of right and wrong are prohibited.

5) Nonjudgmental Behavior

Non-judgment should not be overly conclusive about whether or not the client is responsible for the cause of the client's problems or desires, or to what extent, if any. This is because most clients who come to seek help are often afraid of being criticized, so they can be extremely sensitive to evaluation. However, it is necessary to make an evaluation judgment on the client's attitude, behavior, and value standards. This is not to criticize the client, but to help and understand the client.

6) Self-Determination

Client self-determination refers to the ability of clients to make their own choices and decisions in social welfare facilities and living processes. According to this principle, the job of a social worker is to help clients discover and utilize all the necessary resources, respect client decisions, and maximize their potential. However, the client's right to self-determination is limited by the client's ability, legal and moral boundaries, or the scope of activities of social welfare institutions.

7) Confidentiality

Confidentiality is the basic needs of the client, so social workers have an ethical obligation to protect the client's secrets. If there is no faith in confidentiality, human relationships in social welfare facilities cannot be established, and effective results are difficult to expect. However, there are cases where the confidentiality of the client cannot be guaranteed absolutely. For example, in order to solve the problem, there are cases where it is necessary to request cooperation or support from other experts or related persons, and in this case, the obligation of confidentiality to all employees is expanded and applied. As discussed above, individual social workers should recognize all social welfare recipients as individualized persons with unique qualities, help them with positive emotions and negative emotions(intentional emotional expression), and respond appropriately(control and emotional involvement).

5. Case Management

1) Concept

In advanced welfare countries such as the United States, the United Kingdom, and Japan, the term "**case management**" has been used since the 1980s. The approach is based on the connection between needs and resources, to ensure sufficient care on the client side, and to reduce and streamline costs on the supplier side.

Case management is not a new form of practice that is completely different from traditional social work methodology, but rather an integrated approach or model that provides a more comprehensive and continuous service to clients(Jung, Min-Sook et al., 2009). While traditional social welfare projects are based on institutional services and programs, case management is distinguished in that it emphasizes active community-level service provision and inspection focusing on client needs. Roberts-DeGennaro, 1987 pointed out that "*the concept of case management combines the best direct service practice idea with the best community practice idea for a particular risk object,*" and O'Connor (1988) noted that "*case management is one of the core social business techniques." According to the American Association of Social Workers*(NASW, 1984), "*case management is defined as a mechanism that ensures a comprehensive program that satisfies individual needs by coordinating and connecting elements in the service delivery system.*"

Case management is a client-centered service, and the other is active community protection. Therefore, case management can be said to be a method of continuous and integrated intervention in changing the individual and surrounding environment so that individuals with problems can lead to function recovery and improvement. Casework aims to achieve specific goals through relationships between social workers and clients, while case management is a direct service to establish specific and limited intervention goals and change the client or surrounding environmental intervention.

The importance of case management in the field of social welfare is as follows. ① Provide clients with a minimal regulated environment. ② The goal is for clients to escape facility protection. ③ Try to ensure that clients live in the community as much as possible. ④ Try to reduce the cost of protection provided to clients. ⑤ protect resource acquisition capabilities and rights ⑥ It reduces the perspective of a medical model that defines client problems as 'disease' and 'treatment'. ⑦ It provides complex services and expansion of human service programs.

2) Purpose and Intervention Principles of Case Management

Case management is to organize, coordinate, and maintain a network of formal and informal resources and activities to meet the needs of complex needs, including ensuring continuity of protection, increased service delivery effectiveness and accountability, and integration of client life skills and self-protection systems.

3) Components of Case Management

Case management consists of case management(e.g., clients who need long-term care such as the elderly and mentally handicapped) social resources (e.g., family, relatives, neighbors, friends(colleagues), volunteers, social welfare corporations, social welfare services) case managers(e.g., social workers, nurses, physical therapists, etc.)

4) Case Management Process

The family tree is a diagram of the family relationship of two to three generations to determine the cause of the currently presented problem, and it should be prepared by social workers and clients together. In addition, the family tree is a diagram showing the biological, legal, and mental relevance of each family member from one generation to the next. This describes the relationship between members so that the family type can be grasped in a short time. Ecology is an important tool for planning specific problems and interventions by representing meaningful relationships and systems in a client's situation, and like a family tree, social workers and clients draw together. The ecological map shows how many external systems the family has in the community, the degree of isolation, and the quality of the relationship, allowing them to understand the degree of connection and adaptation with the outside world. Social charts are pictures that express interactions between members in groups using symbols, and are developed by Moreno and Jennings as techniques used to evaluate personal acceptance and rejection between members and interpersonal relationships within the group.

Chapter 6 Social Welfare Practice Techniques

In general, social work tends to be understood in a practical sense, and social welfare tends to be understood in an institutional sense. The purpose and object of social work are aimed at humans and are intended to be supported through technology. Therefore, compared to social welfare, it has a passive meaning, and can be said to be therapeutic, microscopic, and individual.

The social project practice technology method includes individual social projects, collective social projects, and community welfare projects classified around the target, which are called the three representative practice methods of social project technology. However, in modern social welfare practice, it is gradually being excluded from practical technology due to various limitations of individual social projects.

1) Key Model

The main model of individual social work methods is that social workers and clients lead the case process in a 1:1 manner. According to Roberts & Nee(1970), models of individual social work include psychosocial approach models, functionalist models, problem solving models, behavior modification models, and crisis intervention models(Choi, Ok-Chae, 2010).

(1) Psychosocial Approach Model

The perspective of this model is based on system theory. The diagnosis and treatment attempted in this approach focuses on the interaction between humans and their external environment. In this model, it is emphasized that treatment should be changed by the needs. Therefore, social workers should accept clients according to the agreement to improve the welfare of clients, have a "**other-centered**" relationship that prioritizes client needs, and abandon prejudice and understand the client as a scientific form.

(2) Functionalist model

It was developed by professors of the Department of Social Welfare at the University of Pennsylvania in the 1930s. This approach emphasizes an understanding of human nature, an understanding of the purpose of social welfare practice, and an understanding of the concept of the process. Since the functionalist approach is based on growth psychology, change was viewed as client-centered, not social worker-centered, and the purpose of social welfare practice is to influence the healthy personal and social conditions given to clients, and to help the entire process through social welfare practice institutions.

(3) Problem-Solving Model

It means not manipulating people, objects, and the environment to solve the client's difficulties, but developing and promoting exchanges between active social workers, clients, and the surrounding environment. Therefore, one of the points emphasized in this model is the fact that those who feel problems, carry problems, and experience problems are clients who want to get help. The problem-solving model emphasizes that the client's problem-solving is possible through the client and with the client, with the client's power.

(4) Behavior Modification Model

It was naturally developed as individual social workers paid attention to this field as knowledge and practice of behavioral correction emerged. Individual social workers have come to use the behavior modification model to change or sustain the specific behavior of the client. For example, this model is applied to give stickers to children if they model their assignments or daily lives, and to give them sketchbooks when they bring a certain number of stickers. This model is based on the principles of learning theory emphasized in behaviorist theory to change the inappropriate behavior or thinking of clients.

(5) Crisis Intervention Model

It was in the 1960s that the crisis theory and the application of this theory suddenly became interested in the practice of short-term individual social projects. In theory, crisis intervention is based on various theories of human behavior, including psychoanalysis theory. The goal of crisis intervention is to resolve the crisis facing clients. It psychologically resolves the crisis facing the client, so it restores at least the level of functional performance that the client had preserved before the crisis.

2) Process of Individual Social Work

Individual social projects can be expected to be effective by systematically developing them according to a certain process. A brief look at each step of this process is as follows.

(1) Step 1: Acceptance Step(Intake)

The first step(intake) is the step of first contacting a person who has come to get help and determining which institution can satisfy his or her needs. An important part of the first stage is the formation of rapport with clients, which means a 'joint of hearts', meaning a state in which each other's minds are connected, that is, a state in which they communicate with each other. When Rapport is formed, a good feeling and trust can be created, and even deep stories in the heart can be verbalized. Therefore, what needs to be addressed importantly at this stage is, first, to clarify the nature of the problem that the client has, and to identify the importance and cause of the problem. Second, identify the efforts, methods, and expectations that clients have tried so far for their problems. Third, it is to provide guidance on the contents and procedures of help that can be provided by the institution and to arrange institutions that meet its needs.

(2) Phase 2: Evaluation and Planning Phase

In the second step, the problem of the client is diagnosed and information and data related thereto are collected. Here, data refers to information on the development of clients(e.g., history of illness, personality, etc.), basic personal information, and family relationships, and after data and information related to the problem are collected, planning activities for intervention.

Important tasks at this stage include diagnosing client problems(setting scope of resolution goals), collecting data related to client problems, assessment of collected data, and planning for client task assignment for goal selection. Situation is a key step in the social welfare practice process that explores what the problem and cause of the subject is, and what can be changed to alleviate and solve the problem. Therefore, the circumstances provide the basis for establishing an intervention plan for social workers by investigating the subject's needs or resources for solving problems. Household and ecological maps are mentioned as the tools for circumstances. The family tree is to chart the family relationship of two to three generations to determine the cause of the currently presented problem. As a diagram of the biological, legal, and emotional relevance of each family member from one generation to the next, it is a very important tool for finding and insight into repeated types of relationships between generations. Ecology provides a focus on exploring information on the relationship between family stressors and environmental systems and planning interventions in the resource systems needed to help clients. These systems may include expanded families, friends, schools, judicial institutions, social welfare institutions, churches, workplaces, and medical institutions. Therefore, since the ecological map focuses on 'human beings in the environment', it helps to understand from an ecological perspective.

(3) Step 3: Intervention

When the client's problem is assessed and diagnosed, specific activities for problem solving are carried out. In the third stage, which is a core process of the individual social project practice process, social project practice knowledge and skills, and possible community resources are mobilized, and the role of social workers is most important at this stage.

(4) Step 4: Finalization and Evaluation

Considering that the client's problem has been resolved, as a process of closing the consultation, social workers must make sensitive choices at this stage, and they must be able to accurately determine when to close. If it was terminated at an appropriate time, it should take time to evaluate the entire intervention process. In the evaluation, how much the client has changed through intervention, and in terms of time and cost, the evaluation results must be recorded through feedback.

2. Social Welfare Practice Skills for Groups

1) Definition of Collective Social Work

The social group work is a deliberate assistance process conducted through small group activities to meet the needs of objects with a desire to restore damaged social functions or to strengthen their current social functions more actively.

Therefore, since the power of interaction appears actively on the premise that group members exchange dynamic influences, the mindset, behavior, and other self-awareness or lifestyle of the members of the group can be changed.

To this end, experts recognize the power of group interaction and actively and intentionally utilize it to help the subject solve the problems facing the individual or group.

2) Components of Collective Social Work

The basic elements of collective social work are group members, group programs, experts, etc., and there are six components by adding places and purposes to them, but looking at the four components, it is roughly as follows.

(1) Group Membership

Collective social work ultimately focuses on individual group members. Therefore, experts should have sufficient understanding through individualization of each group member.

(2) Group

A group does not simply refer to a state of being a collection of individuals, but a mutual relationship between group members should be premised. A group refers to a group of two or more people who have a certain membership, belong to the same group, have a common purpose or interest, are interdependent in achieving these goals, interact through communication, cognition, and reaction, and have the ability to perform a single action. In the end, since it means a group in which movement as an organism is expected, the dynamic of the group itself has a great influence on individuals belonging to the group.

(3) Program

The program is both the core of the collective social project and the main factor that determines the content of the collective experience. These programs are the entire process from preparation to evaluation, including interaction and my experience as activities that are carefully planned and executed within the group to respond to individual and group needs. Through this, it is possible not only to promote active interrelationships between group members, but also to achieve the purpose of giving abundant group experience and social adaptability to help growth.

(4) Expert

Experts should identify the situation of the group and the needs of their own needs or group members, determine the scope of activities, and develop the program according to the purpose of the group. Therefore, experts play various roles, such as those who make it possible, those who make changes, resource providers, or intermediaries.

3) Social Welfare Practices for Groups

(1) Basic Principles of Collective Social Welfare Practice

The basic principles of collective social project practice proposed by Konopka(1963) are as follows. ① Each individual's unique differences are presented and acted accordingly(individualization of each member within the group). ② To recognize the characteristics of a group and act accordingly (group) characterization). ③ It truly accepts that each member has both advantages and disadvantages. ④ Establish an intentional aid relationship between experts and members. ⑤ Encourage the establishment of cooperative relationships among group members. ⑥ Appropriate modifications are made to the collective process. ⑦ Encourage each group member to participate according to his or her ability and help improve his or her ability. ⑧ Group members are encouraged to participate in the problem-solving process on their own. ⑨ As the members solve the problem, they gradually experience a satisfactory way to resolve the conflict. ⑩ Provide opportunities for new and diverse experiences of personal relationships and achievements. ⑪ Use the program intentionally or differently based on diagnostic assessment of each individual or overall situation. ⑫ For each member, group purpose, and appropriate social purpose, use the program intentionally or differently based on the diagnostic evaluation. ⑬ Continuous evaluation of individual and collective processes is used. ⑭ Utilize the smooth, humane, and well-trained self of experts.

(2) Collective Social Welfare Practice Technique

Philips explained four techniques for making collective behavior efficient as follows. ① It is a technique that utilizes the functions of institutions. It is the role of experts to help individuals and groups develop toward their goals. It is the role of experts to help individuals and groups develop toward their goals. Therefore, the purpose and limitations of the institution must be informed to individuals and groups, ensure that the institution is fully utilized, and have the ability to clearly grasp the function of the institution and use it to achieve the purpose of the individual and group. ② It is important to express and communicate emotions with a technique for communicating emotions. This requires the ability to feel others, so experts must have both an improvisational and outgoing side and a planned, controlled, and introverted side. Experts especially help members find positive emotions and experiences among the emotions they express. ③ As a technique that utilizes reality, activities must start from the interest of reality. Currently, it is a wheel that promotes growth, and everyone has the ability to grow, so experts should have faith in achieving this. ④ It is a technique that encourages and uses collective relationships. Encourage and intentionally utilize group relationships that include experts to achieve individual and group goals. It allows them to discover and occupy their own parts in relationships with other members, and experts should know how to suppress themselves. This can be done on the basis of trust, enabling members to interact and make interpersonal relationships more creative by giving them the opportunity to feel stronger their values and move toward responsibility and contribution as a part of the group.

3. How to Practice Social Welfare for Local Communities

1) Concept of Community Welfare

The concept of a community has long been used in terms of functions and institutions performed by the community, but is used differently depending on the emphasis on its properties. In other words, the definition of a geographic community, the definition of a functional community(referring to common interests and functions such as ideology, hobby, school ties, delay, religion, etc.), and the community as a virtual space of computers and the Internet in the 21st century.

Community well-being is a very comprehensive concept that refers to all social efforts by experts or non-experts to prevent and solve community problems. It is a way of social welfare that requires planning and coordination of health, housing, income, education, and other social services.

In this regard, according to Dunham, community welfare is a conscious process by social interaction and emphasized that it is a method of social welfare that pays attention to several of the following purposes.

① The community solves the problem of widespread use by coordinating and maintaining the needs of local residents and related resources.

② Help develop, strengthen, and maintain the ability of residents to participate, self-determination, and cooperate to effectively cope with their own problems.

③ It is aimed at causing changes in the relationship between the community and the group and the distribution of decision-making ability.

In addition, according to M. Ross, community welfare means that the community discovers its needs and goals on its own and internally mobilizes the resources needed to achieve them to implement them. In particular, it is explained as a process of expanding and developing cooperative and common attitudes and practices in the community.

Taken together, the opinions of scholars can be roughly summarized as follows. Community welfare can be summarized as an activity to adjust the differences between local residents' needs and local resources by mobilizing the internal and external resources of the community as much as possible to solve social problems that all local residents can sympathize with.

Therefore, community welfare can be said to be a kind of technical process that helps local residents systematically solve various problems that arise as a unit of community among professional methods of social welfare. Above all, the ultimate purpose of community welfare is a technical practice method to realize the most ideal society.

2) Understanding of Community Welfare

Community welfare is a comprehensive institutional concept for improving local welfare along with local governments, and is meaningful because it corresponds to community-centered organizational efforts to prevent and solve community problems by intervening at the community level.

In particular, community welfare is significant in that unlike other social welfare fields, state-led social welfare has developed mainly in Anglo-American countries that have emphasized the resource sector rather than a solid European continent.

3) History of Community Welfare

Based on the political and social ideologies of each country, we will examine the historical background of community welfare development through the times and backgrounds that led to the transition to community welfare, and from community welfare.

(1) In the Case of England,

The UK has used community welfare as a concept encompassing community protection and facility protection, but since the 1950s, community care has emerged as a core policy task of community welfare due to negative evaluation of facility protection. In the 1960s, the UK developed community protection centered on the public sector, that is, local government, and in the 1980s, due to the reduction of fiscal expenditure in the social welfare sector under the neo-conservative ideology, the role of the public sector was reduced and emphasized. And the current community welfare is characterized by the appropriate emphasis on the role of the public and private sectors.

The UK has led the legislation of community welfare since the Old Poverty Act, which is the historical origin of community welfare, and has also launched the C.O.S. movement and the settlement movement, the beginning of specialized community welfare in the practical sense of social welfare.

It also shows various processes of developing community welfare ahead of other countries, including the formation of local government agencies to carry out community welfare under state responsibility after World War II, establishment of a professional social project system, and expansion of community protection services. This series of development processes influenced the development of community welfare in Japan.

(2) In the Case of Japan,

Japan uses the term '**regional welfare**' shortly, and the period and background of community welfare have a historical background similar to that of Korea. However, there is a difference in that community welfare is being carried out after institutional support and the need for community welfare has increased as a countermeasure against the aging of the population.

There are these environmental differences. Therefore, if you look at the case of the UK, the historical origin of regional welfare can be found in the charity association and the human resources movement in the late 19th century. And in the United States, it was established as a post-World War I community fundraiser, post-Great Depression public welfare work, and a war on poverty in the 1960s. In addition, the initial form of regional welfare around the world emphasized community organizations. Community organizations cover regional development, social planning, and social behavior, of which community development refers to the government's determination and guidance of policies for the development of the local community. It was proposed by the United Nations in the 1950s as part of a development plan for developing countries, but today there is a tendency to improve welfare through regional activities, including developed countries. It is also in line with the Saemaul Movement in Korea in that it improves social life through local activities.

The new emphasis on regional welfare since the late 1970s is closely related to the shift in social welfare interests from solving economic poverty to solving various life problems. In a traditional society, social welfare had no choice but to make efforts to solve economic poverty. However, due to changes in economic society and changes in people's lives and consciousness, not only economic poverty but also various life problems have emerged as social welfare tasks. Since then, the task of social welfare has been different from the economic deficiency, and its characteristics have been different depending on the form and situation of individuals, families, and communities, and its occurrence has been individual and diverse.

Along with these changes in social welfare needs, the decline in family support functions and lack of social solidarity have emerged as serious social problems, expanding the needs of life to be solved socially, increasing the overall demand for social welfare. In this sense, regional welfare is also a new style of social welfare. In other words, in traditional society, social welfare should be changed to establish a home welfare system(called "home welfare" in Japan) in which everyone, including the elderly, the disabled, and the patients, can live happily in their communities. Therefore, local welfare is characterized by the fact that it is possible to receive appropriate services in the house or region where one lives, not selectively provided to a small number of subjects, but universally provided to most citizens. Local welfare centered on home welfare has been steadily developed because various interpersonal services for the elderly and the disabled in need of care, not response to monetary needs such as poverty, must be provided at all times in the community.

(3) In the Case of Korea

In Korea, it can be said that it has been a professional community organization project in a modern sense since the 1960s based on the spirit of Hyangyak, Gye, and Dure. It began in 1958, when the Community Development Committee was officially established, and in 1972, it was embodied in the 3rd Five-Year Economic Development Plan, and on the other hand, it blossomed with the Saemaul Movement. Through the 1980s and 1990s, professional community welfare or community organization projects began to be implemented as the U.S. professional community education principles and programs flowed into the market.

4) Contents of Local Welfare Service

(1) home welfare service	Preventive Services: Services to prevent falling into protective conditions Professional Protective Services: Higher levels of medical/nursing, rehabilitation, education, counseling and quality new variables Home Protective Services: Family Volunteer Service, Support for Walking, etc. Welfare Promotion Services: Promoting Social Participation of the Elderly/Disabled, Cultural Program Activities
(2) environmental improvement service	Improvement of physical conditions to maintain basic living, such as health and work, improvement of buildings/road, and improvement of institutional requirements to promote social participation, etc. of guardians in need of social welfare services.
(3) organizational activity	Regional organization: Creating a community welfare by promoting participation and cooperation in the welfare of residents and changing consciousness and attitudes Welfare Organization: Organizing and creating services, maintaining the service supply system, and promoting effective operation using social administration techniques.

5) Role of Community Service Workers

The role of community welfare workers in community welfare practice is very important. Looking at the role of community welfare workers, they play the role of guides, assistants, experts, therapists, analysts, planners, organizers, administrators, and actors.

Chapter 7 Social Welfare Investigation

1. Concepts of Social Welfare Survey

Social welfare research refers to a procedure for finding ways to solve social problems and calculating knowledge that can be used to plan and implement social welfare programs as a way to perform the purpose of social welfare. Here, research is generally intended to reveal the causal relationship between natural and social phenomena, and is mainly expanding its scope in social science. In particular, it can be said that it is a process of creating a new theory by proving causality realistically through objective scientific standards. The conceptual characteristics of this combined with social welfare are as follows.

On the premise of the exploratory meaning of social phenomena, the social welfare survey(method) theory aims to objectively investigate the relationship between humans and society because it is a scientific inquiry activity to prove causality to solve social welfare-related social needs and social problems.

Therefore, emphasizing the importance of social welfare investigation theory can be seen as an effort to establish a theoretical system.

2. Types of Social Welfare Survey

Why are we doing research? It is the ultimate purpose of the investigation to seek reliable and systematic knowledge of this question.

Therefore, the purpose of this investigation is subdivided as follows.

1) exploration of specific social phenomena and problems that exist in society
2) description of a group or event or phenomenon
3) explanation of the causal relationship between variables and variables
4) hypothesis verification

5) prediction of future events
6) development of social indicators
7) evaluation

Variables refer to certain characteristics to be studied, and they have at least two or more diverse values and have changing characteristics. It is hypothesis to show the relationship between these variables and variables. Variables, which are elements of the hypothesis, are characteristics of the object to be observed and are divided into several categories such as education level, average monthly income, and gender. Hypothesis is a tentative answer to a research problem and refers to the relationship between an independent variable and a dependent variable. Hypotheses are generally described as 'if ~ if ~, ~' and can be derived from existing theories, constructed through direct observation or intuition, and sometimes synthesized. ① The hypothesis must be clear. ② Hypothesis should be value-neutral. ③ What needs to be specified is not just the presence or absence of a relationship, but also the direction of the relationship. ④ It must be empirically verifiable.

1) Categorization according to the Purpose of the Survey

In this regard, the types of social welfare methods are divided into the following and explained in detail as follows.

(1) Exploratory Research

An exploratory study refers to a preliminary survey and refers to a survey conducted before a full-fledged survey. Therefore, it refers to what is used to gain new insights into the field and hypothesize when there is little known content on the research topic. The results obtained here need to be reconfirmed through new research reflection(Research method). Exploratory research belongs to a preliminary basic process for more systematic research in the future.

Exploratory surveys basically include literature surveys and expert surveys. Literature research is a review of literature related to the research aid to be investigated, also called library research, which can be named because the work is done in the library because it is a process of finding existing published literature. On the other hand, expert research is a method of collecting data by asking experts in the field for opinions on a given topic.

(2) Technical Research

Descriptive study is a description of an individual or social phenomenon, and explains the phenomenon by summarizing and recording a fact at a general level, but does not determine a causal relationship. Unlike exploratory surveys, it is often conducted after research problems and hypothesis establishment, and it takes the form of a fact-finding survey because it describes a simple reality for a phenomenon. Technical research include cross-sectional and longitudinal investigations.

(3) Explanatory Research

It is to clarify the causal relationship by establishing the relationship between one phenomenon and another phenomenon or the correlation between the independent variable and the dependent variable.

(4) Hypothesis-Verifying Research

It is an research to verify hypotheses that contain causal relationships between variables.

2) Breakdown according to Survey time

(1) Cross-Sectional Survey

Cross sectional study is designed to analyze a phenomenon across several parts(class, age, gender, etc.). Mainly exploratory and technical surveys are cross-sectoral studies. The census is a technical and cross-sectional survey of the Korean population at a specific time. The purpose of explanatory investigation is to investigate causal relationships that occur mainly over time. For example, a survey is conducted at some point in time to investigate whether there is a difference in the evaluation of the government's social welfare policy according to class, age, and residential area.

① Longitudinal Study

Longitudinal research is to observe over several points of time.

② Trend Study

Trend study is to study the changes that occur over time in a wide population. For example, the time difference between the 1990 census and the 2000 census is compared, or a monthly poll is conducted during the election period.

③ Peer-to-Peer Research

It is the cohort study that studies changes in any particularly designated population group. Usually, it is divided into groups by age. This is the case when people who were poor in 1990(not necessarily the same person) were surveyed for changes in life in 2000, or when people were surveyed for what they were living 30 years after the war.

④ Repeated Research

Panel study is to study the same person repeatedly. If you re-investigate and study the poor in 1990 in 2000, or if you conduct a monthly survey and study on who to vote for the same voter during the election period, it becomes a repetitive study.

(2) Pseudo-Terminal Study

A similar longitudinal survey is a survey conducted in consideration of the difficulty of investigating by a longitudinal survey method, and is designed to enable cross-sectional research through a one-time survey. For example, by conducting a cross-sectional survey and comparing and studying opinions on specific topics for each age group, it is possible to find out how the consciousness of the subject changes as generations progress from the past. For example, by conducting a cross-sectional survey and researching opinions on caring for parents for each age group, it is possible to infer changes in consciousness over a long period of time.

3) Categorization according to Data Collection Techniques

(1) Quantitative Research

It is a method of collecting quantified data through responses through questions to survey subjects. Quantitative surveys include questionnaire research, interviews, and experiments by controlling external variables and organizing independent variables to identify causal relationships. There are methods of obtaining new information using statistical data).

(2) Qualitative Research

Field studies(mainly small groups of people over a long period of time), in-depth interviews, group discussions, and Delphi techniques are used to collect in-depth data that are difficult to quantify for a small number of subjects or cases. As one of the intuitive prediction methods, it is a technique for predicting the future by synthesizing opinions and judgments of experts in the field. Often referred to as Delphi Technique, it was initially designed to reduce the inefficiency of gathering together and discussing with multiple people, to prevent decisions from being made by influential minority, and to overcome the difficulty of opposing colleagues' opinions. In the first step, a questionnaire is prepared by specifying the subject to be predicted, and experts related thereto are selected. In the second stage, the following questionnaire that organizes the contents of the first response and informs the first respondents is developed to re-research their opinions. In the third stage, various statistical techniques are used to finally organize the contents obtained during a series of investigations and predict the future by interpreting the results.

3. Social Welfare Survey Process

Social welfare research is conducted through a series of scientific procedures. The characteristics of each stage are as follows.

1) Research Plan

Setting up a problem is a step to set the direction of the overall scientific research, and is the most important step to solve problems and seize opportunities that arise in carrying out social activities. If the problem is inappropriate, even if the investigation has been conducted perfectly, nothing can be expected of the results obtained from the investigation. In order to prevent this phenomenon, it is necessary to set a correct investigation problem.

Therefore, the analysis of the problem itself to be solved through the investigation and the background against which such a problem occurred should be clearly.

Once the research problem is set, not only the identification of various variables to be used in a specific research, but also the establishment of hypotheses or literature review of the relationship between these variables should be conducted at the same time.

2) Research Design

The research design can be said to be a blueprint for performing and controlling the entire investigation. Kerringer(F.N., Kerlinger) defines research design in a broad sense as "*the entire process of planning to obtain a valid answer to the investigation problem.*" K.D. Bailey defines the survey design in a narrow sense as "*a step of determining how to measure hypothesis variables and the group to verify hypothesis after survey problems and hypotheses are established.*" The investigation design is to design the entire investigation process, such as planning and determining the investigation targets (population), samples, investigation methods, measurements and scales, data processing and analysis methods, and report results. The survey design is structured with a focus on saving time and money and increasing the efficiency of the survey.

3) Data Collection

The data collection step is a step of directly collecting data according to the data collection method adopted in the research design. Scientific research data are largely divided into primary and secondary data. The primary data are data to be collected directly by the investigator during the investigation, and the secondary data are data already collected by a subject other than the investigator conducting the investigation. Data collection methods include observation method(participatory observation, quasi-participatory observation, non-participatory observation), questionnaire method(open and closed questions), and interview method. Participatory observation guarantees the naturalness and organic overallity of the observation object by entering the inside of the observation object and becoming a part of its members and observing while participating in communal life. Quasi-participatory observation is an observation method in which participants participate only in a part of life, not in all of the life of the observation object, like participatory observation. Non-participatory observation is a method of identifying and observing the status of an investigator, so it is mainly used for organizational observation.

4) Data Analysis

Analysis of data is usually performed using statistical techniques after the editing and coding process of the collected data is completed. Editing is a task to secure complete and consistent data to analyze according to the survey design, and data is corrected, supplemented, and deleted, and coding is a process of assigning a certain number to the observed content to facilitate data analysis.

Statistical analysis of data is selected in consideration of the purpose of the survey and the sampling method, data collection method, and measurement method used to obtain data. Since the statistical analysis method must have the form of data corresponding to it, it must be determined consistently with the nature of the data to be collected from the time the survey design is planned.

5) Report Preparation

The survey report summarizes the conclusions of the survey results in text or diagrams to help information users. At this time, it should be noted that communication between the user and the investigator must be smooth.

Part III Social Welfare Policy and System

Chapter 8 Social Welfare Policy

1. Concepts of Social Welfare Policy

What is social welfare policy? The concept of social welfare policy is defined in various ways by scholars, and the scope of social welfare policy is viewed differently by country. For example, in Germany, social welfare policies are viewed as social insurance, and in the UK, health care policies, education policies, and housing policies are included in social welfare policies.

In general, first of all, policy can be defined as an authoritative activity of the government to solve social problems. Based on this concept, the term policy can be divided into the following. First, all policies have goals, and according to those goals, administrative services are put into practice, so policies can be said to be goal-oriented. Second, it is the concept of a plan(=proposal). As this concept, policy has a plan or proposal to achieve its goal. Third, it is a program. This is a concrete and detailed plan to achieve the policy goals. Fourth, it is the concept of decision-making. All policies are effective because they are made by someone's decision. There can be no policy that does not take this effect into account. Regarding the ultimate research purpose of policy studies, Laswell says that it is to better solve the fundamental problems of human society and realize human dignity more faithfully.

The term social welfare policy has been first used by W.H. Riehl in 1854, and conceptual regulations, or definitions, vary according to the times and countries and according to scholars' opinions. Gilbert and Terrell, renowned U.S. social welfare policy scholars, said that it is a difficult concept to define social welfare policy, and that it is reasonable to understand the concepts of '**policy**' and '**social welfare**' by considering social welfare policy as a complex concept. Nam, Ki-Min said, "*The government intentionally chose the guidelines for action to achieve the goals of social welfare*"(Nam, Ki-Min, 2008).

The existence of these various policy concepts can coexist with social welfare, and since the concept of social welfare includes policy content in consensus, various views can be expressed in defining the conceptual content of social welfare policy.

However, the concept of social welfare policy considering such conceptual complexity generally has content of homogeneity in the following aspects. In other words, when it is said that the concept of social welfare includes policies and institutions, the combined concept can be expressed as one by including this conceptual aspect and the publicity of policy.

Therefore, social welfare policy can be interpreted as an authoritarian activity based on the legitimacy of the government to resolve social inequality.

It can be compared to other policies as a question of whether social welfare policies can exist as an independent academic domain. Different interpretations are required among scholars, but as a result of the long debate process, social welfare policy has not felt the value of research as a discipline. The reason is that in the case of social problems targeted by social welfare policies, it was expected that it would be virtually impossible to solve problems as independent studies due to mutual heterogeneity. In fact, social welfare policies passively mean poor policies, and actively represent almost all government policies based on income security. Therefore, the concept of social welfare policy can be defined in various ways according to the times, countries, and scholars, and the concept belongs to a fairly wide range of areas.

2. Areas of Social Welfare Policy

The concept of social welfare policy is variously defined according to the state, the times, and scholars, and accordingly, the areas of social welfare policy are inevitably classified in various ways. Then, how are the areas of social welfare policy divided, and what are the contents of each area?

In terms of classification, the areas of social welfare policy can be divided into areas of social welfare policy of consultation and social welfare policy of broad meaning. The social welfare policy areas of the consultation include the National Basic Livelihood Security System as public assistance, the public pension system using social insurance, and various allowance systems such as child allowance, old age allowance, and disability allowance. Social welfare policies can be divided into income, health, housing, interpersonal social welfare services, and education policies, including infant care, low-income middle and high school tuition support, school meals, industrial schools, and scholarship systems, and tax policies include negative income tax. And labor market policies include employment policy, wage policy, social security, and corporate welfare. Models for analyzing social welfare policies vary considerably. However, none of them are universally recognized or used in social welfare. This is because each model has different emphasis points, but most of them contain similar elements.

In this regard, the analysis framework of social welfare policies by Gilbert and Terrell is as follows.

1) What should be provided as a social provision?

Salaries provided with social welfare policies today can traditionally be divided into cash benefits and in-kind benefits. However, in reality, there are various forms and types of social welfare services. Therefore, there are six things: planning, services, goods, certificates, cash and power.

(1) Cash Benefits and Payment - In -Kind

Cash benefits can maximize the utility of recipients, so efficient allocation of social resources can be achieved when paying in cash. It is also an aspect of freedom of choice and consumer sovereignty. Cash benefits not only can reflect various tastes by expanding the range of recipient choices, but also protect the right to freedom or self-determination, which is a value that is very important in a democratic society itself. In addition, cash benefits are superior to payment - in-kind benefits to maintain human dignity, and the program costs less to operate than in-kind benefits, and it costs a lot to store, manage, and deliver in-kind benefits.

On the other hand, the advantage of spot benefits is that the target efficiency of the policy can be improved. Therefore, it is possible to more reliably increase those with needs and select those with needs, so that salaries can be intensively provided to those in need. It is also preferred in terms of politics over cash benefits. In general, taxpayers are interested in what purpose their taxes are used and what goals they have achieved, because in-kind benefits are relatively clear compared to cash benefits. In addition, cash benefits have a large economic effect on scale due to mass production and mass consumption, which can reduce program costs. For example, constructing large-scale public housing to pay recipients is less expensive than purchasing homes on the market by giving housing allowances.

(2) Six Types of Social Benefits

① Opportunities

In social welfare policy, opportunity benefits are in the form of direct social benefits, but they are ambiguous and abstract. Because social welfare policies relate to the creation and allocation of opportunities, unlike goods and services, opportunity benefits relate to citizenship or special allocation.

② Services

Services refer to all activities such as in-home protection, counseling, case management, and vocational training for clients. The service does not have a specific shape but is intangible, so it does not give immediate market value to beneficiaries. The commonality between case work and case management is that appropriate assessments are made for clients and resources, and individualization, client self-determination, and confidentiality are applied. The difference is that individual social projects focus on client problems, solve problems through personality development, and focus on social adaptation. Case management focuses on the complex needs of clients, and focuses on satisfying their needs and improving social functions through connection and coordination between clients and social resources.

③ Goods

Goods refer to products with specific shapes such as food, clothing, and housing, and the wages of goods have limited transfer and exchange values, so they are limitedly used within a limited range.

④ Certificate(Vouchers)

A ·certificate is a method that allows recipients to freely select the goods or services they want within a certain purpose. For example, food exchange rights in the United States can exchange a variety of food products, and education certificates can receive educational services at the institution of their choice.

⑤ Cash

Cash is a salary that provides unlimited purchasing power to purchase certain goods and services at any time, such as public assistance, child allowance, and social insurance.

⑥ Power

Power refers to the influence that can affect the control of goods and resources. For example, power can be obtained by transferring policymaking authority to a small number of people. Power is not consumed in a way such as cash or certificate, but it provides much more control over the socio-economic choices themselves than goods, services, and opportunities. Power has a fluid exchange value.

2) Who should be Provided with Benefits?

Social welfare policies mainly deal with intentional redistribution. In this regard, the principle is presented as attributive needs, compensation, diagnostic differences, and asset investigation needs in relation to the selection criteria for determining social welfare service targets.

(1) Attributive needs

Salary qualifications based on attributive needs depend on whether they belong to a group of people with common needs that have not been met under the current socioeconomic system.

(2) Compensation

Compensation-based salary qualifications are determined by whether they belong to a specific category or group. These include those who have made social and economic contributions, such as those who have paid insurance premiums, or those who suffer from social injustice such as racism or gender discrimination.

(3) Diagnostic Difference

Salary qualifications based on diagnostic differences are given to subjects judged by experts for individuals who need specific goods or services, such as physical and emotional disabilities. According to the Welfare of the Disabled· Act in Korea, the disability of the disabled is judged by disability classification and grade. In addition, various benefits are provided to the disabled through this judgment process.

(4) Property Investigation Needs

Salary conditions based on asset survey needs are given to individuals who cannot organize goods and services. Access to social benefits depends on individual economic conditions rather than the environment.

3) How should the Delivery System Pay be Provided?

In social welfare policy, when the target to be paid is determined, the question arises as to how to properly provide these benefits or services to the target. In other words, the importance of the social welfare delivery system is required, and the reason why the social welfare delivery system is important is because of public welfare provided by the government and private welfare provided by private institutions.

Public welfare refers to various social welfare policies implemented by the government. Income security, medical security, and housing security are included, and public elderly care systems have been introduced for the elderly in need of long-term care. Private welfare refers to non-governmental social welfare activities conducted by the private sector, such as individuals, non-profit social organizations, and companies. These include charity projects, the operation of social welfare institutions and facilities, and corporate social contribution activities.

4) How will Finance be Covered?

In social welfare policy, it is very important how to reasonably establish the financial resources necessary to achieve the organization's goals.

The financial resources of social welfare policy can be largely divided into public sector financial resources and private sector financial resources. Taxes account for the largest portion of the public sector's financial resources, while the private sector's financial resources include voluntary contributions, user burden, and occupational welfare. These resources are mainly raised and operated by the government and private organizations for the operation of social welfare organizations, but are not sufficient in reality.

4. New Trends in Social Welfare Policy

1) The Emergence of Neoliberalism Transforms Welfare into Pluralism.

Neoliberalism emerged when Keynesianism, which served as a driving force for the continued growth of the Western economy and the development of a welfare state, failed and faced a rapidly increasing fiscal crisis. After World War II, advanced Western countries achieved political stability and full employment with confidence that they could control capitalism's essential problems through Keynesian state intervention.

- The market is good, the country is bad.
- Strong trade unions and excessive social welfare have exhausted the vitality of capitalism.
- The neoliberal ideology is summarized as anti-socialism, anti-unionism, and repetitive nationalism.
- Neoliberalism systematically corroded the welfare state.
- The representative strategy of neoliberalism in social welfare policy was privatization.

As neoliberalism criticized the welfare state, it became an opportunity to bring about a change in the existing state-centered welfare supply system. The British Thatcher government and the U.S. Reagan government, which emerged in the 1980s, boldly reformed the line of state interventionism under the name of a welfare state and strongly introduced the elements of marketism in the public sector. These governments carried out strong institutional reforms aimed at a small government through market-oriented restructuring and tax reduction policies. At the government level, public sector reform, restructuring, and deregulation were carried out to eliminate administrative inefficiency, privatization of state-owned enterprises, and market openness were promoted. The welfare sector also transformed the welfare supply system into a form in which companies(market) and volunteer organizations are in charge of certain sectors rather than the state being fully responsible for the area of social welfare as in the past. Individual choices and market functions were emphasized in welfare, and welfare privatization and marketization were promoted. These actions by the British and American governments were ultimately intended to create a strong nation by pursuing small and efficient governments. This reform of the welfare system based on neoliberalism brought about well-being pluralism in which welfare creation and delivery are dominated by the mayor, civic groups, and family units in addition to the national domain. It is to diversify the subjects of welfare, but to avoid the supply of welfare centered on the existing central government and to make non-profit sectors, companies, and local governments as the subjects.

2) Seek a Third Way Based on Neoliberalism

Thatcher's Conservative government, which carried out major reforms in social welfare policy based on neoliberalism, handed over power to the Labor Party government led by Tony Blair in 1997. Blair promoted social welfare policy under the slogan The Third Way, theoretically organized by Anthony Giddens, who served as his brain. The 'third path' is a new policy line that integrates the past social democratic welfare policy line(first path: pursuing social equality) and the neoliberal welfare policy line(second path: emphasizing market efficiency).

Looking at the third path from a policy perspective, the basic policy line is to maintain and develop economic growth and social welfare at the same time while pursuing market efficiency and equity in social welfare(Moon, Soo-Yeol et al., 2010). In terms of welfare policy, collectivism, or decommodification, is pursued simultaneously within the capitalist market economy by pursuing individualism, that is, by pursuing commercialization, while realizing fair equality of opportunity and distributive justice. In this respect, the third path is pursuing a market economy. In addition, the third path emphasizes the role of welfare recipients as a leading entity in producing economic wealth while paying attention to social security and redistribution. In other words, in contrast to passive welfare recipients in the Beveridge era, the focus of policy is on establishing the status of active welfare citizens.

The active welfare strategy on the third road is the "social investment strategy." Representative examples of social investment strategies are measures for the elderly population and measures for unemployment. It is argued that the fixed retirement age should be abolished and the elderly population should be recognized as a resource rather than a problem. In unemployment measures, the government should actively support companies' job creation efforts, emphasize lifelong education, and support education necessary for job change. In addition, the active welfare strategy advocated on the third road can replace each passive element raised by Beveridge with an active one. They include autonomy instead of poverty, vitality, not disease, education instead of ignorance, well-being rather than filth, and initiative instead of laziness. The core of Blair's welfare reform is "**WELFARE TO WORK**." This is a transition from "**dependent welfare**" to "**independent welfare**," restoring the dignity of anyone to work, and ensuring that household income after employment does not decrease from social security benefits.

Chapter 9 Social Welfare Law

1. Concepts

The term social welfare law is a complex term of social welfare and law, and the concept of social welfare law is variously defined by scholars, so it is difficult to define it as one.

2. Purpose of the Social Welfare Act

1) Guarantee of Minimum Living Security

The primary purpose of the Social Welfare Act is to protect individuals from unexpected social risks and ensure that they can live at the lowest level. The state and society must provide public guarantees to meet the welfare needs of all citizens. The purpose of the Social Welfare Act is to ensure that all citizens can lead healthy and cultural lives and maintain a minimum of life through the Social Insurance Act, the Public Aid Act, the Social Welfare Service Act, and the Social Welfare-related Act.

2) Income Redistribution

In the purpose of the Social Welfare Act, if the resolution of wealth inequality is made in the process of income redistribution, social equity and integration can be achieved through indirect income transfer.

Article 34 (1) of the Constitution stipulates that "*all citizens have the right to live a human life*," and paragraph (2) of the same article stipulates that "*the state is obligated to guarantee this and strive to promote welfare.*" How actively each country practices social welfare is closely related to how much interest it has in social welfare laws. In practice, in order for the people to satisfy their social welfare needs through the exercise of welfare rights, it must be realized in detail through the Constitution and specific social welfare-related laws.

3. Legal System of Social Welfare Law

Korea adopts written law and focuses on the Constitution at the top, and the Framework Act on Social Security is enacted in its lower laws, and can be classified into the Social Insurance Act, the Public Aid Act, the Social Welfare Service Act, and the Social Welfare-related Act.

1) Constitution

The Constitution is a basic law on the rights and obligations between the state and the people, and the provisions of the Constitution on the right to live serve as the basis for the enactment of the subordinate law and serve as the highest law suggesting the direction of enactment. The Korean Constitution emphasizes the state's social policy obligations to ensure the effectiveness of this right while guaranteeing the right to live a human life for all citizens(Article 34 (1). In other words, the state has an obligation to strive to improve social security and social welfare(Article 34 (2)), to protect people without living ability(Article 34 (5)), to strive to improve women's welfare and rights(Article 34 (3)), and to prevent disasters.

2) Basic Social Security Act

The Framework Act on Social Security is a sub-concept of the social welfare regulations of the Constitution, the highest social welfare law in Korea, but other social welfare laws can be said to be a detailed expression of the contents of the Framework Act on Social Security. The Framework Act on Social Security aims to contribute to the promotion of the welfare of the people by defining the rights of the people and the responsibilities of the state and local governments regarding social security systems.

3) Social Insurance Act

The Social Insurance Act is a law on the operation and implementation of the social insurance system. Social insurance refers to a system that guarantees national health and income by coping with social risks arising from the public through insurance methods(Article 3, Article 2 of the Framework Act on Social Security). Korea's representative social insurance includes the National Pension Act, the National Health Insurance Act, the Industrial Accident Compensation Insurance Act, and the Employment Act, and from July 2008, the Long-Term Care Insurance Act for the Elderly was enforced and reborn as one of the top five social insurance countries. In addition, special job pension laws such as the Public Officials Pension Act, the Private School Teachers Pension Act, and the Military Pension Act are also in effect.

4) Public Aid Act

The Public Aid Act refers to a law that stipulates matters related to the implementation of a public assistance system. Public assistance refers to a system that guarantees the minimum life and supports independence of people who are unable to maintain their lives or have difficulty living under the responsibility of the state and local governments(Article 3, Paragraph 3 of the Framework Act on Social Security). In Korea, the National Basic Livelihood Security Act, the Medical Benefit Act, the Disaster Relief Act, the Act on Honorable Treatment and Support for National Merit, the Act on Protection and Settlement Support for North Korean Refugees, and the Act on Life Stability and Commemoration of Japanese Army victims.

5) Social Welfare Services Act

The Social Welfare Service Act refers to a law related to the direct provision of social welfare services. The term "social welfare service" specified in Article 2 Subparagraph 1 of the Social Welfare Service Act refers to various welfare activities, such as social welfare counseling, homelessness, vocational reporting, free accommodation, community welfare, medical welfare and so forth.

6) Social Welfare law

Social welfare-related laws refer to various welfare systems that support human-like living, such as the Public Health Management Act, the Rental Housing Act, the Minimum Wage Act, the Employment Equality and Work-Family Compatibility Support Act, and the Special Education Promotion Act.

4. Social Security Rights

1) Level of Social Security Benefits

Article 10 (3) of the Framework Act on Social Security stipulates that "*the state or local government should determine the level of social security benefits in consideration of the minimum cost of living and the minimum wage under the Minimum Wage Act.*" In this case, the level of social security benefits guaranteed by the state shall be the level of salary at which all citizens can maintain a healthy and cultural minimum life in order to specifically realize the "*right to live a human-like life*" under Article 34 (1) of the Constitution. The Minister of Health and Welfare announces the minimum living expenses for the following year after deliberation and resolution by the Central Living Security Committee by December 1 every year, and conducts a measurement survey necessary to determine the minimum living expenses every three years. Minimum wage refers to the minimum wage determined and promulgated by the Minister of Labor after deliberation by the Minimum Wage Committee in consideration of workers' living expenses, wages of similar workers, and labor productivity in order to contribute to the sound development of the national economy.

2) Application for Social Security Benefits

Article 11 (1) of the Framework Act on Social Security in Korea provides social security benefits based on applicationism by stipulating that "a person who intends to receive social security benefits must apply to the state or local government as prescribed by relevant laws and regulations. However, for the vulnerable who do not understand the purpose of the system, public officials sometimes decide the right to receive ex officio. The beneficiary must apply to an institution with legitimate authority, but if the beneficiary incorrectly applies to another institution, the institution must protect the right to social security as much as possible by transferring it to the legitimate institution without delay. In this case, the application for social security benefits is deemed to have been filed on the date of transfer to an institution with legitimate authority.

3) Protection of Social Security Benefits

The right to receive social security cannot be transferred or provided as collateral to another person as prescribed by relevant laws and regulations, and it cannot be seized, thereby providing full protection to the right to receive social security.

The right to receive social security cannot be restricted or suspended unless prescribed by law.

Even if restricted or suspended by laws and regulations, the restriction or suspension shall be limited to the minimum necessary for the purpose. In other words, the social security system achieves its legal purpose in terms of guaranteeing the right to live for the socially disadvantaged as much as possible, but allows recipients to restrict supply and demand requirements if they are illegal or contrary to social justice and style. Social security recipients may waive social security recipients by notifying legitimate authorities in writing unless the waiver of social security recipients damages others or violates related laws and regulations on social security. However, if the waiver of the right to receive social security benefits damages others or violates related laws and regulations on social security, it cannot be waived.

Chapter 10 Social Welfare Administration

1. Understanding Social Welfare Administration

1) Rise of Social Welfare Administration

Economic growth, low growth, labor shortages, and mass unemployment have been experienced in any industrial country, but Korea has not reflected such obvious historical lessons as a policy.

In particular, the lack of social security systems is causing great pain to both the people and the government in today's economic crisis. Each of the previous administrations made a loud slogan of welfare and social construction, but they did not achieve much development except for the medical security system and social welfare services.

The biggest reason why our economic and social conditions have become difficult is that leaders have always put only economic logic first in establishing national policies and have been too obsessed with the goal of high economic growth even if they overdo it.

The perception that appropriate social welfare policies are indispensable for improving the quality of life of the people should be firmly rooted in policymakers such as politicians and bureaucrats.

The fact that there were no questions about social welfare services or medical services in the nine-hour policy debate during the 1997 presidential election shows that people are insensitive to social welfare, which differs greatly from advanced foreign countries. Along with a new thinking shift in social welfare, the proportion of welfare in the national budget should be corrected as soon as possible. In developed countries, 20 to 30% of the total budget is distributed to the welfare sector, and Korea was only 6% in 1997, and the fact that it is the lowest among OECD member countries does not need to be explained for a long time.

It is also necessary to change the public's perception of social welfare.

Regarding the aging population, the precedent of significantly strengthening the social security system should not be overlooked in advanced Western countries when the elderly population aged 65 or older reaches nearly 5% of the total population. Korea's medical security system has succeeded in targeting the entire nation after Japan in Asia. However, due to the national financial burden and ability to bear insurance premiums, it was inevitable to be satisfied with the developing country-type medical insurance system of low insurance premiums and limited benefits.

In particular, it is clear that the burden on the government is too small for a country that provides national health insurance. Unlike the initial promise, government assistance for local medical insurance subscribers remains at the 30% level of insurance premiums. Above all, for the participation of residents in social welfare in the era of local autonomy, efforts of local governments are required to form a new social welfare committee and support activities in cities and counties.

Finally, social welfare work will have a real meaning and can be expected to develop only when the passionate heart and tears for the weak and suffering people, regardless of the status quo, the people, and the workers.

Our welfare system remains in place even if times change. It's just that you have to give the least help to the poor. The issue of welfare administration is that it has not yet escaped from charitable and poverty-oriented policies. Budget allocations are also stingy. Even many people worry that if social welfare is too good, it will end in a European way that "**play and eat.**" There is also a huge lack of expertise in social welfare. First of all, even measures to measure this are not properly prepared. All standards are created by the central government and uniformly applied across the country. Regardless of the region or personal characteristics, the selection of subjects also pays more attention to numbers than effects.

Therefore, government statistics on the disabled are hovering around the 1 million mark a decade ago. This is a huge difference from the four million people identified by private organizations. Support for those eligible for living protection is also centered on living expenses. This is in stark contrast to Britain's long-standing departure from the poverty-oriented social welfare policy in the process of enacting the Poor Law. Our general view of welfare is passive and even negative. Welfare, however, is not a problem, but a process of solving it. And it is basically not charity, but our duty and right.

Regarding social welfare, institutional improvement is more important than emotional motivation. This is because neglecting this will add to the enormous social problems and burdens in the future. Therefore, just because economic problems are in an era of overcoming the more urgent IMF era and making a new leap forward does not mean that they will be neglected. However, it is important to have a perspective for long-term and systematic social welfare. First of all, we should aim for professional social welfare. Professional counseling and treatment program development for individuals and effect measurement evaluation should also increase expertise.

Vocational training for children or people with disabilities subject to life protection should also be expanded to jobs with high added value and high self-support effects, and the level should be raised. To realize effective welfare, regional welfare must be strengthened. Programs suitable for local conditions and personal characteristics should be developed, and in particular, human and material resources that can be mobilized should be utilized. There are bound to be limitations in the uniform programs and standards of the central government. In the future, welfare activities of local governments will determine the level of national welfare.

2) What is Social Welfare Administration?

The fundamental reason why it is difficult to clearly define administration is that the administrative phenomenon subject to conceptual regulations is human behavior, unlike natural phenomena, and second, conceptual regulations are made by having a certain idea or idea through recognition of phenomena(Park, Dong-Seo, 2005).

Recently, as social welfare organizations have increased in Korea, the importance of administration to maintain and develop the organization has been recognized. Social welfare administration is an activity related to the process of converting abstract social welfare administration into specific social welfare services and delivering them to people in need of services.

Social welfare administration in this sense can be largely divided into the concept of consultation and the concept of broad meaning. In the concept of consultation, administration is viewed as a practical method, and from this point of view, social welfare administration refers to a systematic intervention process such as interdependent tasks, functions, and related activities performed by managers to facilitate the achievement of social welfare organizations.

On the other hand, in the broader administrative concept, administration is viewed as a cooperative and coordinated effort of members of the organization who contribute variously to all activities of the organization, in this sense, social welfare administration refers to the overall activities of social welfare organizations. The social welfare administration of consultation is mainly related to the activities of social welfare organization managers, and deliberately applies social work knowledge, skills, and values to task activities such as goal setting, program, planning, resource mobilization and evaluation. Social welfare administration refers to the overall activities of a social welfare organization, the responsibility to achieve the goals is shared by all members of the organization, and all activities within the social welfare organization are important in the administrative process.

2. Comparison between Social Welfare Administration and General Administration

Administration exists not only in social welfare administration, but also in various forms such as corporate administration, government administration, and education administration. Administration has different characteristics depending on the characteristics of the organization. In Korea, administration is usually recognized as a public administration performed by the government, but in advanced foreign countries, administration tends to be used in the same way as the term management(Park, Cha-Sang, 2010). Spencer explains the similarities and differences between social welfare administration and other administrations as follows.

1) Common Ground

Administration is a problem-solving process that mainly encompasses identifying problems, researching aspects of problems, developing resolvable plans, implementing plans, and evaluating effectiveness.

2) Administration is a System Made Up of Interrelated and Interactive Parts.

① Administration uses value judgment in alternative choices.

② Administration is considered a process that allows individuals and groups to function more effectively.

③ Administration is very much related to the future.

④ Administration consists of creative use rather than uniform use of knowledge and technology.

⑤ The administration is interested in organizing programs, services, and employees to ensure optimal efficiency and ease the production of products or services.

⑥ Administration, whether large or small, is related to putting public will into practice.

⑦ Administration maintains an appropriate balance between the objectification of management and management and the use of human resources.

⑧ Administration is interested in the status and stability of individual employees, and I think that employees need to actively have a sense of unity in the goals, values, and methods of the organization.

⑨ Communication, collective relationships between employees, and participation in administration are major areas of administration.

3) Difference

Administration in social welfare organizations exists to help satisfy perceived needs in the community. Services provided by social welfare organizations through administration are largely classified into three categories: recovery of damaged social functions, provision of social personal resources for more effective social functions, and prevention of social dysfunction.

A typical social welfare organization, the venue for social welfare administration, generally has a board representing the local community. The size, scope, structure, and program form of social welfare organizations are wide and diverse.

Social welfare administrators are responsible for associating the internal operation of social welfare organizations with local communities as they become de-institized. There is a need to continue making choices about resource utilization. Social welfare organizations should avoid deficit management of resources for the survival of the organization. Social welfare administrators are responsible for creating, maintaining, and protecting the optimal function of the organization. In services performed by social welfare organizations, the nature of professional social work is gradually increasing.

3. Social Welfare Administration Process

1) Social Welfare Administration Theory

The main task of social welfare administration is to efficiently operate and manage social welfare organizations to convert social welfare policies into social welfare services. In the theory of organizational management, there are three basic models: a classical model, a human relations model, and a structuralist model, and there is a system model that compromises these three models into one. Here we will look at these models.

(1) Classical Model

The classical model begins with the fact that members of the organization are mainly economically motivated. Individuals strive for organizational goals when they are given economic incentives. Therefore, if an organization can provide economic compensation to an individual, it is believed that the individual's goals and the organization's goals can coincide. The classical model has borrowed all families from scientific management, public administration, and bureaucratic models, and the core assumption is that organizations are rational systems and can be planned just like machines. The classical model was created based on the research of the organization and the prediction that the ideal organization should be rather than the actual function of the organization. The classical model recognizes the importance of the environment to the organization, and is sometimes criticized for not considering human elements, subsystems, and informal systems within the organization, especially for social welfare organizations. It still remains the dominant model in the field of organizational management.

(2) Relationship Model

The human relations model is a model developed to compensate for various defects in the classical model. This model was created through experiments at Western Electric's Hawthrone plant near Chicago, with Mayo at the center, emphasizing the importance of human elements in the organization. For example, how the brightness of fire affects work productivity. The study found that, as expected, the productivity of the factory's bright working group was higher than that of the non-light working group, but surprisingly, some working groups found that lowering the brightness of the fire steadily increased(Han, Dong-Il et al., 2009). This model emphasizes unplanned and irrational factors within the organization to satisfy individual needs. Despite the differences between the relationship model and the classical model, the relationship model is the same as the classical model in the basic assumption that if individual needs are satisfied, individuals within the organization will work for the goals of the organization. If you show interest in individual needs, organizational goals and individual goals can be matched. Therefore, the human relations model is in the spotlight by managers of social welfare organizations.

The characteristic of the relationship model is that workers' work efficiency is largely influenced by human relationships with colleagues or above, secondly, informal groups exist separately in organizations, thirdly, workers act as members of groups. However, although the human relations model has great significance in that it emphasizes the human aspect of the organization, it is subject to criticism in the same logic as the criticism applied to the human view of the classical model. Real humans are also criticized for having both rational and irrational aspects at the same time.

(3) Structuralist Model

The structuralist model is a synthesis of a classical model and a human relationship model. The structuralist model arises from criticism raised against the human relations model. According to structuralists, the interpersonal approach does not provide a complete view of the organization, suggesting that the partial view favors managers while misleading workers. The structuralist model differs from the human relations model and the classical model in that it does not assume that the goals of individuals and organizations can be consistent. Rather, structuralism emphasizes that conflict in an organization is inevitable. In contrast to the classical model and the human relations model, the structuralist model sees conflict as more functional than dysfunctional. Conflict can function socially by exposing problems and finding solutions accordingly. Trade unions, complaint handling committees, and other trial proceedings are believed to have occurred as a mechanism to mediate conflicts in the organization due to the inevitability of conflicts within the organization, but there is widespread resistance to the use of conflict as a constructive strategy. However, those who argue for the human relations model criticize that the structuralist model does not fully consider human factors. Relationshipists argue that conflicts arise in organizations, but they can be resolved through open communication and trust.

(4) System Model

The system model is based on the assumption that the three models discussed above, the classical model, the human relations model, and the structuralism model, can be integrated into one model. The system model sees an organization as a complex composed of many subsystems that perform specific functions based on various dynamics and mechanisms. The system model provides managers with a method for analyzing and diagnosing organizational problems. This model can be used to find and correct which part of the organization is functioning incorrectly. In other words, the performance of a specific organization can be compared and evaluated with that standard by presenting standards for what functions, dynamics, and mechanisms each subsystem performs.

The system model consists of the following five subsystems.

2) Social Welfare Administration Process

The process of social welfare administration generally consists of planning, organizing, personnel, directing, coordinating, reporting, budgeting and evaluation.

(1) Planning

Planning is the first process carried out by administrators and can be said to be a process of making a series of decisions about future actions to achieve goals. The plan consists of setting specific goals, collecting related information and reviewing available resources, finding alternative methods to achieve the goals, evaluating alternative implementation and expected effects, selecting final alternatives, and establishing specific action plans.

(2) Organization

The second process of the administrative process is an organization, which requires the establishment of a formal structure in which work allocation is defined and coordinated. When roles and responsibilities are not clear, conflicts arise between employees and become inefficient institutions. In order to maintain a strong and vibrant organization, the administrator must clearly understand the organization to all employees and keep pace with changes in institutional objectives, capabilities, and tasks and methods required accordingly.

(3) Personnel Management

Personnel management refers to management activities that motivate employees to hire, develop their abilities, and devote themselves to the organization with a willingness to work. Personnel management has three tasks: recruitment, employee development, and motivation. Recruitment means the recruitment of new employees as appropriate personnel as employees of a social welfare organization, and is divided into recruitment, selection, and appointment based on the process in which this is carried out. Employee development is an educational and training activity to develop the knowledge and skills of employees working in social welfare organizations, improve knowledge and skills necessary for job performance, and change values and attitudes in a desirable direction. Motivation is an important factor in managing social welfare and services and can inspire motivation to work.

(4) Directing

The administrative officer should be a leader who effectively directs the institution by demonstrating the following capabilities. These capabilities include the ability to make rational decisions after reviewing all relevant facts possible, the active interest in the organization's purpose and commitment to achieving it, the ability to praise other employees' contributions and improve their status in the organization, and the ability to inspire individual and collective creativity.

(5) Mediation

Mediation is the work of correlating various parts of institutional activity. In order for an administrator to function as a coordinator, there must be effective communication channels between various departments and employees of the institution. It is effective to activate committee activities for communication channels.

(6) Reporting

Reporting refers to informing the institution's employees, board of directors, local communities, and institutions that provide financial resources of the institution of the situation occurring in the institution. Administrator activities to perform these functions include maintaining records, regular audits, and research.

(7) Finance

Finance, like other organizations, is the most important resource for social welfare organizations. Social welfare organizations receive financial support from the government, various private organizations, and individuals, but it is not sufficient. Therefore, administrators need knowledge and skills in preparing budget statements, financial execution plans, and managing accounting procedures to receive financial support.

(8) Evaluation

Evaluation is a process of evaluating the results of activities in the light of the institution' Evaluation is understood as a concept of reward and punishment for something wrong because it has a negative image in Korea, but in reality, evaluation is a positive factor in that it is a starting point for a new project rather than a concept of reward and punishment for something wrong.

4. Social Welfare Administrator

1) Concept

Social welfare administrators not only manage the organization to achieve the goals of the social welfare organization, but also engage in many activities in relation to the external environment. To that end, sufficient knowledge, skills, experience, and command, supervision, and ability for organizational management are required. Skidmore(1980) classifies 17 management behaviors that social welfare administrators should practice. First, social welfare administrators must accept the reality that employees and clients, as well as other professional staff and leaders in the community they work with. Second, social welfare administrators should have a warm heart and ensure that employees work with a sense of belonging. Third, social welfare administrators must be creative and must be a person who likes to pioneer and establish employee relationships with innovative policies, methods, and procedures to improve organizational services. Fourth, social welfare administrators are advocates of the democratic process. Fifth, social welfare administrators should always trust their employees. Sixth, social welfare administrators must understand that employees or clients are very anxious for praise and recognition. Seventh, social welfare administrators should strive to enjoy a smooth life, including work, rest, play, and religious life. Eighth, social welfare administrators must have planning skills. Ninth, effective organization should follow after sound planning is established. Tenth, competent social welfare administrators should understand that any of the various goals is more important and that the process of prioritizing them is important. Tenth, competent social welfare administrators must realize that the responsibilities of social welfare organizations must be shared and provide opportunities for other employees to be willing to give responsibility and authority. Eleventh, a competent social welfare administrator must realize that the responsibilities of the social welfare organization should be shared and provide an opportunity to give responsibility and authority to other employees. Twelveth, it is important for social welfare administrators to maintain good relationships with the public. Thirteenth, it is necessary to understand the overall process and individual measures to be taken to make decisions that will benefit social welfare organizations and communities. Fourteenth, social welfare administrators must open their minds wide and do everything possible so that employees can move in the direction they want and need to move forward. Fifteenth, the most important of the actions of social welfare administrators is the communication of thoughts and emotions. Sixteenth, social welfare administrators show significant differences in how to deal with employees. Seventeenth, effective social welfare administrators must have the ability to motivate and move their minds in exercising their abilities and performing the functions of social welfare organizations.

2) Attitudes of Social Welfare Administrators

Social welfare administrators must maintain an expert attitude along with professional knowledge. Even if professional knowledge changes, attitudes are difficult to change, which is very important because it is linked to values and becomes the basis for action. The challenges and attitudes as a social welfare administrator presented by Han, In-Young et al.(2011) are as follows. ① Social welfare administrators, above all, require balanced thinking and action. ② Social welfare administrators must recognize that administration and management are both science and art. ③ Social welfare adminstrators understand the various activities and targets of social welfare administration according to the integrated area. ④ It is necessary to accurately grasp the organizational culture and the stage of organizational development. ⑤ Professional and specific knowledge and skills for management should be acquired. ⑥ The administrator faithfully plays the role of a bridgehead and strives for arbitration and communication. ⑧ Depending on the position, wear a hat according to the situation. ⑨ He or she maintains a constant learning attitude, develops himself, and strives to develop employees.

Part IV Social Security Theory

Chapter 11 Significance of Social Security

1. Concepts

The first use of the term social security originated from the 1935 US Social Security Act, enacted as part of overcoming the 1929 global panic. The U.S. Social Security Act of 1935 defines the Social Security Act as a law that implements federal-controlled old-age benefits to promote general welfare, supports state-controlled welfare for the elderly, the blind, children with disabilities, public health and unemployment. The International Labor Organization(ILO) defines the purpose of social security as "*social insurance, public study assistance, social welfare services, and related welfare systems provided to protect all citizens from social risks such as disease, disability, old age, unemployment, and death.*" The principles on social security of the International Labor Organization presented in various ways emphasize the rights of the insured and the responsibilities of the state, and suggest three main points. First, as a universal protection principle for beneficiaries, social security should target not only wage workers but also the entire public. Second, the principle of commonality of the cost burden is that the social security cost burden should not exceed a certain level, with the state, employer, or bilateral joint burden on workers. Third, as a principle regarding the salary level of insurance, it presents the principle of proportion of benefits that are paid in proportion to the recipient's previous income and the principle of uniform benefits that guarantees the legal minimum.

2. Purpose

The purpose of social security is generalized and summarized as follows.

1) Minimum Human Livelihood Security

According to the Framework Act on Social Security, "**Social security guarantees the minimum life so that all citizens can live a human life**," stipulating that the primary purpose of social security is to guarantee the minimum life of the people. Here, "minimum living" means guaranteeing basic living by satisfying basic human needs, and "guarantining the basic living of the people" means guaranteeing the basic needs of the people, the right to live and the right to pursue happiness.

2) Income Redistribution

Income redistribution refers to income or salary considered as income transferred from one individual or group to another. One of the important purposes of the social security system is income redistribution. The types of income redistribution are as follows.

3) Growing Sense of Social Solidarity

Social solidarity is a term that has the dictionary meaning of "*doing something or taking responsibility together with two or more people.*" Therefore, solidarity implies a belief in human sociality and emphasizes responsibility for each other(Yoon, Chul-Soo et al., 2011). One of the goals of the social security system is to guarantee basic living for those exposed to the risk of income loss and act as an important mechanism for social solidarity or social integration.

3. Principles of Social Security

We examine the principles of the Beveridge Report, which have made an important contribution to the development of social security. Beverage believes that social insurance should be the main method of social security in order to solve social problems, and suggested the following six basic principles as the principle of social insurance.

1) Flat Rate of Subsistence Benefits

The first principle of social insurance is that in the case of loss of income due to unemployment, disability, and retirement, the amount of insurance benefits must be the same regardless of the amount of income received before loss of income. However, exceptions are made to occupational accidents or diseases.

2) Flat Rate of Contribution

Second, the contributions paid by workers or employers are the same regardless of their income level.

3) Unification of Administrative Responsibility

Unify the administrative system in consideration of efficiency and economic feasibility(country).

4) Appropriateness of Benefits

It is appropriate in terms of the amount and timing of the salary. The amount of salary should be appropriate to guarantee the minimum livelihood, and the payment of salary should be paid as long as there is a desire without a survey of needs.

5) Comprehensiveness

It should be applied as comprehensively as possible in the population covered by social insurance and its application needs.

6) Classification

Although it is a unified and comprehensive social insurance, various lifestyles within the community should be considered.

Chapter 12 Public Aid

1. Concepts

Public assistance refers to a system that guarantees a minimum living for those in need of life as public servants based on laws and regulations under the responsibility of the state. The financial resources of public assistance are financed by taxes from the people and other national and local public organizations, and the eligibility for benefits is determined based on the fact that they are "**living difficulties**" and the period of benefits is not particularly fixed. Article 2 of the Framework Act on Social Security in Korea defines social security as public assistance provided by social insurance and free of charge. It can be said that Korea's social security system consists of social insurance and public assistance as its two major shareholders(Kim, Ki-Tae et al., 2009).

2. Fundamental Principles

1) Principle of Guaranteeing the Right to Live

The purpose is to contribute to the improvement of social welfare by providing necessary protection to those who do not have the ability to maintain their lives or are in need of living to ensure their minimum lives and create self-support(Article 1 of the National Basic Living Protection Act). All citizens have the right to claim protection from the state when their lives are poor, and the state is obligated to guarantee these rights of the people.

2) Principle of Equal Security

The equality of protection given by the public assistance system means that the minimum standard of living guaranteed as a result of protection is substantially the same, recognizing the difference in meaningful living conditions of each minimum life security line.

3) Principle of Minimum Living Security

Although each citizen may differ in income, job differences, and family size, it is a principle that excludes the causes that threaten this guarantee so that all citizens can be objectively guaranteed a minimum of life. The case of the constitutional petition of an elderly couple in Korea is too similar to the Asahi lawsuit in Japan. Shim, Chang-Seop(then 85 years old) and Lee, Geum-Soon (then 83 years old) living in Jungnim-dong, Jung-gu, Seoul filed a constitutional petition in 1994. The elderly couple argued that the living protection standards announced by the Minister of Health and Welfare were unconstitutional because the monthly living protection benefit amount of KRW 65,000 was less than the minimum living cost. However, grandfather Shim, Chang-Seop died without seeing the results of the constitutional petition. And on May 29, 1997, the old couple's claim was dismissed. What was even more sad, however, was that the logic of the Constitutional Court's rejection of the constitutional petition was too similar to that of the Supreme Court in the Asahi lawsuit.

4) Principle of Complementarity

As a prerequisite, a person who intends to be protected by this law should personally mobilize all resources as much as possible to maintain his or her life, and if such efforts are insufficient, the lack should be protected through the system of this law. This principle best represents the nature of public assistance as a final or comprehensive means of living in a capitalist society based on personal responsibility or self-responsibility in life. This emphasizes that poverty or responsibility for living lies primarily with individuals and families in a capitalist society, and is a principle that secondarily supplements the responsibility of the state or society for this.

3. Types of Public Assistance

1) National Basic Livelihood Security System

The national basic living security system guarantees the minimum life and creates self-support by providing necessary benefits to those in need of living. The National Basic Livelihood Security Act was enacted in 1999 and implemented in 2000 as the need to establish a social safety net required fundamental changes to protect low-income families living in blind spots of the social safety net in 1997. The legal rights of beneficiaries to the right to live were emphasized by recognizing the rights of those receiving benefits by law that recognized the right to receive public assistance as a legal right. As a comprehensive poverty measure, the requirements for supply and demand were simplified to poverty, and active self-support policies were implemented by providing benefits to beneficiaries with working capacity under working conditions.

2) Medical Benefit System

The medical benefit system aims to improve national health and social welfare by providing medical benefits to those in need of living. The medical benefit system is implemented as part of the public assistance system as a medical aid system that contributes to the promotion of national health administration and social welfare for low-income families who do not have income or have a certain income. In addition to health insurance, this is an important means for the medical welfare of the low-income class as a medical security system to ensure a healthy life for the people. The Living Protection Act was enacted in 1961 and medical protection was enacted for the first time, but the enactment of the Medical Protection Act in 1977 laid the foundation for medical protection projects to settle as a public assistance system.

3) Basic Old-Age Pension System

Considering that the elderly have contributed to the raising of descendants and the development of the country and society, the Senior Pension Act was abolished and enacted on April 25, 2007 to support the elderly's living stability and welfare. It targets 70% of the elderly, and although the name of the basic old-age pension is pension, it corresponds to public assistance, not social insurance.

Chapter 13 Social Insurance

1. Significance of Social Insurance

Social insurance has also grown with the development of the capitalist economy even if it does not pursue the purpose of the for-profit economy. In other words, social insurance, which was implemented to guarantee and secure the economic life of the working class with the advancement of the capitalist economy, expanded its target and scope as their living risk increased, and the increase in the number of wage earners simultaneously expanded the scale of social insurance.

In the process of growing the capitalist economy, private insurance and social insurance have been operated by different entities from different purposes at first, but as the scope of social insurance expands, it was necessary to introduce the principles and technologies of private insurance limitedly.

The social insurance system is to systematically protect individual citizens from various life risks or economic instability that threaten the lives of the people with the responsibility of the state and society. Therefore, social insurance aims to minimize social or economic inequality and increase equity, stability, and efficiency by preventing and eliminating worsening factors of national living conditions.

Since July 1995, Korea has established four major social insurance systems along with pension insurance, medical insurance, and industrial accident insurance by implementing employment insurance. Social insurance-related ministries include five(Ministry of Health and Welfare, Ministry of Education, Ministry of Public Administration and Security, Ministry of National Defense, and Ministry of Employment and Labor), and five management agencies(Medical Insurance Management, National Pension Service, Private Pension Service, and Labor Welfare). And from July 2008, the long-term care insurance system for the public elderly will be fully implemented, so it will become a welfare state.

As the four major insurance collection sectors were integrated into health insurance in 2011, wages, which are the basis for calculating employment insurance and industrial accident insurance, were also changed from "**wage**" under the existing Labor Standards Act to the concept of "**reimbursement**" under the Income Tax Act. In the case of insurance premium payment, other industries, except for the construction industry, have changed from the current annual voluntary reporting and payment method to the monthly bill imposition and payment method. The criteria for calculating national pension and health insurance premiums were maintained as remuneration(earned income subject to income tax), and the criteria for imposing employment and industrial insurance premiums were changed from the current wage to income tax.

Since the employer is not a worker, it is not included in the industrial accident insurance employee employment information report. A person with less than 60 hours of working hours per month and foreign workers(workers subject to voluntary employment insurance) may not be reported.

2. Categorization of Social Insurance

In general, the management and operation methods of the social insurance system can be divided into a single type and a separate type. The unified social insurance management operation is a method of collectively managing various social risks such as old age, disease, disaster, and unemployment under a single management and operation system, and the UK is a representative example.

Separation type is a form in which various risks managed by social insurance are managed separately by guarantee function or by function and region, and Germany is a representative example.

Similar to the type of Germany, Korea adopts a separate management method for each function, but manages pension insurance by function and medical insurance by function and region.

3. Background of the Introduction of Social Insurance

In the 19th century, many countries in Europe competed and began to introduce social insurance systems. For advanced capital countries, the introduction of such a social insurance system means a breakthrough in the history of social security. To compare and explain the implementation of the social insurance system with the poor law,

First, social insurance focuses on preventing poverty through everyday means, while the poor law is limited to temporary relief. Therefore, the social insurance system means the beginning of an institutionalized intervention method on the poverty problem.

Second, the social insurance system allows the subject to maintain their past income even in special circumstances, but the poor law system is limited to a small number of fixed services.

Third, the social insurance system mainly targeted male workers, while the poor law system focused on necessary protection targets such as women and children. This means that the main method of social security shifts from selective to universalist services.

Fourth, in the social insurance system, salaries are provided by the payment of insurance premiums, forming legal rights, while the old poverty law provides unilateral benefits to the subjects.

Therefore, the social insurance system provides an opportunity for social security to be converted into citizenship of the subjects, rather than unilateral benefits by the state.

However, the social insurance system, which replaces the poor law system, was introduced by different countries depending on the degree of capitalist development, the degree of growth of the labor class, the political situation, and the degree of development of the national state.

In general, if the factors that had a great influence on the introduction of social insurance systems in many countries are largely classified into three categories, it can be examined as follows.

① The progress of industrialization and the establishment of capitalist production relationships has led to large-scale movement and concentration of population in cities, resulting in social problems such as poverty, unemployment, housing, and environmental problems. In other words, the social insurance system presupposes permanent workers with a certain income source every month, and rapid industrialization at the end of the 19th century expanded these prerequisites.

② The growth of the working class is also often mentioned as a factor for the establishment of the social security system.
In other words, in order for capitalist citizens, who have increased significantly due to the progress of industrialization, to convert to practical political power, the general election system must be premised. The right to vote for men has gradually expanded since the mid-19th century, which is also the result of various struggles of the labor class, including the chartist movement. It had a great influence on the expansion of social insurance programs targeting the political labor class of the overall labor class.

③ In other words, when a crisis occurred in the lives of the people, the state appeared as a crisis manager, which can be seen as a great influence of the panic that periodically attacks capitalism.

4. Social Insurance in Korea

Social insurance currently being implemented in Korea is largely divided into five areas. Since it is very important as (1) national pension for retirement security, (2) national health insurance, (3) industrial accident compensation insurance for industrial accident compensation, (4) employment insurance for unemployment, and (5) long-term care for the elderly.

1) National Pension

(1) Outline

The national pension system stipulated in Article 1 of the National Pension Act stipulates, "*If there is a risk of suspension or loss of income due to social risks such as aging, abolition, or death of the people, special corporations under the state or law become operating entities.*" In addition, the national pension system, which is implemented in Korea as one of the public pension systems, is divided into a national pension system for the entire people, and a special occupational pension system for special workers such as civil servants pension, military pension, and private school faculty pension.

The introduction and development of the National Pension Service are divided into three stages: preparation stage for introduction, implementation stage, and expansion stage, and these detailed changes by period are as follows.

First, the National Welfare Pension Act was enacted and promulgated in 1973 as a solution to social problems caused by industrialization, urbanization, nuclear familyization, and aging as an economic development plan promoted in the 1960s. However, due to the economic recession caused by the oil shock that occurred in 1973, the national pension system, which was scheduled to take effect in January 1974, was postponed indefinitely. The 1973 Middle East War caused an oil crisis in which oil production decreased and prices soared, and Western welfare states, which had expanded under the boom of global capitalism and political stability until the 1960s, faced a crisis.

Second, as the introduction and implementation stage(revised the National Pension Act in 1986 and implemented the system in 1988), the national pension system will be implemented from January 1988 by revising and supplementing the previous national welfare pension system from 1986 as of January 1988. This national pension system established the National Pension Service as an independent institution in September 1987 for efficient management and operation such as fund management, and first of all, workers and employers under the age of 18 to 60 working in workplaces with 10 or more employees.

Third, the national pension system, which was promoted around 10 or more workplaces in 1988, expanded to 5 or more workplaces in need of income security benefits in 1992, expanded the national pension system to rural areas in 1995 as part of the new five-year plan and World Trade Organization(WTO).

(2) Subject to Application

Those eligible for the National Pension Service are citizens under the age of 18 to 60 living in Korea, including foreigners working at workplaces and foreigners living in Korea, but those who are enrolled in special occupational pensions(public service pension, military pension, private school faculty pension) are excluded. In addition, the type of subscription to the National Pension Service is largely divided into those subject to natural subscription (mandatory subscription) that must be subscribed to and those subject to voluntary subscription by their own choice.

As for the types of national pension subscriptions in 2009, as shown in the following table, the explanation is as follows: workplace subscribers, local subscribers, voluntary subscribers, and voluntary continuous subscribers.

First, business subscribers and workers under the age of 18 to 60 who are users and workers under the age of 18 to 60 who are subscribed to the National Pension Service and who use one or more Korean workers as foreign institutions in Korea naturally become business subscribers. Therefore, when a local subscriber is employed in a workplace, he or she automatically becomes a business subscriber, and his or her qualification as a local subscriber is lost.

Second, local subscribers are citizens under the age of 18 to 60 living in Korea, and those who are not business subscribers naturally become local subscribers. However, recipients of other public pensions, such as retirement pensions(temporary payments), retirement pensions receiving disability pensions, recipients under the National Basic Livelihood Security Act, and business subscribers who are not engaged in income activities cannot be local subscribers.

Third, voluntary subscribers can become voluntary subscribers if they apply for membership at their own wishes before the age of 60 even if they cannot become business subscribers and local subscribers. In other public pensions, beneficiaries such as retirement pensions(temporary payments), disability pensions, recipients under the National Basic Livelihood Security Act, business subscribers who have not paid insurance premiums, and those under the age of 27 may become voluntary subscribers.

Fourth, if a subscriber with a subscription period of less than 20 years loses his/her eligibility for the national pension due to reaching the age of 60, or if he/she wants to receive more pensions by extending the subscription period, he/she can become a voluntary subscriber until he/she reaches 65.

(3) Type of Salary

The national pension is paid as social insurance that guarantees income by paying a certain salary when income decreases due to age, disability, or death. The types of benefits are: old-age pension, which is the basis of the national pension, survivor's pension, survivor's pension for the survival of the bereaved due to the death of the subscriber, or survivor's pension or return payment.

National health insurance is social insurance aimed at contributing to improving national health and social security by providing insurance benefits for prevention, diagnosis, treatment, rehabilitation, childbirth, death, and health promotion of citizens' diseases and injuries. Articles 34 and 36 of the Constitution stipulate the right of all citizens to live a human life, the obligation of the state to promote social security and social welfare to realize it, and the protection of the state on public health(Health Insurance Research Center, 2005).

It began with the enactment of the Medical Insurance Act in 1963, but it can be said that it was nominal at the time as a voluntary application method. In the 1970s, the "**Medical Protection Act**" was enacted for workers, public officials, and soldiers, but even the enforcement decree was not prepared due to difficulties such as problems caused by compulsory application. After that, medical insurance for residents of rural areas was implemented in January 1988, and medical insurance for residents of urban areas was implemented on July 1, 1989, opening the era of national medical insurance. In 1988, the integrated discussion on medical insurance began in earnest, and the current National Health Insurance Act, which aims at integrated medical insurance, was enacted in 1999, and the medical insurance system has been integrated into national health insurance since January 2000. At that time, the medical insurance system simply dealt with medical services that treat diseases, but the National Health Insurance is an active system that deals with the scope of health examination, rehabilitation, and prevention, including disease treatment. On July 1, 2000, the medical insurance system, which was centered on the existing union, was changed to a method of integrating the whole, and the name of the system was also changed to the health insurance system. The management and operation organization was unified into one National Health Insurance Corporation, and an independent Health Insurance Review and Assessment Service was newly established to handle the medical expenses review function.

(2) Subject to Application

The coverage of the national health insurance is for all citizens living in Korea, and the national health insurance classifies those eligible for workplace subscribers and local subscribers, but excludes those eligible for medical benefits that are public assistance.

A workplace subscriber is a person who has been appointed or hired as a worker at a workplace with one or more employees, a public official, and a private school teacher. In addition, dependents of workplace subscribers are dependents who mainly live by workplace subscribers, such as spouses, direct descendants(including spouse direct descendants), and siblings, and those without income or remuneration become dependents. In other words, the dependent must meet two conditions that must be in a kinship relationship and a livelihood maintenance relationship with the insured. In addition, local subscribers are agricultural and fishing workers and urban self-employed people, excluding workplace subscribers and their dependents.

(3) Type of Salary

It refers to medical services provided by the Corporation in various forms for prevention, diagnosis, treatment, rehabilitation, childbirth, death, and health promotion of subscribers and dependents subject to the National Health Insurance.

Salaries are divided into legal and voluntary benefits, which are benefits that must be naturally supplied by law, whereas voluntary benefits refer to wages paid arbitrarily, not by law.

The types and contents of the in-kind benefits and cash benefits of the national health insurance, which are actually paid, are described in detail as follows. In other words, in-kind benefits include medical care benefits, delivery benefits, and health checkups as direct medical services are received at designated nursing institutions during illness, injury, and delivery. In addition, cash benefits are paid equivalent to medical care benefits when treated at a medical institution or pharmacy other than a designated nursing institution for emergency or other unavoidable reasons, including medical expenses, childbirth expenses, disability security benefits, funeral expenses, and personal compensation.

(4) Financial Burden

The management and operation system of health insurance in Korea is handled by the National Health Insurance Corporation, an organization under public law, and an integrated method is adopted. The financial burden of the national health insurance is operated with insurance premiums paid by subscribers and some government support, and insurance premiums are calculated and applied differently by workplace subscribers and local subscribers.

3) Industrial Accident Compensation Insurance

(1) Outline

Industrial accidents are social insurance systems designed to protect workers and their families from industrial accidents, as well as making it difficult to make a living for workers in the socially and economically disadvantaged position(Ministry of Labor, 2007).

In general, industrial accident insurance was introduced first in many countries, which can be seen as having a significant impact on the introduction of other social insurance systems, and it was enacted in 1963 and implemented in Korea from 1964. In particular, in the case of Korea, industrial accident insurance is very important as 90% of the disabilities have acquired disabilities such as industrial accidents and traffic accidents in modern times.

Unlike other insurances, industrial accident insurance is mainly covered by employers only, and workers are the main targets. In addition, the biggest feature of industrial accident insurance is that employers' intention or negligence is considered a requirement in accordance with the principle of no-fault liability, which is considered as a protection target, even if the victim has negligence. In other words, the compensation for industrial accident insurance adopts and applies the principle of no-fault liability that pays compensation to industrial accident workers only if the requirements based on the cause of the accident are met, rather than judging the liability of employers or workers.

(2) Subject to Application

Industrial accident insurance protects only workers who have suffered accidents due to work while performing their duties at workplaces covered by industrial accident insurance. In other words, in order for a person who suffered an accident while performing his/her duties to receive industrial accident compensation. Workability must be recognized under the Industrial Accident Insurance Act, and Injury, disease, physical disability, or death(labor corporation, 2009).

The scope of industrial accident insurance gradually expanded to apply to all businesses or workplaces using more than one full-time worker from July 1, 2000, but in principle, industrial accident insurance is not applied in consideration of the risk rate, size, and location.

① Industrial accident insurance is compulsory for businesses or workplaces with more than one full-time worker, so even if the employer does not subscribe to industrial accident insurance or does not want to be treated as industrial accident insurance, it can be compensated. ② The voluntary application of industrial accident insurance depends on the employer's free will, but if the employer of the project No. 3 to No. 6 arbitrarily applies to the Korea Workers' Compensation and Welfare Service to approve insurance coverage.

(3) Type of Salary

Payments for industrial accident workers are medical care benefits(payment for medical treatment or illness due to industrial accidents), suspension benefits(payment for non-employment due to industrial accidents), disability benefits(in the event of death by accident workers), injury compensation benefits(for 2 years or more).

(4) Financial Burden

Industrial accident insurance was originally managed and operated by the Ministry of Labor in 1995, but it was divided into policy and execution of industrial accident insurance, and the Labor Welfare Corporation is in charge of determining insurance premiums and insurance benefits. In other words, it is an obligation(forced) insurance that the state is responsible for to guarantee the lives of industrial accident workers and their families, and to guarantee the employer's liability for accident compensation, a predetermined premium is collected only. In addition, insurance premiums are calculated by multiplying the total amount of wages for the relevant insurance year by the insurance rate for each business diagnosis in accordance with the differential burden principle according to the risk of accidents at workplaces.

The industrial accident insurance premium rate is directly related to the insurance premium burden of insurance subscribers, and the insurance rate is subdivided into business diagnosis(by industry) classified according to the risk of disaster based on the ratio of the total wage over the past three years as of September 30 every year.

4) Employment Insurance

(1) Outline

Employment insurance is a social insurance system that promotes the stability of life and reemployment of unemployed workers and their families when workers are unemployed. The purpose of such employment insurance is to prevent unemployment, promote employment, develop and improve workers' vocational skills, strengthen the national job guidance and job placement function, and promote the stability of workers' lives and job search(Article 1 of the Employment Insurance Act).

In August 1991, when the need for unemployment insurance was raised due to the high unemployment rate experienced in the early 1980s, the 7th Economic and Social Development Plan(1992-1996) decided to introduce employment insurance.

Employment insurance is a social security insurance that is integrated by actively linking labor market policies such as unemployment insurance projects, employment stabilization projects, and vocational competency projects in the traditional sense as shown in Figure 9 below.

(2) Subject to Application

From October 1, 1998, employers with one or more workers are obligated to subscribe to employment insurance and are applied to businesses and workplaces employing one or more workers.

However, considering the size of the project and the characteristics of each industry, the application is excluded for some projects that are deemed very difficult to manage the workplace and the insured. Among agriculture, forestry, fishing, and hunting, non-corporate employees hire less than four full-time workers, and construction works with a total construction amount of less than 20 million won per year(after 2004) by the Minister of Employment and Labor.

Employment insurance, such as industrial accident insurance, is divided into general natural application projects and voluntary subscription projects for businesses subject to exclusion. First, insurance relationships are automatically established regardless of the will of the employer or worker when the project is initiated or the project meets the application requirements. Second, a voluntary subscription project refers to a project that is not subject to the mandatory application of the Employment Insurance Act(excluding application) and whose employment insurance subscription is entrusted to the employer's free will. In this case, the employer must submit an application for employment insurance to the competent Labor Welfare Corporation with the consent of more than half of the workers(excluding workers subject to application) to sign up, but cannot sign up only for unemployment benefits.

(3) Type of Salary

Employment insurance in Korea is largely divided into employment security and vocational competency development projects and unemployment benefits. Support services that individuals can benefit from such employment insurance include training support for incumbent workers, training support for unemployed workers, unemployment benefits, parental leave benefits, and postpartum leave benefits. In addition, support services that companies can benefit from are classified into job creation support area, employment adjustment support area, employment promotion support area, construction worker employment stability support area, workplace childcare facility support area, and vocational training support area.

(4) Financial Burden

The management and operation of employment insurance is directly managed by the Ministry of Employment and Labor, but the management of insurance subscribers is delegated to the Korea Labor Welfare Corporation, which manages industrial accident insurance for workplaces. Since both employment insurance and industrial accident insurance are social insurance for workplaces, cooperation between the Ministry of Employment and Labor(Employment Support Center) and the Korea Workers' Compensation and Welfare Service is essential.

As in the 2011 employment insurance premium rate and calculation, unemployment benefits are borne by workers and employers, respectively, and workers' share(5.5%) of unemployment benefit premiums can be deducted at the time of monthly wage payment. In addition, in the case of employment stability and vocational competency development projects, the employer is entirely responsible, and the premium rate is differentiated according to the size of the workplace, and the larger the size, the higher the premium rate. Rather than a regulation to induce SMEs, it can be interpreted that the larger the size of the workplace, the more likely it is to use it, so that equity can be secured.

5) Long-Term Care Insurance for the Elderly

(1) Concept

It is a social insurance system that provides long-term care benefits such as physical activity or housework support to the elderly who have difficulty living alone for more than six months due to old age or senile diseases (http://www.longtermcare.or.kr). Article 1(Purpose) of the Long-Term Care Insurance Act stipulates that "*This Act provides long-term care benefits such as physical activity or domestic activity support to the elderly who are unable to perform their daily lives alone due to old age or senile diseases.*" The "**Long-Term Care Insurance Act for the Elderly**" was promulgated on April 27 after virtually unanimously passing the plenary session of the National Assembly on April 2, and the long-term care insurance system for the elderly was implemented from August 1. The long-term care insurance system for the elderly, such as dementia and stroke, which have been entrusted to the family domain, shares long-term care issues with the state and society according to the social solidarity principle. The long-term care insurance system for the elderly benefits not only the elderly, but also all generations, including middle-aged and children, who were directly in charge of long-term care. The elderly can no longer burden their children and receive planned and professional long-term care services, allowing them to spend their retirement with more dignity. Middle-aged people who were directly in charge of long-term care can focus on economic and social activities away from mental, physical, and economic burdens. Children can also receive better education and care at home where the burden of long-term care has been lifted.

(2) Grading Criteria and Procedures

① Rating Criterion

Ratings are "**very unhealthy**" and "**I have a serious illness.**" It is based on the long-term care recognition score that indicates "how much help(long-term care) is needed in daily life according to the functional state of mind and body?" rather than a subjective concept such as such. The rating is determined in five grades based on the long-term care recognition score.

② Door-to-Door Survey

When applying for recognition, long-term care staff from the Corporation, consisting of nurses, social workers, and physical therapists, visit in person and investigate the following items according to the following Long-Term Care Recognition Survey Table.

③ **Calculation of Long-Term Care Recognition Scores**

The "**long-term care recognition score**" is calculated by entering the results of a survey of 65 items indicating the applicant's mental and physical condition.

④ **Deliberation and Judgment by the Rating and Judgment Committee**

The Rating and Judgment Committee deliberates and judges the applicant's functional status and the degree to which long-term care is required based on the results of the visit survey, doctor's note, and specialized matters as follows.

- It deliberates whether it falls under the state of need for medical care.
- If medical care is necessary, the grade shall be determined according to the rating criteria.
- If necessary, the opinions of the rating committee may be attached.

(3) Application Procedures for Long-Term Care Accreditation

Those aged 65 or older and those under 65 with senile diseases are eligible. When the application investigation is completed, the Corporation shall submit the investigation results, applications, communication opinions, and other materials necessary for deliberation to the Committee on the Judgment of Long-Term Care Ratings. If it is deemed difficult to perform daily life alone for more than six months, the Rating and Judgment Committee determines the long-term care grade according to the mental and physical condition and the degree to which long-term care is required. When the Rating and Judgment Committee completes deliberation on long-term care recognition and rating, the Corporation shall prepare and send a long-term care recognition letter containing the following matters to the recipient without delay(Article 17). Standard long-term requirements for the Corporation to ensure that recipients can smoothly use long-term care benefits within the monthly limit when sending a long-term care certificate. A quantitative use plan is prepared and sent together(Article 17).

(4) Implementation of Long-Term Care Benefits and Types of Benefits

① Implementation of Long-Term Care Benefits

Long-term care benefits may be received from the date the long-term care certificate is reached(however, if there are unavoidable reasons prescribed by Presidential Decree, such as no family to take care of, long-term care benefits may be received during the period until the long-term care certificate is reached).

② Type of Salary

Long-term care benefits are largely divided into home care benefits, facility benefits, and special cash benefits.

A. Home-Based Benefits

A long-term care worker visits the recipient's house to take a bath, excretion, toilet use, changing clothes, washing hair, cooking, purchasing daily necessities, cleaning.

B. Facility Benefits

It is a medical care benefit that provides education and training to support physical activity and maintain and improve mental and physical functions by entering medical welfare facilities for the elderly(excluding hospitals specializing in the elderly).

C. Special Cash Benefits

There are family care expenses and special care expenses.

i **Family Care Expenses**: A person who lives in an area where long-term care facilities are remarkably scarce(books and remote areas), or a person who is deemed difficult to use long-term care benefits provided by long-term care institutions due to natural disasters, etc. Paid to a person whose family, etc. needs long-term care due to mental, character, etc.

ii **Special Nursing Expenses**: If the recipient receives long-term care benefits equivalent to home care or facility benefits from institutions such as long-term care facilities not designated as long-term care facilities, etc., some of the long-term care benefits are paid.

iii **Nursing Hospital Nursing Expenses**: Part of the expenses used for long-term care when the recipient is admitted to a nursing hospital under the Elderly Welfare Act or a nursing hospital under the Medical Service Act.

(5) Long-Term Care Worker

It is a job that provides physical and household support services at elderly care and home facilities for the elderly who are unable to perform independent daily life due to senile diseases such as dementia and stroke. The long-term care insurance system for the elderly, which took effect in July 2008, trains manpower through the newly established national qualification system to strengthen the level of skills and knowledge compared to family volunteers and life instructors.

Part V
Theory of Individual Social Welfare

Chapter 14 Welfare of Children and Youth

1. Introduction

Child welfare and youth welfare have developed independently and segmentally based on different promotion systems, but the Lee, Myung Bak government was established in February 2008 and the child care policy of the Ministry of Health and Welfare was integrated into the Children and Youth Policy Office. On October 27, 2008, the Minister of Health and Welfare announced a legislative notice of the 'Act on the Revision of the Child Welfare Act' Therefore, the revision of the Child Welfare Act to the Child and Youth Welfare Act is an attempt to break down the boundaries between the existing child and youth policies and redefine them as child and youth activity policies. However, in recent years, government organizations are being promoted in the direction of separating child and youth policies from integration(Park, Cha-Sang, 2010). According to this trend, this book will divide child welfare and youth welfare and systematically describe them.

2. Child Welfare

1) Significance and Characteristics of Child Welfare

Child welfare is a combination of children and welfare, and it can be understood as a combination of the concept of welfare with the concept of children. The conceptual definition of other social welfare fields may be the same way, but child welfare is a combination of the meaning of welfare with the noun child, and in fact, the scope of the conceptual regulations may widen or narrow depending on how you understand the meaning of the child. From this point of view, children are slightly different from the concepts of infants, children, and adolescents, and are similarly used, and are recognized in various ways depending on the changes in the times and society, and the perspectives of scholars. In developmental psychology, it is subdivided into newborns, girls, infants, children, and adolescents according to age, and in an pedagogical sense, children can be seen as children with a broad meaning.

In other words, it includes newborns and infants, and refers to until puberty and adolescence are reached. However, strictly speaking, it is a principle to say the period of elementary school, that is, between the ages of 6 and 12. On the other hand, in the field of child welfare, it is mainly classified by age, but the focus is different according to related laws, so it is specified somewhat differently as follows. The contents presented by the relevant laws are as follows.

Children are beings whose mind and body grow, develop, and need social protection, and although they vary according to age, they are still immature physically and mentally, and are insufficient to live independently by themselves. Physical strength is weak, social life experience and learned knowledge are absent or insufficient, and personality is incomplete and cannot handle the role of an adult. Looking at the characteristics of children, they can be divided into six categories as follows.

① In general, the mind and body are immature compared to adults and the elderly.
② It matures through various stages of growth and development throughout human life.
③ It should be dependent and protected for a longer period of time than any other mammal.
④ Physiological and personal needs must be satisfied together.
⑤ They are very sensitive and are becoming more and more socialized at the beginning of the family.
⑥ In order to grow into a social human, it is necessary to learn the ability to adapt to the social environment.

In this way, children are beings with the characteristics of dependence, maturity, sensitivity, desire, adaptation, and learning. Therefore, children must rely on adults to meet these needs, and adults must take care of children.

Child well-being has been defined slightly differently depending on scholars' perspectives, but in general, child well-being refers to organizational activities in which all children with special disabilities, as well as public and private organizations or institutions in the field of social welfare, cooperate and implement.

In other words, interpreting child welfare in a narrow sense refers to welfare activities centered on children who need to be protected, which refers to activities centered on individuals or private organizations. However, child welfare in a broad sense means that various welfare entities systematically conduct welfare activities for general children and their families, and general children are used to mean all children, including children with care.

Among scholars, Friedlander said, "*Child welfare is not just about children with poverty, neglect, abandonment, diseases, defects, or delinquent children who cannot adapt to the environment. Child welfare is social, economic, and health activities conducted by all institutions of the corporation to protect and protect all children from risks so that they can be safe and happy in physical, intellectual, and emotional development*," he said. Taken together, he argues, it can be seen as physical, economic, and health activities conducted by all children in public or private institutions.

Therefore, child welfare has no choice but to pay primary attention to the welfare of children who are protected while pursuing the happiness of all children.

Overall, the subject of child welfare is changing from children with needs due to parents' deficits and poverty to children with needs due to parental employment, and from the protection of some children to the protection and development of all children. These changes are closely related not only to changes in the parenting environment of parents, but also to changes in children's perspectives. In other words, children change from the subject of protection to the subject of enjoying rights, and the adoption of the

International Convention on the Rights of Children in 1989 is spreading the view that they are the subject of realization of rights.

In response, the Child Welfare League of America takes the position of 'child welfare as a substance' by saying, "Child welfare is to provide social services to children and adolescents whose parents cannot fulfill their parenting responsibilities or the community cannot provide the resources and protection required by children and their families." If you look at the meaning of this concept, it can be seen that it is also a consultative meaning, and the core of the concept of child welfare is to represent and supplement the functions of families with disabilities in carrying out child rearing responsibilities. If the function of child welfare services is in operation, children in need of protection are allowed to continue to be protected in their original environment, and if possible, do their best to help them return to their homes. It is also to cultivate the ability of the community he has grown up to do so.

In addition, Kadushin explains the minimum service direction and individual service direction for child welfare. These two directions can be expressed differently in a residual approach and an institutional approach. The former is specific in that it targets people who need it a lot, but the service is not efficient or fair. In a society that recognizes and is not ready to respond to children's new needs, it is natural to consider priorities under conditions of insufficient social resources, and in this case, a minimum approach is inevitable. The latter emphasizes agency protection.

In modern times, society and the state have tended to shoulder some of the responsibilities of child rearing, not only for children in need of special protection, but also for the healthy development of ordinary children.

In summary, the child welfare activities of the consultation refer to public and private services, such as protection, aid, guidance, support, and treatment, mainly based on public responsibility, and child welfare activities are conducted directly or indirectly.

In a broad sense, child welfare refers to dealing with the general welfare of children and promoting the development of children's physiological, psychological, and social possibilities in harmony with community needs and dealing with countermeasures.

In this sense, child welfare is interpreted as a broad meaning due to the complexity of economic life and the development of public and private organizations in the field of social welfare.

2) Modern Child Welfare Process

(1) Contemporary Children's Problems

A. Family Problems

In referring to family problems that cause child problems, there is often a saying, "*There are problematic families or problematic parents behind problematic children.*" The economic instability of the family due to poverty or unemployment, defects in the family structure, and defects in parenting of parents cause child problems. In a society where parents' educational background or social status is favored, parental poverty and unemployment can have a very negative effect on children. In addition, malnutrition and unclean living conditions caused by poverty are obstacles to the healthy growth of children. This can lead to deprivation of educational opportunities and further flight. Children who have no choice but to passively accept their parents' divorce experience psychological conflicts due to their parents' divorce.

B. Problems in the Social Environment

Modern society provides a surrounding environment that is inappropriate for children's growth. In other words, environmental pollution, pollution problems, traffic problems, slum areas, and dangerous areas have a negative effect on children. In particular, the influence of the public media, the form of intemperated adults, as well as child abuse and sexual assault are emerging as serious social problems. Accordingly, intervention for the development of healthy growth of children is urgently required in terms of social environment.

C. Problems of Maladjustment

In the case of disabled children with special needs among children's problems, special social welfare services appropriate for them should be provided. In general, special protection is required for mentally retarded children because they are psychologically likely to cause problematic behaviors such as self-abuse, suicide, and academic abandonment. In addition to their own problems, problems with children with these needs may be caused by indifference and neglect of the family or social environment, so appropriate service intervention is required.

D. Lack of Support Systems

Today, child problems are spreading due to the increase in nuclear familyization, the increase in dual-income families, and single-parent families. This phenomenon is more pronounced in low-income families, and due to the absence of a social support system, children are left alone at home, causing various child problems. In order to solve such a child problem, a social support system is urgently required.

E. Economic Issues

Economic stability has a great influence on children in family life. The economic instability of the family is an obstacle to robust growth and development as the minimum needs of children are not satisfied. In other words, not only does it harm their bodies due to economic problems, but it also deprives them of educational opportunities, which greatly hurts their intelligence and emotions. Therefore, for children, consciousness, diet, and maintenance problems become essential factors for mental and physical development, so economic benefits and stability must be guaranteed through public and private programs.

(2) Child Welfare Development Process

A. Child Protection in Traditional Society

Industries related to child protection, which were carried out in traditional society, had their own projects that began in Korea, but were also influenced by the ideas and institutions of neighboring China.

In the Koryo Dynasty, as Buddhism flourished, orphans, hunger, and poor children were protected in the form of consignment in temples by the basic spirit of Buddhism, and the country provided consignment protection for raising poor or helpless women.

During the Joseon Dynasty, laws and regulations were enacted to protect orphans, hunger, and poor children in advance compared to the Goryeo Dynasty. However, overall, since the Joseon Dynasty was not only a strict status society, but also dominated Confucianism, children were treated differently according to status or gender. In other words, children from families with high status were considered to be in charge of family successors and ancestral rites, and the idea of preference for boys became an important cause of the early development of the quantum system. However, children from low-income families were treated as subordinate humans and exploited the labor force, and were often discriminated against in other cases in terms of job choices and national examinations such as the past.

B. Contemporary Child Protection

It can be seen that the social and national sense of responsibility for the welfare of children has become more solid compared to the traditional society, and at the same time has been relatively and systematically implemented. To summarize the development of Korean children's welfare after the traditional society, modern child welfare projects such as the establishment of Korea's first orphanage in Myeong-dong Catholic Church by a French priest in 1888, and Gyeongseong orphanage by Korean Lee Pil-hwa in 1905. These child welfare projects began to be systematically and practically strengthened and expanded to solve various child and family problems caused by rapid industrialization from the 1960s. However, until this period, child protection or child welfare remained post-mortem and emergency relief, and it was only after the enactment of the Child Welfare Act in 1981 that it sought to switch to preventive measures to foster all children soundly.

3) Principles and Areas of Child Welfare

(1) Principle of Child Welfare

A. Principles of Rights and Responsibilities

In the healthy growth of children, parents, and society are based on the establishment of rights and responsibilities, respectively. In this sense, it can be seen that the subjective meaning of child welfare means the responsibility for child welfare. This responsibility is gradually spreading from home to society and the country, and recently, it has also emphasized children's responsibility as an active subject for welfare, not as an object of benefit.

However, it is recognized that child welfare does not take unilateral responsibility in any one subject, but takes its own responsibility within the scope of the social roles assigned to each other, and at the same time shares responsibilities with each other in an organic relationship. It stipulates the responsibilities of children, parents, families, society, and the state in various child welfare laws.

B. Principles of Universality and Selectivity

The universality of all children and the selectivity for which help is requested should be applied complementarily. In this sense, the principle of universality and the principle of selectivity can be classified as follows.

The principle of universality is that all children are provided with the same type of business at the same level without any conditions or restrictions. Therefore, this principle is premised on the assumption that children's problems and social problems are prevented through healthy and sound fostering along with the ideology of equality.

The principle of selectivity is also called the principle of sensationality, which refers to limiting the subject of child welfare projects under various conditions or standards. In most cases, the degree of parenting ability of parents is the standard. In other words, when it is difficult or almost impossible for parents to fulfill their parenting responsibilities, so-called protected children are the targets.

C. Protection and Individual Principles

The principle of protection means that children are immature and lack judgment, life on their own is inevitable or very difficult, and they are almost impossible to act for their rights and interests, so children are subject to top priority protection and relief. The Declaration of Children's Rights(1959) also declared that children should receive protection and relief first in any case.

D. Principles of Inclusiveness

In terms of administrative organization, programs, policies, and services for stable family life, economic stability, education, health, etc., which are the premise of child welfare, should be implemented comprehensively and complementarily.

E. Principles of Professionalism

For the sound development and growth of children, specialized organizations and personnel with professional knowledge or skills related to their needs, thoughts and behaviors, and problems are required.

(2) Field of Child Welfare

There are various types of child welfare programs. This is because the subject of child welfare has not only been expanded to all general children, including protected children, but also the needs and problems of each child are very diverse. Various child welfare projects can be classified based on targets, locations, and functions.

A. Categorization Based on the Subject

① Child Care and Welfare Services

It mainly refers to children who grow up in an inappropriate parenting environment for poor or poor families and children with developmental problems or disabilities, and not only includes their parents. Various businesses are provided through parents. Most of these projects are provided from a therapeutic perspective according to the principle of selective service.

② General Children and Welfare Services

Welfare services for general children refer to children who can live without receiving special help from outside the home, including their parents. This type of project is widely implemented in developed countries with developed social security systems.

B. Categorization by Location

It can be classified into domestic and non-home businesses, focusing on the place where child welfare is delivered.

Home business refers to a business in which children live in their own homes with their parents and other family members and provide various help from the outside. Examples include counseling, family education and treatment, and childcare projects. Off-home business refers to a business in which children leave their own home and live in other families or facilities to provide various help. Examples include adoption projects, home consignment protection projects, and facility protection projects.

C. Categorization Based on Functionality

Kadushin says that child welfare services are supportive services(e.g., child counseling, home counseling, single-parent counseling, community mental health counseling, abuse) based on how and to what extent children can be raised at home. Type into neglect child protection, supplementary service (supplementary service, income supplementation project-aged, family incompetent insurance, required child family allowance, daycare project, home creation project), and substitute service(adoption project, home consignment protection, facility protection).

① Business that Supports Parental Parenting Skills

Projects to support and strengthen parental parenting functions are provided from the following perspectives. In other words, if knowledge and skills for child development are insufficient, parent-child relationships, marital relationships, and other family relationships are not smooth, and proper parenting is not possible due to poor surroundings. However, these problems are almost insurmountable with the help of child welfare institutions and society, so the institution only helps parents and families raise their children properly and is not responsible for any(primary line of child welfare).

② Business that Complements Parental Parenting Skills

The projects included in this classification are childcare, income supplementation, and home adjustment projects, and their significance is that society is partially responsible for raising children(second line of defense for children's welfare) to ensure that they can live at home and with their parents.

③ Business Representing Parental Parenting Skills

The projects included in this classification include foster care(abuse children, unmarried parent children, single parent children by death, divorce, and separation), adoption projects, facility protection projects(orphans, mentally and physically handicapped children, delinquent children), and society guarantees children's right to live. If society is not responsible, the survival of children becomes impossible, so it is called the third line of defense for child welfare. In other words, this is the last measure.

4) Child Rearing Support Policy

(1) Dream Start Business

The "**Dream Start Project**" is a child rearing policy that supports children's overall development by providing customized integrated services such as health, welfare, and childcare to low-income pregnant women living in vulnerable areas(http://www.dreamstart.go.kr). In principle, priority support shall be provided to children from basic supply and demand and the next-highest-class families, families with deficits, victims of sexual assault, and single-parent families. As for the service content, it is a customized integrated service that provides essential services necessary for the growth and development of poor children through case management through home visits, and provides optional services according to the individual needs and circumstances of children. The Dream Start Center is directly managed by cities, counties and districts. Therefore, the center belongs to cities, counties, and districts, and consists of three dedicated public officials and three private professionals.

(2) Child Development Support Account(CDA) Project

Child Development Account(CDA) support aims to overcome the reality that children cannot stand on their own feet even after the age of 18 and pass on poverty even when they become adults. Starting in April 2007, children in need of protection, such as children in facilities and children in need of protection, will be supported by guardians or sponsors, and children up to 30,000 won per month will be eligible for self-reliance(www.adongcda.or.kr, 2009).

(3) After-School Care and Activity Support

A. Community Children's Center

Around 1975, educational activities and community movements in the form of unlicensed daycare centers for children before school age were developed. With the growth of children, study rooms for school-age and middle and high school students have been developed since the 1980s as part of the demolition struggle and organized community movement, taking the lead in solving local children's problems. The local children's center, rooted in the local movement, is a child welfare facility that provides comprehensive welfare services for the healthy development of children, such as protection and education of local children, provision of sound play and entertainment, and connection between guardians and the community(Han, In-Young et al., 2011). Article 52 (1) 8 of the Child Welfare Act stipulates that local children's centers are "a facility that provides comprehensive child welfare services for the healthy development of children, such as protection of children in local communities, education, provision of sound play and entertainment, and linkage between guardians and the community." Local Children's Center's functions include ① ensuring children's rights, protecting them safely, and supporting meals in the community. ② Educational functions: improving children's learning ability. ③ emotional support. ④ Cultural support.

B. After-School Academy for Youth

The after-school academy aims to support healthy growth of adolescents through comprehensive learning support, such as fostering learning skills, hands-on activities, meals, health care, and counseling for teenagers spending time alone after school classes of low-income, double-income, and single-parent families.

(4) Youth Study Room

Youth study rooms are established and operated to provide learning opportunities to teenagers with poor learning conditions and to grow into healthy members of society by operating learning support programs and supporting cultural and experiential activities(Children and Youth White Paper, 2008).

5) Child Abuse

(1) Definition

Child abuse is defined as "*an act of physical abuse against a child deemed to have intention*". According to the management guidelines for child abuse stipulated by the Ministry of Health and Welfare, child abuse refers to "physical, mental, and sexual violence, harsh acts, and abandonment by children's guardians that can harm children's health and welfare by adults, including guardians."

(2) Type

A. Physical Abuse

It includes all actions except accidental accidents that allow guardians to cause physical damage or physical damage to children. Physical damage refers to bruises or burns, tears, fractures, organ ruptures, and functional damage caused by beating or violence, as well as damage caused by other methods such as shock, penetration, heat, chemicals, or drugs. For any reason, physical punishment imposed on infants under 12 months of age is considered abuse.

B. Emotional Abuse

It includes physical restraint or confinement, verbal or emotional threats, and other sadistic acts imposed on children. It refers to the act of severely ignoring or insulting a child's personality, existence, emotion, or mood, threatening or harming physical or sexual abuse, including cruel and abusive treatment, intentional repetition of food, clothing and shelter, or commercial use of a child.

C. Sexual Abuse

It refers to physical contact or interaction applied to children for the purpose of satisfying adults, such as rape, sexual behavior, sexual exposure, self-defense, and sexual play, including sexual or other physical contact.

D. Negligence

It refers to all behaviors that can harm children's health or welfare or hinder normal development by neglecting child rearing and protection by intentional repetition. Neglect includes improper supervision, educational neglect, and emotional neglect, such as refusal of therapeutic treatment.

6) Child Problems and Improvements

(1) Contemporary Society and Children's Problems

Since the 1960s, Korean society has experienced rapid changes in political, economic, social, and cultural aspects. Among the experiences of these changes, the social aspect caused family dissolution, nuclear familyization, and employment simulation increase due to changes in social structure due to urbanization, industrialization, and eventually, this weakened the family's function and caused child rearing problems.

A. Family Disbandment

Family dissolution means the destruction of family bonds, such as unity, loyalty, agreement, and breakdown of the normal function of the family unit, and narrow marriage relationships are destroyed due to separation, divorce, abandonment, and hope. One of the most representative family dissolution is divorce. Divorce among Koreans is on the rise from 5.5 percent in 1974 to 18.5 percent in 1996.

B. Nuclear Familyization

As industrialization progressed, adolescents were forced to separate housing and work from the land-oriented large family lifestyle and transition to a parent-child-centered nuclear family. The proportion of these nuclear families increased significantly from 71.5% in 1970 to 79.8% in 1995. This phenomenon of nuclear familyization has had a great impact on raising children. In other words, the mutual influence between families has been reduced, and the decrease in the number of children has led to a lack of emotion to take care of brothers and children, and it has become difficult for grandparents and relatives to take care of grandchildren.

C. Employment of Women

Employment of women with children, especially infants, is rapidly increasing. The participation rate of Korean women in economic activities increased significantly from 26.8% in 1960 to 48.6% in 1969. The increase in the number of employed mothers is also a change in women's awareness of work and social advancement, although there is a reason to improve the economic level of families.

However, because the mother is engaged in social activities, children who have been left to day care mothers or who have grown up in rural areas without their mother taking proper care of their children due to farming cannot grow emotionally sound. In the end, women's social advancement is an inevitable phenomenon, but it causes defects in children's development and eventually causes children's problems.

D. Bad Friendship Group

Another factor that caused the child problem is the increase in the number of delinquent friends. Children who experience family dissolution due to divorce or separation are experiencing mental pain or bitter life such as anxiety, conflict, and anger. As a result, it has a great negative effect on the child's personality and emotional formation, making it suitable for a group of delinquent friends outside the family. They are more likely to cause problems such as runaway crimes to survive or remain loyal to the group.

(2) Improvements in Child Welfare in Korea

Some factors that have formed Korea's child welfare at a low level are as follows.

First, there is a strong patriarchal tradition. The solid patriarchal tradition resulted in a strong sense of ownership of household members by the head of the household, and in particular, the concept of ownership of their children was more explicit, making most adults conscious and unconscious.

Second, the firm survival of Confucian customs played a role in making the status and rights of children irreplaceable in front of adult authority. The feudal Confucian tradition, symbolized by the long will, played a major role in establishing children's self-consciousness, independent thinking, and independent status.

Third, because children have no political bargaining power, they have no influence on the introduction and development of welfare policies. The limitations of such a child group can be solved only when a mature sense of welfare and civic consciousness with a subjective interest in children's rights and welfare is premised.

Fourth, as a group that is actively interested in child welfare in society, it reveals fundamental limitations in responding to child welfare issues due to the facility selfishness and the tendency to maintain vested rights of child welfare facility operators, but rather hinders the development of child welfare.

Fifth, the lack of social awakening to the consciousness of children's rights and the lack of dynamic movement groups representing children's rights and children's welfare are the causes.

3. Youth Welfare

1) Concept of Youth Welfare

Adolescence is derived from the Latin word 'Adolescere' and has the meaning of '**growth**' or '**mature**'. In general, adolescence is a period located between childhood and adulthood that requires parental dependence and protection in the human development stage, and refers to adolescence ages 12-13 to 22 or 23. Before the word 'youth welfare' was used in Korean society, youth welfare was included in child welfare or dealt with as an extension of child welfare. In the university curriculum, youth welfare was also dealt with in child welfare, but gradually reorganized into child and youth welfare, and only recently, an independent curriculum called youth welfare was established. The controversy over youth welfare depends on how to distinguish between adolescents and children's ages and how to secure the identity of youth welfare.

Focusing on the views of major scholars, the definition of the concept of youth welfare is as follows.

The understanding of youth welfare from an institutional standpoint is in line with Friedlander's position of seeing "**child welfare**." Children's welfare is not just about children with poverty, neglect, disease, defects, or delinquent children who cannot adapt to the environment, but is social, economic, and health activities conducted by the corporation to protect all children from safety and happiness in physical, intellectual, and emotional development, he said.

In Korea, the concept of youth welfare and child welfare is not clearly distinguished from the concept of youth welfare in the Korean Social Welfare Review(1977), and it is assumed that there is some confusion and difficulty in compiling the title of youth welfare separated from child welfare. He tried to present issues that must be considered for the future by reviewing the current situation at the welfare level, such as the educational environment, health, occupation, humanity recovery, and leisure use, which have an important influence on youth personality formation with youth welfare. Although he did not systematically attempt to define youth welfare, his view of youth welfare as a "**factor influencing youth personality formation**" has implications.

Lee, Soo-Min has various meanings, and it is said that it generally means various actions to promote the welfare of children and adolescents through various supportive, protective, and supplementary slogans and services. In order for all adolescents to be healthy and achieve personality, planning and practice of volunteer work are required, and all institutions and facilities in the community, especially in the fields of health, education, and social welfare, must be mobilized for this work. His definition emphasizes the practical aspects of youth welfare, suggesting that youth welfare originated from practice in the field rather than discussion by the platform.

When defining youth welfare, it is worth noting that adolescence is in the process of moving from child to adult in the cycle of life. Everyone has a developmental task that must be achieved at that stage at each stage of development, and adolescence is a time to seek physical maturity, make friends of the same sex and reason, and prepare to become economically independent. Therefore, youth welfare should be a social service that helps adolescents overcome social problems such as deviance, inequality, and social dissolution while satisfying more desperate social needs such as education, health, and job.

Adolescents are growing up, and they are gradually influenced by peer groups, teachers (or) schools, and society, away from the influence of their born families or parents. Adolescents can grow up with less parental protection compared to children, but they satisfy basic needs such as food, clothing, and shelter and rely almost entirely on their parents for living expenses such as school education. Therefore, changes in family and society directly affect the lives of adolescents, and conversely, changes in adolescents can also affect families and society. Because of these attributes, youth welfare is generally developed in the following three cases.

First, the state or local governments intervened when it was impossible to satisfy basic human needs such as income, health, education, and housing from the family where adolescents were born. A typical type is when the family is economically poor and the living expenses required for adolescents to live are insufficient, and when the family cannot be properly protected due to the death or divorce of parents.

Second, it is difficult for parents to guide adolescent children due to running away from their families, habitual drug abuse, and sexual problems. When physically out of the parental protection network, such as running away from home, social protection is required, and the recent increase in drug abuse and sexual problems is requested by experts such as medical treatment.

Third, welfare is also necessary to reduce harmful things in the living environment where adolescents live and to create a beneficial environment. As adolescents' play culture is commercialized, appropriate regulations on violent and obscene electronic entertainment, cartoons, videos, television, and computer programs are being requested, and social welfare services are being developed to expand healthy play spaces and opportunities for teenagers. In addition, as seen in the International Convention on the Rights of Children, it is necessary to guarantee the 'best interests' of adolescents as an independent person while emphasizing the human rights of children and adolescents. Youth welfare is not determined by one of the above three factors, but rather works in combination.

2) Conceptual Provisions of Adolescence

Adolescence, an intermediate stage between childhood and adulthood, is a transitional period in which children who relied entirely on their parents grow into independent adults. The word adolescence in English, which means adolescence, means "**growth**" in Latin. During this period, rapid development takes place not only in physical development but also in intellectual and emotional aspects. In general, adolescence is thought to start in adolescence and take on adult responsibility, but the beginning and end of adolescence vary slightly depending on the academic field and scholars.

(1) Physiological Adolescence

Adolescence begins when reproductive organs and secondary sexual characteristics appear and ends with the full maturity of the reproductive system. Therefore, it can be said that the beginning of adolescence is the beginning of adolescence, and the period of obtaining fertility due to the regular production of fertilized eggs and the establishment of menstrual cycles is the end of adolescence.

In addition, even if adolescence is defined from around the 11th century when the beginning of adolescence begins to around the 20th century when it enters adulthood, the people in between can be divided into various subgroups. In terms of school age, the early teens who are just starting adolescence are high school students, the mid teens are middle and high school students, and the late teens are college students or office workers. Therefore, it should be viewed as a group with growth potential with a wide variety of properties rather than a group of storm and stress.

(2) Economic and Legal Adolescence

The period of economic independence from parents varies from individual to individual, and the legally eligible age varies from country to country. For example, young people in the United States and Europe are economically independent and legally treated as adults around the age of 18, but most of the 18 years old in Korea rely on their parents economically and do not have the right to vote legally. As such, the beginning and end of adolescence should consider the social environment along with physical maturity.

In this respect, middle and high school students, who are of social interest, are in the middle of adolescence and still have a beginning to go crazy in adulthood. Therefore, middle and high school students are distinguished from college students who want to become economically, emotionally and socially mature social workers while being independent from their parents, and it can be said that it is a time to spend their living time mainly on learning activities. Therefore, all adolescents must face the next period while performing development tasks suitable for their development stage. Here, '**development task**' is a skill or ability required for an individual to adapt to the environment at each development stage, and if the achievement of the development task at one stage is not satisfactory, the development at the next stage is hindered. Havighurst is a development task in adolescence, and it emphasized emotional and social development as follows.

① acknowledge one's physique and accept one's gender role

② Create a new relationship with friends of the same gender or opposite sex.

③ Emotional independence from parents and other adults.

④ feel the need for economic independence

⑤ Choose a job and prepare.

⑥ acquire intellectual skills and concepts that must be equipped as a competent citizen.

⑦ They want socially responsible behavior and practice it.

⑧ Prepare for marriage and family life.

⑨ Form a value system according to the appropriate scientific worldview.

3) Characteristics of Adolescence

(1) Physical and Sexual Development

A. Physical Development

During adolescence, the body of a child changes into the form of an adult, and the physical and sexual differences between men and women are established. In general, height, weight, and rapidly increasing growth rates occur between the ages of 10 and 11 in girls and 12 and 13 in boys, and then continue to grow afterwards, and when they reach around the age of 20, height almost stops and weight slowly increases.

The rapid growth phenomenon in adolescence is also remarkable in areas other than height and weight. The forehead becomes wider and higher, and the skull looks like an adult. The lower jaw and nose become longer, the mouth becomes larger, and the lips become plump. The increase in the proportion of boy's muscle tissue and girl's adipose tissue gives boys a tough look and girls a round look. The activation of the genders widens the shoulders of boys and widens the pelvis of girls, giving them the appearance of typical men and women. However, as a result of asynchronous growth, the hands and feet may be temporarily imbalanced compared to the arms and legs.

Korean adolescents' height and weight are continuously increasing as their nutritional status improves. 〈1997 Student Physical Examination Results〉 In the case of middle and high school seniors, the average height of male students was 172.15 centimeters, growing 3.25 centimeters from 10 years ago, and the average weight increased to 64.1 kilograms. As such, his physique grew, but his physical strength measured by running, push-ups, and sit-ups continued to decrease.

B. Sexual Maturity

In adolescence, secondary gender characteristics begin to appear along with rapid growth. Secondary gender characteristics are the characteristics that distinguish men from women, such as physique development, chest development, body hair distribution and voice change, but are not essential factors for reproduction. On the other hand, primary sexual characteristics such as male testicles and penis, female ovaries and uterus, which are essential factors for reproduction, mature slightly later than secondary sexual characteristics. In general, the time when primary sexual characteristics begin to develop is viewed as the beginning of puberty, and the growth of sexual characteristics continues, so girls, on average, are completed around the 17th century and boys around the 21st century.

Changes in hormone secretion with the onset of adolescence arouse adolescents' interest in sex. Adolescents sometimes suffer from problems with sexual institutional development, sexual emotion, and sexual impulses. One of the important developmental tasks of adolescence is to learn how to deal with sexual impulses and emotions in a socially acceptable way. Europeans, who are somewhat fast in sexual development and open in sex, learn how to deal with sexual impulses and emotions in middle and high school, but Koreans are strongly suppressed in this period. In the process of attending middle and high schools separated by men and women, sexual behavior between opposite sex is prohibited, and there is little time to date opposite sex due to the burden of studying for college entrance exams.

For this reason, middle and high school students often fail to learn how to deal with sexual impulses and emotions in a socially acceptable way and fall into sexual problems. In particular, in the global trend of gender openness, the flooding of various pornography is changing attitudes and behaviors toward sex more openly, but more and more adolescents suffer from sexual problems such as premarital sex, premarital pregnancy, and venereal disease due to their inability to responsible sexual behavior.

(2) Cognitive Development and Study

A. Development of Cognitive Abilities

Cognition can be defined as a higher mental process such as thinking, imagination, creativity, reasoning, problem-solving skills, conceptualization, and categorization, including the composition, acquisition, maintenance, and utilization of knowledge. Piaget is a representative scholar who comprehensively explains the composition of human knowledge and the use of it, and Piaget says that cognitive development is not entirely done by internal maturity according to age change, nor is it influenced by post-birth experience or external education. He viewed it as an active composition process that establishes a more differentiated and comprehensive cognitive structure through active actions as well as the timetable already determined when a child is born.

Piaget viewed the cognitive development stage as four stages: sensory motor(about 2 years old after birth), precursor(between 2 and 6 to 7 years old), specific manipulator(between 7 and 11 to 12 years old), and formal manipulator(starting between 11 and 15 years old). He saw that even if it was not specifically performed on a formal manipulator, it could potentially apply mental representation to think, and that various reversible possibilities cooperated to enable a higher level of thinking. Therefore, the thinking characteristics of this period can be thought logically about hypothetical things, can create multiple hypotheses, systematically verify all possibilities, and can think hypothesis deductively.

In this sense, in adolescence, thoughts change from reality-oriented to possibility-oriented. Possibility-oriented thinking is the driving force behind solving problems with alternatives in many aspects, rather than just conventional thinking. Formal manipulators examine the logic of a series of beliefs, which tend to take into account one's beliefs in religion, politics, morality, and education with consistent logic. Therefore, when one belief is challenged, all other beliefs are consistently questioned and attacked more severely. Therefore, adolescents are outraged by the inconsistency that is suddenly found in various thoughts that were previously the eldest son, and challenge the adults around them to explain it. It can be explained that the characteristics of young people who are controversial and prone to rebellion stem from the characteristics of thinking that insist on this logical consistency.

In the case of Korea, since entrance examination-oriented knowledge education is emphasized, it is easy to reserve logical thinking and critical behavior suitable for the cognitive development stage in middle and high school students. Just as a reservoir without proper sluice collapses when the bank is filled, college freshmen are free from regulations and are likely to criticize the existing order at once. Rather than seeking a reasonable alternative, excessive attitude of ignoring and criticizing the older generation may lead to violence.

B. Academic Problems

According to a survey of 1,245 middle and high school students nationwide conducted by the Youth Painting Plaza(1992), academic problems are the biggest problems for middle and high school students. Academic problems include study, career choice, study method, and grades, and studies are the main interests of students more than any other problem.

(3) Personality Formation and Changes in Values

A. Character Formation

In adolescence, dramatic changes in body proportions occur, emotional and inappropriate feelings increase, and self-centeredness increases. In addition, changes take place in attitudes and behaviors along with changes in values.

Regarding the personality change during adolescence, some scholars argue that it is only a phenomenon(birth simultaneous group effect) that occurs because the birth group is the same or that it reflects the effect of the measurement period. However, many scholars have studied the simultaneous birth group several times, and believe that individuals' self-intensity and impulse control skills continue to develop from the beginning of adolescence, and self-intensity gradually improved with an increase in age. The self-defense mechanism used by teenagers also changes into a more mature defense mechanism with age increase.

Since adolescence is a time to experience various events that have not been experienced in childhood, the scope of adolescents' emotional experiences expands and the depth of emotions deepens. Representative positive emotions experienced during adolescence include feelings of happiness and love. Teenagers experience the beauty of nature, the purity and seriousness of friendship, and the vivid happiness that love brings. Also, interest in reason makes you experience love. Representative negative emotions experienced in adolescence include depression, fear and anxiety, loneliness, guilt, and anger.

B. Changes in Values

Values are more generalized and organized concepts than attitudes or values, and are principles and central beliefs that present order and direction for human behavior and thinking. Therefore, values function as standards or guidelines for behavior, criteria for preference, and evaluation.

The important values that become the standard of behavior in adolescence are religious values and political and social values. Individual religious values are an important factor in shaping his sense of identity. Cognitive changes in adolescence and exposure to diverse and broad views stimulate adolescents to consider religion from a more abstract and personal perspective than in childhood.

Fowler suggested six stages of religious belief development, according to which middle and high school students(from 12, 13 to under 18) uncritically accept certain groups' beliefs and unconditionally ignore information that does not match them. This is because individual beliefs play a role in giving consistency and meaning to their lives at this stage. However, after the age of 18, people can evaluate and criticize religious doctrines and principles based on their own experiences and values.

The formation of individual political and social values takes place over a considerable period of time. Scholars generally take place between the ages of 10 and 17 ~ 18. Scholars generally believe that the basis of political and social attitudes is formed between the ages of 10 and 17~18. Positive political socialization occurs in the upper and middle school years, and in the middle of adolescence, individual political socialization begins to take on a negative and skeptical color. From the middle of adolescence, when formal manipulation skills are developed, attitudes toward political institutions or authoritative groups change critically and cynically.

Although they learn politics, economy, society, and culture in middle and high school, their desire to participate may erupt as young people who were controlled by the entrance exam-oriented educational environment enter college. For this reason, first and second-year university students are attracted to criticizing real politics with interest in political and social issues as part of their identity formation.

(4) Building a Sense of Self-Identity and Career Choice

A. Formation of a Sense of Self-Identity

Self-identity is a relatively stable feeling for one's uniqueness and is the consistency we have for ourselves despite changes in behavior, thinking, and emotions. Erickson stressed that the individual's feelings about who he is should be consistent with the view that others see him. He presented eight stages of development and considered that an individual's unique personality was formed depending on how to solve the psychosocial crisis at each stage. Adolescence(11 to 22 years old) is a period of self-identity versus role confusion, and seriously agonizes and conflicts to get answers to the questions of "**Who am I**" and "**What can I do?**" If you are confident about your existence and the value you will pursue, you will gain an identity, otherwise you will fall into role confusion.

The establishment of an identity in adolescence is not a universal phenomenon that can be found in any society, and the larger the cultural discontinuity between childhood and adulthood, the longer adolescence. The more technologically advanced society, the longer the learning period is because the technology acquired in childhood is not useful in adulthood and has to be constantly newly learned.

Erickson's psychosocial development stage is divided into eight stages, focusing on the quality and mental function of interpersonal relationships that humans have in relationships with society, and is explained by conflicting crisis concepts.

B. Career Choices

The vast majority of middle and high school students in adolescence prefer college, so they worry about career choices. College students are also deeply interested in many studies and careers because it is a time to prepare for a job along with major learning.

4) Prospects and Challenges for Youth Welfare

(1) Outlook for Youth Welfare

Until the mid-1980s, youth welfare was treated as one of child welfare, and areas of interest were also limited to juvenile delinquency and problems. Over the past decade or so, social interest in youth welfare has increased quantitatively and intensified qualitatively, and is expected to change as follows.

First, as civic groups related to youth welfare emerge, the areas of interest will be subdivided. Youth runaway, school violence, and human rights issues have already become social concerns, and in the future, parenting of children with parents, school social welfare projects, and youth unemployment will draw attention.

Second, interest in youth welfare will be further amplified as academic organizations subdivided by areas of interest lead research. Social interest in adolescents was systematized by the creation of the Korean Youth Association(1991), and recently, professional academic gatherings such as the Korean School Social Work Association, the Korean Youth Welfare Association, and the Korean Society for Children's Rights have emphasized research on youth welfare.

Third, as youth welfare facilities that provide youth welfare services are expanded, facility users' needs and interest in services will increase.

Fourth, youth welfare will not be limited to some problematic adolescents or protected adolescents, but will spread to the learning and life of all adolescents. Student volunteer activities, youth human rights improvement, compulsory education of secondary education, expansion of school meals, and emphasis on various youth experience activities will pay attention to the "quality of life" of all adolescents.

(2) Youth Weltare Challenges

The task of youth welfare should be to find alternatives that can solve youth needs and problems in the near future and improve the quality of life of adolescents.

First, information should be taught to children and adolescents the contents of rights stipulated in the International Convention on the Rights of Children, and revised if existing domestic laws contradict the contents of this Convention. In particular, a system that can guarantee the human rights of adolescents who are not sufficiently protected from parental divorce, adoption, or dissolution should be established.

Second, it is necessary to appropriately adjust the responsibilities of guardians and the responsibilities of the state and local governments for youth in need. When a juvenile is required to be protected, the head of the City/Gun should fully consider the parenting conditions of the guardian and the needs of the youth so that in-house protection and facility protection have an organic connection.

Third, current youth welfare facilities often do not receive government support due to the absence of related laws, so legal supplementation is necessary. In other words, protection facilities that temporarily raise protected adolescents without families to return to family deficits or dissolution should be expanded, and at least one therapeutic protection facility should be installed or designated per city and province to treat adolescents who abuse drugs or engage in problematic behavior.

Fourth, youth projects should be implemented for each living area unit. Given that one of the biggest desires of teenagers is "no time to play and no place to go," it is necessary to reduce the burden of entrance exams to secure leisure time, build youth facilities to benefit from leisure time, recruit more professionals and secure project costs.

Fifth, in order to institutionalize various youth welfare programs, regulations on youth welfare and youth welfare facilities must be specified in the Framework Act on Youth or Youth Protection Act, and youth welfare projects must be included in the Social Welfare Act. Although the Framework Act on Youth stipulates 'promoting youth welfare', the definition of youth welfare and youth welfare facilities is omitted. Therefore, it should be defined as youth welfare facilities by establishing treatment facilities for abused children and drug abuse treatment facilities, including youth counseling rooms, youth shelters, and youth study rooms that are currently engaged in youth welfare projects.

This proposal recognizes that adolescents are also citizens of this land and intends to devise youth welfare projects that suit their needs and problems. Existing youth projects were mainly intended to provide minimum welfare services to youths who were protected, but now they should be developed in a way that selectively provides services to adolescents with more needs, while developing universal welfare services for all adolescents.

Chapter 15 Welfare of Persons with Disabilities

1. Concepts and Types of Persons with Disabilities

1) Concept of Disabled People

In Korea, expressions referring to the disabled are often vulgar. These expressions were even exposed to the public without being purified even in the media. In the case of the law, the worst expression for the disabled was the unification of terms, from the expressions of "**disabled**" to the disabled and sometimes blind people. Meanwhile, the Joint Task Force, which led the revision of the existing Act on the Welfare of Persons with Mental Disabilities in 1988, insisted that the term "disabled" should be adopted as an official legal term, citing the negative perception of the general public.

In the Declaration of the Rights of Persons with Disabilities, declared in 1975, the United Nations said, "*A disabled person, whether born or acquired, means a person who cannot fully or partially secure what is necessary for daily personal or social life due to incomplete physical and mental abilities.*" According to Article 2 of the Welfare of Persons with Disabilities Act, "*a person with disabilities is defined as a person who is significantly restricted in daily life or social life over a long period of time due to mental defects such as physical disabilities, visual impairment, hearing impairment, speech impairment, or mental retardation.*"

Legally, the disabled are set differently according to the will and level of a country's welfare policy. In the United States, Canada, and Australia, even patients with organ diseases are classified as disabled until treatment is completed.

When defining the disabled, the cause or disease name is irrelevant. The International Labor Organization's recommendation on vocational rehabilitation for physically disabled people also stipulated that physically or mentally disabled people are significantly reduced in their chances of finding a suitable job or continuing it as a result of physical or mental damage. Article 2 of the Framework Act on Persons with Disabilities stipulates that a disabled person refers to a person who is significantly restricted from daily life or social life over a long period of time due to physical disability, mental weakness, or mental disability.

Article 3 of the Special Education Promotion Act in Korea classifies the scope of the disabled into visually impaired, hearing impaired, mentally handicapped, physically handicapped, emotionally handicapped, speech impaired, and other mentally and physically handicapped people. In Chapter 1, Article 2 of the Welfare of Persons with Disabilities Act(revised in 1989), the term "**disabled person**" refers to a person subject to considerable restrictions such as physical disability, visual impairment, hearing impairment, speech impairment, or mental retardation.

This law was revised in February 1999, and Article 2 of the same Act stipulates the following for the disabled. In paragraph (1), a person with disabilities refers to a person who is significantly restricted from daily life or social life over a long period of time due to physical and mental disabilities. The disabled subject to this Act under paragraph (2) refer to those with disabilities falling under any of the following subparagraphs 1 and who meet the types and standards of disabilities prescribed by Presidential Decree, so that those with physical disabilities or mental illness can be included in the category of disabled.

Physical disability refers to disability of major external physical functions and disability of internal organs.

Mental disability refers to a disability caused by mental retardation or mental illness(implementation date: January 1, 2000).

In the past, the criteria for the disabled were mainly set to the degree of physical or intellectual defects, but in recent years, the disabled are being judged and classified due to the ability to work and the degree of discomfort in family life and social life, and Korea also defines the disabled. In recent years, as awareness and understanding of disabilities have intensified and their understanding has expanded, efforts to subdivide and understand disabilities have been made.

This reflects the continued spread of rehabilitation activities and improved expertise, while at the same time having a cause in terms of policy. The World Health Organization(WHO, 1980) proposes a hierarchical concept in the International Classification of Impairs(ICIDH), which classifies disabilities, showing the usefulness of rehabilitation activities according to the condition of the disabled. Therefore, it is classified into I, D, and H disorders and presented. ① Impairment(I code): It refers to structural and functional damage to the mind and body itself, and refers to mental disorders such as retardation, visual impairment, hearing impairment, mental retardation, memory, accident, emotion, epilepsy, etc., internal and skin disorders, and loss of body structure. ② Disability(D code): It refers to a disability that appears in daily life activities at the individual level due to functional constraints, and has difficulty in activities in a state in which daily behavior is impossible or limited. ③ Handicap(H code): It occurs at the social level and refers to disadvantages, prejudices, and discrimination caused by relationships with others by people with mental and physical damage or functional limitations. This includes the living environment of the disabled, which means physical, cultural, and social barriers, and means that the disabled are restricted or deprived of the opportunity to participate in society equally(Park, Sang-Ha et al., 2009).

In Korea, the Special Education Promotion Act was enacted in 1977, followed by the Welfare of Persons with Disabilities Act in 1989, and the Employment Promotion of Persons with Disabilities Act in 1990. In developed countries, welfare for the disabled, centered on mentally handicapped children, was enacted early on, and the UK, Sweden, and Denmark are considered the best countries with welfare systems for the disabled. The types of pension benefits of the National Welfare Pension include disability pensions, and pensions are to be paid according to the degree of disability(grade 3) caused by injury.

2) Causes and Types of Persons with Disabilities

(1) Cause of Disability

According to a World Health Organization(WHO) survey, the number of people with disabilities in a country is roughly 10 percent of the total population. According to the Ministry of Health and Welfare(currently, the Ministry of Health and Welfare) survey on the disabled in 1990, Korea announced that it was 2.2% of the total population. In order to understand the number of people with disabilities, economic conditions, health conditions, and welfare needs, a five-year survey has been conducted since 1985, and the number of people with disabilities in Korea is estimated to be 1,398,000, 3.09% of the total population. On the other hand, the average monthly income of disabled households is about 1,082,000 won, which is only 46.4% of urban worker household income(KRW 23.31 million in the second quarter of 2000), and disability treatment, rehabilitation services, and special education for transportation are the main causes of poverty.

The difference in the number of people with disabilities in each country seems to be due to differences in the category and method of investigation of people with disabilities, and the expertise of those surveyed.

As the WHO announced, it is a global trend to see 10% of the total population as disabled, and scholars cite the figures because there is no reliable survey report.

The causes of disability vary from traffic accidents, industrial accidents, pollution, diseases, drug misuse and abuse, general accidents, and genetic factors. In our case, there are no official statistics on the proportion of people with disabilities, but according to an analysis by a disabled welfare institution called the Institute for the Rights of the Disabled, it is estimated that about 40% of traffic accidents, 30% of industrial accidents, 20% of diseases, and 10% of others.

(2) Type of Disability

A. Function and Form

Functional and morphological disorders, which are characteristics of an individual, are the primary level of disability. It occurs directly from a disease and is a disorder(I code) identified at the biological level(long-term level) based on the site or function of the disorder.

B. Dysfunction

The state in which the ability to form activities in the normal range of life as a human being is limited or deficient by function and morphological disorder is the secondary level of disability due to disability. It is an obstacle(D code) identified at the level of a human object based on its ability to perform as an individual.

C. Social Disability

It is the tertiary level of disability, which is caused by illness, damage, or social disadvantage, and is the social consequence(H code) of competency disorder. In other words, even if the disability is the same, there is a big difference in the actual life of the disabled in a society where the understanding of the disabled, the easy-to-action urban environment, and measures for social return or rehabilitation are sufficiently taken. Focusing on the disadvantages of the disabled as such a social being, the disability identified at the social level is called a social disability. This view takes the view that people with disabilities not only have mental and physical disabilities, but also lead social lives. The amputation of the lower extremity or the mental development retardation itself is a function, form, disability, or damage. Such damage is the same whether the person is Korea or the United States. Even those who have the same damage but have no lower limbs can walk or get a job if they are educated or trained or motivated. In some cases, even mental development delays can be performed without protection. On the other hand, even with the same degree of damage, the person's motivation and educational opportunity are not sufficient, and even if the person's damage is not sufficient, the person's motivation and educational opportunity are not sufficiently exercised. Of the two, the former person is less damaged than the latter. Even if the degree of damage is the same, for example, if physical environmental preservation or social prejudice such as indoor renovation is removed, the social obstacles that the person has in his or her social life will decrease. In short, it is possible to make the lives of the disabled more convenient through social efforts. The rate of progress in social policies, in particular the rate of living conditions and environmental improvement, reduces social obstacles for the disabled.

3) Concept of Welfare for the Disabled

Welfare for the disabled refers to welfare services at the institutional, policy, and clinical levels to ensure human life for the disabled and improve their quality of life. This welfare for the disabled stems from respect for human rights and is based on humanitarianism based on the idea of human respect. Welfare for the disabled is also important for realizing democracy, which is equality of opportunity.

There are two perspectives on defining the concept of welfare for the disabled. First, welfare for the disabled as a concept of purpose. In other words, it refers to a desirable social state(social situation) for the disabled, and is an objective concept called an ideology or goal. No matter what obstacles you have, human life itself is valuable, and you exercise your ability and lead a faithful life. To that end, it is the ideology and goal of welfare for the disabled to ensure opportunities for human development. Second, welfare for the disabled as a substantive concept. This refers to the system of social policies such as policies, institutions, and aid, which are divided into welfare for the disabled in consultation with current welfare policies, systems, and aid activities, and welfare for the disabled, including related policies such as education, hygiene, and labor.

Article 1 of the same Act stipulates that "the welfare of the disabled is to promote comprehensive welfare measures for the disabled, such as prevention of disability and medical care, training, protection, education, employment promotion, and allowances for the disabled.

Therefore, welfare for the disabled is based on the ideology of dignity of the disabled, human rights recovery, efforts to stand on their own feet, and social participation.

Social welfare refers to the guarantee of individual welfare, the disadvantages of disabled people in light of the former ideology and goals are mitigated, resolved, and secured equal living conditions and stability with human, psychological and physical disabilities and social bias.

2. Ideas and Objectives for Welfare of Persons with Disabilities

1) Philosophy of Welfare for the Disabled

One of the most difficult things that people with disabilities feel is alienation and unequal treatment, recognizing and enjoying equal opportunities as equal neighbors within the social community, and full participation and equality are what people with disabilities today want the most. There is no controversy over this social integration itself, and the problem can be said to be a way to achieve social integration. In other words, it means that practical completion can be achieved only when the three processes of social integration are mainstreamed, normalized, and equalized. Here, mainstreaming means that the disabled should not be isolated in education, occupation, and cultural life, and should be considered to be at the center as much as possible. Methods to achieve this include integrated education, compulsory employment for the disabled, and community-based rehabilitation(CBR). Until now, mainstreaming has meant the process of attracting the disabled to the center of the general society. This is because the wall is too high for the disabled to enter the center of society through overcoming disability without social change, which is much more likely to give up and frustration than the joy of success. However, rather than transforming the disabled to fit into society, the need for mutual change to embrace the disabled and develop the remaining ability of the disabled to enter the center of society is called reverse mainstreaming. In addition, the meaning of normalization originated from the welfare problem of mentally disabled people in Scandinavia in the late 1960s, and then elaborated, generalized, and systematized in North America. Wolfensberger defines the principle of normalization as "*using culturally valuable means to acquire, organize, and maintain social roles that are as valuable to people as possible.*" In other words, normalization refers to the recognition of disabled people as normal and ordinary members of society by bringing their living environment and conditions as close as possible to the living standards and prototype of the general public(Park, Sang-Ha, 2009). Normalization refers to treating any child or disabled person as an ordinary human being. Disabled people are basically equal personality subjects, except for the visible nature of disability. No matter how precious the disabled are, if it is formed in the idea of isolation or exclusion, the personality of the disabled is not respected. Normalization is the principle of equal living in which people with disabilities are equally responsible for their rights and obligations as humans despite the presence or absence of disabilities without overprotecting or special treatment.

We can say that the disabled are integrated into society only when they are recognized as ordinary people who are not treated inferior to the non-disabled or who have physical disabilities but are capable of fulfilling their responsibilities and duties as members of the community. The ultimate goal of welfare for the disabled is to achieve full participation and equality of the disabled in this form.

(1) Principle of Equality of Human Rights

Society's perception of the disabled has long been veiled with discrimination and prejudice. In response to these issues, paragraph 2 of the United Nations World Action Plan on the Disabled points out that people with disabilities have the same rights and equal opportunities as everyone else, and paragraph 26 states that "*disabled people have equal rights and obligations.*" According to Article 34 (1) of the Constitution of the Republic of Korea, "*all citizens have the right to live a human life,*" *and Article 10 stipulates that "all citizens have the right to dignity and value as human beings and pursue happiness.*" In this way, the disabled are considered as subjects of rights and obligations without special treatment.

(2) Individualization Principle of Disability

Even if they have the same disability name and cause of disability, it never has the same meaning for individuals with different personalities, situations, and tasks in life. In paragraph 8 of the United Nations World Action Plan on the Disabled, there is no homogeneous group for the disabled. For example, the so-called mentally handicapped, visually impaired, hearing impaired, speech impaired, and mobility have different properties and must overcome them in different ways, suggesting that there is a high degree of individuality in the meaning of disability and problem solving. Even in the treatment process of the disabled, it is very important to identify the individual meaning of the disability, find a solution suitable for the individual, procure resources, and conduct mediation activities. Therefore, it is absolutely necessary to eliminate the stigma of the same kind of disorder or to treat irresponsible people without fully understanding them.

(3) Principle of Development Security

Even if the mental and physical functions are impaired, for example, for the visually impaired, as hearing, tactile, and olfactory development other than vision, humans' ability to survive, that is, the function of other organs, is improved overall. A person who is delayed in intellectual development is slow in development, but he or she grows in his or her own way. Therefore, it is very important not to give up from the beginning, but to find the possibility of individual development and growth of remaining abilities. Dr. Goodman, the founder of Paralympic sports, points out the importance of finding what is possible, not lamenting the loss compared to others, and believes that rehabilitation philosophy is to see each person's personality and characteristics as a whole and increase its potential. All individuals change and develop. Efforts to trust that possibility and intervene in human potential are the principles of humanization that aim to ensure development.

(4) Principle of Commonality of Needs

In general, people pay attention to the difference in the properties of the average personality of disability, but they should know that the commonality of human needs shared by the disabled and the non-disabled is greater. Everyone tries to achieve the common demand for advancement, employment, marriage, etc. with other means such as studying for the disabled. If there is a limit to making efforts on one's own, developing and helping other methods is the principle of welfare for the disabled that the disabled want.

(5) Principle of Participation and Equality

Disabled people who are awakened to their dignity have the right to live as the same human being, excluding eternal discriminatory treatment. No matter how free the hands and feet are, integrated education that allows students to study with other children in general schools has led to the claim of integration into society and the flow of the trend. Nevertheless, schools, workplace and public facilities have created and maintained a physical and mental framework that rejects coexistence by overlooking the existence of a minority called the disabled. The idea of participation and equality against such a caring society began to challenge a society with barriers as the self-liberation goal of the disabled. When the complete participation and equality of the disabled progresses, the state in which the disabled and the non-disabled become friends without being separated is called integration. It cannot be realized unless anyone participates on the premise of equality. The United Nations warns that if society fails to accept everyone, it will become a social organization that excludes the disabled, and a society that excludes the disabled will eventually become a society with defects. Article 3, Paragraph 2 of the Welfare of Persons with Disabilities Act stipulates that "*No one is discriminated against in all areas of political, economic, social, and cultural life on the grounds of disability*" and Paragraph 3 stipulates "all persons with disabilities are guaranteed opportunities to participate in political, economic, social, and cultural activities".

Organizations with disabilities are united in a joint struggle to acquire their human rights. They are demanding active government intervention in the right to move and education. The disabled have formed a general association of disabled groups and are actively moving as they speak out on their own welfare issues. Therefore, I think it is time for the government and experts to change their perspective on the disabled. In advanced countries such as the UK, the parties who say "*the biggest enemy of the disabled is the government and experts*" are very high in voice, which suggests a lot. From the perspective of the disabled, the government establishes and implements policies according to the opinions of experts, and there is also a perception that experts are always on a special track for them.

To this end, the following points must be improved.

The first is the division of labor and specialization of business. Until now, the perception that the disabled's work is related to the disabled is dominated by the Ministry of Health and Welfare. However, the government should now provide programs based on the perception that the disabled are one of the people. The Ministry of Health and Welfare should boldly link the sports issues of the disabled with the National Sports Function of the Ministry of Culture, Sports and Tourism to consider the variables of disabilities, and the Ministry of Knowledge Economy should establish and execute specialized services.

Second, the problem of unemployment for the disabled is solved. Even if the employment promotion project for the disabled has been carried out for more than 12 years, it has yet to meet half of the mandatory employment rate, which is 2%, and in a high unemployment rate of about 30%, a groundbreaking alternative must be prepared.

(6) Principle of Equalization and Normalization of Opportunities

Equalization of opportunities is a process that makes the entire social organization, including physical environment, housing and transportation, social services and health services, educational and labor opportunities, and sports and recreational facilities, available to all. This society shared by everyone should be open to the disabled, and it is not desirable to accommodate and isolate the disabled only in separate living areas and special facilities. Based on the principle of equal opportunity, the mission of welfare for the disabled is to open up general social relations to the disabled.

Normalization is a recognition that it is natural for the disabled to be in society, and it is the fact that they exist just like the so-called non-disabled and should be treated as human beings. The disabled should not be regarded as a special group with different needs from the rest of the society, but as ordinary citizens with special difficulties in satisfying their ordinary human needs. Criticism is normalized that the disabled have been rejected in many social lives, including education and labor.

Mainstreaming is the first possible discussion of disabled children in the United States and has been in effect since October 1975, and all disabled children, regardless of their degree of disability, should be educated in an environment as limited as possible. The law requires educational mentally retarded children to return from special classes to ordinary classes.

2) Characteristics of Welfare for the Disabled

Welfare for the disabled can be classified into several characteristics as follows.

First, it is the complexity of the problem of the disabled. The disabled are suffering not only from medical and physiological discomfort but also from various problems derived from the fact that they are disabled, that is, disadvantages on school, employment, and marriage. The problems experienced by the disabled are not only multi-layered, but also have a complex structure. In addition, at the root of this pattern, there is a false view of the disabled throughout society.

Second, it is a problem of integration of welfare for the disabled. The problem of the disabled is not satisfied with only one side of the solution. This is because welfare for the disabled is not only a social welfare problem, but also a welfare that requires integration related to studies in medicine, education, psychology, sociology, and other fields.

Third, it is a matter of mobility of welfare for the disabled. In the case of developed countries, at the beginning of the implementation of welfare for the disabled, it was centered on politicians and experts, but gradually the awareness of the rights of the disabled increased and this began to develop as a social security movement. This movement deepened citizens' understanding of the disabled and had a consensus, thereby securing the subject of the rights of the disabled.

3) Welfare Targets for the Disabled

The target of welfare for the disabled is, of course, the disabled in a broad sense. Disability does not mean that all people with disabilities are eligible for welfare for the disabled. Article 3 of the Act on the Promotion of Special Education in Korea(1977) classifies the scope of the disabled as blind, deaf, mentally handicapped, physically handicapped, emotionally handicapped, speech-impaired, and other mentally and physically handicapped. In Chapter 1, Article 2 of the Welfare of Persons with Disabilities Act(revised in 1989), the term "**disabled person**" refers to a person who falls under the standards prescribed by Presidential Decree for a long period of time due to mental defects such as physical disability, visual, hearing, speech, or mental retardation. According to this definition, internal organ disabilities and mental illness are excluded from the target. With the revision of the Disabled Welfare

Act in 1999, the first category of disability, which took effect on January 1, 2000, has included brain lesions, developmental disorders, mental disorders, kidney disorders, and heart disorders in the category of disabled people. Following the expansion of the primary scope, secondary expansion preventive diseases include respiratory disease, chronic liver disease, chronic alcohol and drug addiction, organic brain syndrome, and other mental development disorders. Article 2 of the Enforcement Decree of the Disabled Welfare Act presents standards for each type of disabled person, and the Ministry of Health and Welfare divides the grade into six grades according to the degree of disability.

4) Rehabilitation for the Disabled

Rehabilitation can be said to help the disabled live a self-sustaining life by developing the maximum functional recovery and potential possible by integrating and cooperating with medical, social, educational, and vocational retraining for the disabled. The types of rehabilitation are as follows. ① Medical rehabilitation is a rehabilitation process that aims to minimize disability status and maximize residual capacity to return to society. It plays a role in preventing disability, accurate diagnosis, treatment, hearing tests and hearing training, and vocational rehabilitation. ② The purpose of educational rehabilitation is to foster the remaining capacity of the disabled to maximize and exercise as much as possible. Depending on the specificity of the target, there are special schools, special classes in general schools, circuit education, integrated education, and early special education. ③ Vocational rehabilitation is an important area of rehabilitation that can find and nurture the abilities of the disabled as much as possible to have the right and obligation to work like a normal person to change from dependent life to independent life. It leads to vocational training, job placement, and follow-up guidance. ④ Social and psychological rehabilitation is a mental rehabilitation in which the disabled can overcome their obstacles, return to society, and adapt smoothly as a member of society. ⑤ Rehabilitation engineering is a new field of rehabilitation and refers to rehabilitating the lost parts of people with mental disorders through engineering technology.

3. Contents of Welfare for Persons with Disabilities

The budget for social welfare in Korea has steadily increased every year, but it is still about 6% of the national budget. The social welfare service budget accounts for about 22.8%, of which the Ministry of Health and Welfare's budget for welfare for the disabled was only 39 billion won in 1992, up 3.7 times from 143.4 billion won in 2000, but only about 2%.

1) Income Security

Income security measures for the disabled can be largely divided into direct income security measures and indirect income security measures through economic burden reduction. Direct income security measures include social insurance and public assistance.

Social insurance includes salaries and disability benefits under the Industrial Accident Compensation Insurance Act(1963), and disability pensions under the Public Officials Pension Act(1960), the Military Pension Act(1963), the Private School Teachers' Pension Act(1973), and the National Pension Act(1987).

In the public assistance sector, living protection, including living benefits, has been provided under the National Basic Livelihood Security Act(1999), and living subsidies have been paid since 1990, but the National Basic Livelihood Security System has been disabled.

2) Medical Security

The medical security system for the disabled includes national health insurance, a social insurance system, a public assistance system, a medical protection system, medical expenses support for low-income disabled people, and free issuance of guarantees. The medical protection system allows only the disabled who are designated as eligible for life protection to receive medical protection benefits.

3) Housing Security

As a housing security policy for the disabled, housing benefits under the National Basic Living Protection Act have been paid to the disabled under the National Basic Living Protection Act since 2000, and a system that gives additional points to permanent rental housing tenants has been in operation since 1997. A system is being implemented to specially sell part of the total volume when supplying apartments of 85㎡ or less sold by national housing and public institutions to disabled householders without homes. However, the housing security policy for the disabled is very insufficient.

4) Social Service

Home care services are supported by the government to install and operate facilities that can be used to help people with disabilities receive treatment, education, jobs, and training services while living at home.

When looking at facility services by type of disability, accommodation facilities for mental retardation are the largest, followed by facilities for physical disability, facilities for hearing and speech disabilities, and facilities for the visually impaired. While other facilities have not changed much, the number of accommodation facilities with mental retardation is steadily increasing, and the number of nursing facilities for the severely disabled has increased significantly, but it is insufficient so far.

4. Directions for Welfare of Persons with Disabilities

1) Guarantee of the Rights of the Disabled

Welfare for the disabled can no longer be a grace under the government's policy. It is the right to guarantee a human life guaranteed by the Constitution from the state. Therefore, society must first strive for social integration of the disabled. Social integration is to integrate people who have deviated from society into the community. People deprived of value should be able to live with normal people, be educated with colleagues, work with others, and be included in religious life, recreation, shopping, and all other activities. There should be a social system established and guaranteed to protect their rights and interests to those who are alienated from social life due to disabilities. However, the first thing to do is to change the way normal people think about the disabled. Watching them use sarcastic language, you can realize that ordinary adults do not have adequate education for the disabled. I don't know if it's the result of a uniform educational environment, but in order to advance to a better society in the future, it is essential to establish a mature perception that can respect the underprivileged and the disabled. To that end, it is necessary to establish a system that can reliably establish consideration and correct perception of the disabled from our educational environment.

In particular, in order to integrate the disabled into society and expand the foundation for self-reliance, it is necessary to discover physical, mental, and economic availability through the welfare of the disabled as much as possible to enhance the dignity of individuals with disabilities.

Therefore, welfare for the disabled requires a professional and individual delivery system.

2) Establishment and Operation of Welfare Facilities for the Disabled

Various facilities should be operated by recognizing the necessity of living facilities for the disabled. In other words, facility protection should be provided as an optional data to ensure a human-like life in the disabled or their families and to select appropriate social welfare services for the disabled themselves. Due to certain circumstances, disabled people who cannot adapt to the family environment have been created, and inevitably, a system called facility protection is needed. In other words, in any case, it can be called facility protection to take care of and protect disabled people who cannot be raised at home. Therefore, the purpose of facility protection is to provide collective protection and treatment for the disabled who cannot properly meet their needs at home.

As can be seen from the specific purpose of facility protection, facility protection is not just to protect accommodation, but to provide various experiences and provide good opportunities through group life programs or special services according to the needs of disabilities.

Facilities protection should be provided to the disabled themselves so that they can choose appropriate social welfare services to ensure a human life for the disabled or their families, and living facilities for the disabled for healthy personality development and various problems. Therefore, living facilities for the disabled must perform the functions of these problematic life, technology, and aid services. In addition, the necessity of living facilities for the disabled is increasing to enhance the dignity of individuals with disabilities and to secure human dignity by discovering the personality development of the disabled and physical, mental, and economic availability as much as possible.

3) Measures to Improve the Operation of Residential Facilities for the Disabled

According to the results of several studies, living facilities for the disabled have many operational problems. This problem is expected to act as a factor that hinders normalization and social integration for people with facility disabilities. In order to improve these problems, improvement measures such as improvement of the delivery system of living facilities, activation of organization and operation, realization of finances, improvement of manpower and working conditions, and revitalization of relations with local communities were proposed.

First, the results of the survey on the delivery system showed a lot of dissatisfaction with the government's policy support, support for the disabled, timing, and delivery system. To improve the delivery of services to disabled living facilities, special cities, metropolitan cities, counties, and districts. In addition, reinforcement of local front-line organizations should be prioritized in the administrative system. The timing of government subsidies will also be appropriate for monthly living expenses and quarterly support for labor and management and operation costs. In addition, the timing of support should be adjusted so that living expenses, labor costs, and management and operation costs are supported at the beginning or before the execution cause occurs. In particular, government subsidies supported at the beginning of each year tend to be provided late, and local governments should secure and support government subsidies at the beginning of the year to prevent distortion in facility financial management.

Second, the results of the survey related to organization and operation showed that most of the facilities were poor or free of certification holders, facilities and equipment, and most of the facilities were not operated by the Operation and Personnel Committee, and few programs were provided for exchange with local communities. In addition, it was found that modernization of facilities, recruitment of professionals, exchange with local residents, and expansion of financial support are the most necessary factors in achieving business goals depending on how the organization is operated. Therefore, in order to operate the facility in a changing environment, the operator requires disabled-centered thinking, more scientific thinking, and open thinking. In addition, in order to respond to the diverse needs of the disabled and society, it is necessary to give responsibility to employees, improve appropriate work division and personnel system, and to boost employee morale and secure competitiveness between facilities.

A reasonable and realistic placement standard for facility employees should be prepared. In addition, with the introduction of a two-shift work system for rehabilitation teachers, the number of rehabilitation teachers has doubled, and it is inappropriate to maintain the current status of staff placement standards for other occupations. The criteria for staff placement should be considered so that hiring employees of similar occupations can be a criterion for exercising the discretion of facility managers when preparing. Rehabilitation for the disabled is by no means of the nature that can be done with one person's professional power. Therefore, the purpose of the service can be achieved depending on whether the team of many experts is organized and operated complementarily.

Residential facilities for the disabled should not only be operated through the agreement of the CEO of the corporation, facility operator, local maintenance and local governments, but also establish fairness in personnel organizations to operate the facilities. Therefore, it is necessary to establish efficiency, democracy, and fairness by revitalizing the steering committee and the personnel committee rather than formally operating them.

Efforts should be made to improve the level of facility protection in the future to ensure the human-like life of the disabled. These efforts should be made jointly not only by the government, but also by facility officials, local residents, facility disabled people and their families. In addition, diversification of programs in facilities will improve the quality of facility protection, individualization of the disabled, psychologically and socially, and improve the perception of local residents. Therefore, it is necessary to invest a lot in facilities and equipment of facilities.

In order to develop various programs to satisfy the needs of the disabled, the enthusiasm and expertise of the investigators are required, and the awareness of employees to improve their quality of life through the program must precede. In addition, considering the position of the staff in charge of the program and the circumstances of the facilities, there is a tendency to ignore the opinions of the disabled. Therefore, it is most important to understand the needs of the subject when conducting the program. One of the problems with the program is financial support, and the quality of service varies depending on the finances.

Third, the results of the financial survey were dissatisfied with the financial status of the facility and corporate transfers, the proportion of national and local expenses was absolute, and everyone was dissatisfied with government subsidies and city and provincial subsidies. As a way to realize the finances, facilities should improve the quantitative or qualitative aspects of resources by strengthening resource development and self-help efforts through profit projects and sponsorship organizations, not relying entirely on government subsidies.

Local governments also set aside a certain percentage of local taxes as a welfare fund for the disabled and invest in welfare projects for the disabled to support welfare projects, equipment and functional reinforcement projects or program development costs suitable for local conditions. In corporations and facilities, efforts should be made at the same time, such as strengthening their own profitable classes and seeking ways to mobilize community resources, breaking away from the practice of relying solely on government subsidies.

Fourth, in the results of the survey on manpower and working conditions, the biggest grievance of workers was the low remuneration system, many workers did not know or encounter operating regulations, most of them were dissatisfied with the recreation system, workplace communication, decision-making system, creativity, and expertise. In addition, most of the Gangwon-do special welfare benefits were dissatisfied. As an improvement plan for this, operators, workers, and the disabled should all make efforts to actively support the government in order to secure professional manpower in the facility. In addition, facility workers should have a good rest system, democratic decision-making, and grievance handling procedures so that they can trust each other and exercise their creativity and expertise.

The biggest reason for the employee's turnover was the low remuneration system. Therefore, labor costs should be realized and increased support should be provided to at least become labor costs based on public officials. Such measures to increase labor costs must be preceded for the specialization of facility workers. In addition, conditions will be difficult in Gangwon-do, which aims to foster welfare demonstrations for the disabled, but special welfare allowances similar to those of other metropolitan organizations should be paid to foster demonstrations and boost workers' morale. In addition, corporations and facilities should pursue rationalization of management by creating a separate allowance system and paying it to workers.

Fifth, the results of the survey on exchanges with the local community said that due to the lack of facilities, many facilities were not satisfied with the exchange and response of the local community, and many volunteers simply worked hard. In addition, most of the facilities did not have a sponsorship. As a way to revitalize this, the ultimate purpose of living facilities for the disabled is to normalize the disabled and integrate society. Accordingly, measures to expand community relations for facilities include the utilization of community resources, the utilization method in facility operation, and the opening of facilities to the community. In addition, the installation and operation of a group home can be said to be an improvement in the quality of life and social integration for the disabled. For such a relationship with the local community, the perception of facility operators should be strengthened, and a suitable number of employees should be secured for facility operation. In addition, public relations activities of facilities should be strengthened, and facilities should be reinforced. Therefore, in order to establish a relationship with the local community, the government's various support, facility operator's consciousness, worker's awareness, and local residents' participation consciousness are the most important.

Sixth, it has been proven that many variables influence each other in facility operation through correlation. First, the more appropriate the time of support for the facility in the operation of the facility, the more efficient the facility-related delivery system is, which requires a review of the efficient support system related to the characteristics of the area and facility. In addition, the operation of the steering committee appears to be correlated with the timing of the support, the delivery system, and satisfaction of the government and city/province subsidies, which proves the importance of the steering committee for efficient operation of facilities. In the working environment of workers, the employee's identity and recreation system, communication and decision-making system and grievance processing procedures were highly correlated, followed by the worker's awareness and participation consciousness.

Chapter 16 Welfare for the Elderly

1. Concepts of the Elderly

In order to know the concept of welfare for the elderly, it is necessary to define the concept of the elderly first. The concept of the elderly cannot be concluded in one word because it can be defined according to the national, social, economic, and cultural background and social customs, and the tradition and history of the society. And the concept of the elderly should consider both human function and relationship with society. Therefore, in this book, the concept of the elderly is divided into two ways as follows.

First, there may be a practical method of considering that aging has reached a certain stage according to changes in mental and physical function, that is, a method based on life age.

The gradual change that occurs in the cells, tissues, or the entire organism over time is aging, and defining an aged person as an elderly person simplifies only the change in physical conditions and does not fit the current concept of the elderly as a member of society. This is because considering the regulations of the elderly simply considering the biological aspects, it overlooks the function humans are doing and their relationship with society.

In this sense, aging is a part of the entire normal growth and development process of humans, and the process of change in at least three aspects - biological aging, psychological aging, and social aging - should be understood in a broad sense.

Here, biological aging means that the structure and function of the body's organs and systems change over time, psychological aging means that behavior, sensory and awareness, and self-awareness change over time, and social aging means changes in norms, expectations, social status, and roles.

2. Concepts of Elderly Problems and Occurrences of Elderly Problems

1) Elderly Problem

Among the various modern social problems, the elderly problem, one of the top priority problems to be solved, can be said to be various social difficulties arising from old age, and difficulties refer to the state in which basic needs of human social life are not satisfied. In addition, basic needs can be said to be economic stability, professional stability, family relations stability, medical and health guarantees, educational opportunities, opportunities for social cooperation, opportunities for cultural and entertainment, etc. In other words, the core of the elderly problem can be summarized as the elderly's accident, that is, illness(losing mental and physical health), poverty(economic dependence), loneliness(discontinuation of human relationships), and ignorance(lost social role).

In this way, the basic needs and thoughts of the elderly are not treated or cared for, and the state of becoming a social problems.

2) Occurrence of Elderly Problems

(1) Aging Population

The reality is that the increase in the elderly population is remarkable worldwide due to medical technology that has achieved prosperous development along with the development of science and technology. Such an increase in the elderly population is called aging. There is a fundamental factor in the elderly problem that the elderly population is relatively increasing in terms of the population composition ratio.

In Korea, the average life expectancy increased from 53.0 years for men in 1960 to 57.8 years for women, 62.7 years for men in 1980, 67.1 years for men and 73.6 years for women in 1990. And in 2002, men were 73.4 years old and women were 80.4 years old, extending their lifespan. And the average life expectancy of Koreans is 15 years longer than 30 years ago. He turned 64.5

years old in 1977, 72.8 years old in 1993, and 78.5 years old in 2005.

Moreover, the elderly population aged 65 or older exceeded 7% of the total population for the first time in 2000, entering an "**aging society**" classified by the United Nations. Of course, the proportion of the elderly population is still not so high, as compared to Italy, Japan, and Germany, which accounts for 18.2%, and Germany, which accounts for 16.4%. However, Korea's population aging is getting faster and the population-related outlook shows that the elderly population is expected to enter an aging society in 2020, according to population is expected to enter a super-aged society is expected to enter. It takes 20 years and 10 years for Korea to reach an aging society from an aging society to an aging society, and from an aging society to an ultra-aged society, respectively, which is almost unprecedentedly faster than in developed countries. This fact suggests that Korea's aging phenomenon can be a serious social problem.

(2) Industrialization and Urbanization

Unlike the advanced industrial society in the West, it has undergone a rapid industrialization process in a short period of time, as it led to economic and social development in the 1990s from the start of the first economic development plan in the 1960s. As a result, the number of industrial workers increased rapidly and the urban concentration of the rural population became clear. The urbanization rate rose from 28% in 1960 to 50.9% in 1975, 62.5% in 1981, 64.2% in 1986, and 73% in 1991, showing an urbanization rate at the level of advanced countries.

If industrialization and urbanization progress beyond the traditional social structure, various problems arise in society, especially due to imbalances within social organizations. In other words, there are imbalances between industries, regional imbalances, and social imbalances by social class, gender, or age, and this phenomenon causes social problems by differentiating and diversifying social functions to promote heterogeneity among social members.

In particular, in an industrial society where the person is evaluated according to the individual's ability and achievements, the role of the elderly is excluded or greatly reduced, which causes the elderly problem.

Industrial society lowers the status of the elderly as an authority in the traditional society, pushes them to become incompetent in society, and replaces the traditional society's pathology based on recognition and love with individualism and materialism.

(3) Change in Family Concept

The traditional society, which was based on agriculture, had little social change, and the experiential experience and knowledge of the elderly were respected by the younger, so they were unconditionally followed. Therefore, in traditional society, senior filial piety was valued as a social virtue, and the elderly were in the position of a prophet who predicted the future as a leader who guided young people with wisdom.

However, in an industrial society, where the proportion of industries has shifted from primary to secondary and tertiary industries, the large family system of traditional society has changed to a nuclear family system, and functions as a principle of equality for all, including marital and relatives. Under the nuclear family system, patriarchal rights are significantly weakened and the role of the elderly is also weakened, which is perceived as uncomfortable rather than help with the sex life of sons and couples, does not help economic life, and results in only a secondary role in education. In other words, in terms of functionality, the role of the elderly in modern families becomes a burden rather than a help to the family. Therefore, the life of the elderly has no choice but to be an unstable life, which soon caused the elderly problem.

(4) Elder Abuse

Elder abuse refers to the fact that the elderly do not take care of themselves, or that a caregiver in charge of supporting or caring for the elderly intentionally or unintentionally causes physical, emotional, sexual, financial damage to the elderly or neglects their duty to support them. The subtypes of elder abuse are summarized as follows.

3. Significance and Problems of Welfare for the Elderly

1) Concept of Welfare for the Elderly

Welfare for the elderly, which is understood as a comprehensive concept, is generally interpreted in a broad sense to refer to the overall guarantee of life for the elderly, or in a narrow sense to mean a nursing home or minimum livelihood.

However, in general, welfare for the elderly means that the elderly satisfy basic needs as a human being and maintain their cultural life. The basic idea of elderly welfare is to recognize that the elderly should maintain normal interpersonal relationships with others through social activities, perform certain social roles to have satisfaction and meaning in life, and satisfy the elderly's desire for social activities.

In old age, everything retreats mentally, physically, economically, and socially, so the status and alienation of the elderly generally occur, so it has emerged as an international common interest at that time and has established itself as a social problem to be solved. In 1948 the UN issued the World Declaration on Human Rights as part of its senior citizens' policy, and stipulated the protection of the elderly, the guarantee of freedom and dignity of the elderly, and the right to receive cultural benefits outside of livelihood in Articles 22 and 25.

In this sense, it can be said that welfare for the elderly contains various aspects such as the economic, physical, mental, and social aspects of elderly life. Therefore, a comprehensive policy that can satisfy the overall needs of life, not only some aspects of elderly life, should be called elderly welfare.

2) Characteristics of Welfare for the Elderly in Korea

The characteristics of the elderly population in Korea are important clues to the elderly problem and welfare policy for the elderly. It is also an important matter to be reviewed in the process of implementing countermeasures against the elderly problem. Examining the elderly population is a basic matter for understanding problems related to the elderly and countermeasures, and efficiency and effectiveness can be improved in the practice of welfare policies for the elderly by understanding the overall context.

The average life expectancy of each country in the world was 97.11 years in Japan, 77.6 years in Sweden in 1990, and 74.04 years in France in 1990. Korea is expected to reach the level of advanced countries by 2020.

(1) Pluralism of Needs

Desire mostly means what is good, necessary, or essential for a purposeful. In other words, it refers to a state in which what is necessary or essential for a purpose is lacking. Even if Abraham Maslow's theory of human needs is not explained, it can be said that humans face difficult problems such as economic poverty, health weakness, loss of role, and loneliness, especially as they grow older. In addition, the desire to be treated as an adult for the future of descendants has a pluralistic character.

(2) Universality of Objects

Unlike other welfare, the universality of the subject should be understood as an attribute in that all humans become the elderly and all people are soon subject to the welfare of the elderly.

(3) Object Multiplicity

In modern society, the level of living has improved and the average life expectancy has been extended due to the development of science and technology, the development of medical technology, and the natural increase of the population, resulting in an aging population. As an object of welfare for the elderly, the elderly population is rapidly increasing due to such increasing factors. In addition, the elderly are rapidly increasing due to institutional treatment of the elderly according to artificial policies such as new technology development, industrialization policy, and retirement age system, and the need for welfare for the elderly is increasing.

(4) Pre-Servic and Post-Comfort

Currently, the elderly have contributed to insurance finances and national finances through insurance premiums or tax payments during their economic activities, and have the right to be supported by today's economically active population in their later years.

3) Problems of Welfare for the Aged in Korea

(1) Shortage of Welfare Facilities

Currently, among the living facilities for the elderly in Korea, it can be said that nursing homes are common. Except for nursing homes, institutions and facilities for accommodation and protection of the elderly or medical rehabilitation are still insufficient compared to advanced foreign countries. However, there are senior citizens' centers, senior schools, and senior citizens' centers as facilities to use leisure, not directly to protect the lives of the elderly. In other words, it is not a certain subsidy or support from the state, but is simply a place for autonomous leisure use by the private sector.

(2) Fiscal Compactness

Finance related to welfare for the elderly is largely divided into public and private finances, which are divided into those supported by central ministries and those supported by local governments. Among the welfare finances for the elderly, in general, the public sector is often financed by taxes, and the private sector mobilizes various forms of private funds. Today, public and private resources are mixed together, and facilities or institutions are operated by combining these resources. Public finances refer to public charges or subsidies(including social welfare project funds) by central and local governments, and private finances include user charges, corporate charges, inheritance(money, securities), community donations, and other private funds.

The proportion of social security budgets in the government budget is relatively low, and in particular, the public sector budget for welfare for the elderly is very small compared to other budgets.

(3) Inadequate Medical Service Delivery System

Medical services for the elderly at home should be sufficiently provided by the medical protection and medical insurance system, which is actually very difficult. Therefore, basic medical services should be guaranteed by these two systems, but everyone in the elderly has a disease or deteriorated mental and physical function, so they have their own health vulnerabilities. Therefore, it is necessary to look at Korea's medical service delivery system for the elderly who are sick and spend lying down and those who do not have diseases but need observation and prevention at all times.

4. The Development Direction of Welfare for the Elderly in Korea

The government's policy requires workplaces to be installed in welfare facilities for the elderly, including senior citizen centers. By working according to the aptitude and ability of the elderly, the installation of such workplaces may provide opportunities to increase income as well as leisure use. When the government intends to install a workplace in welfare facilities for the elderly, it would be desirable to support basic installation and operation costs.

1) Expansion of Healthcare Services for the Elderly

A system to continue to apply workplace medical insurance to retirees according to retirement age, etc. should be introduced, and measures should be prepared to reduce the personal burden of elderly medical insurance premiums and medical expenses. In addition, medical insurance benefits should be provided for equipment essential for maintaining the healthy life of the elderly due to deterioration of physical function, such as dentures, glasses, and hearing aids. In addition, various cancer tests such as liver cancer and stomach cancer have been added to the free health examination items provided to national basic living recipients aged 65 or older since 1996, and the items are gradually expanding.

Specialized elderly care facilities for the elderly with dementia and stroke are gradually expanding. The number of elderly people who have restrictions on their daily life was about 140,000 in 1995, and is estimated to be 260,000 by 2010. Among them, specialized elderly care facilities with enhanced medical functions should be expanded and operated nationwide for the elderly who cannot live at home.

In particular, since July 2008, as nursing facilities have become larger due to the implementation of long-term care insurance for the elderly, they have been fiercely competing with the latest facilities.

However, dementia-specialized nursing facilities should be further expanded, dementia remote medical information and communication networks should be established and operated, dementia-specialized personnel such as dementia specialists, nurses, caregivers, and counselors should be trained. In addition, it is necessary to actively review the revision of related laws and systems so that these facilities can be designated and activated as medical insurance institutions. Therefore, a private elderly hospital should be established and the installation cost should be supported. It is necessary to provide low-interest financial benefits so that specialized elderly hospitals for the elderly who can be treated but need long-term inpatient treatment or those who are recovering from surgery can be operated at lower medical costs than general hospitals.

Personnel and equipment for physical therapy will be reinforced at public health centers to foster them as primary care institutions for senile diseases, and dementia counseling and reporting centers will be established and operated at each public health center.

2) Expansion of Home Welfare Services

Home welfare services should be expanded and strengthened not only for the low-income elderly and the elderly with mental and physical disabilities, but also for the elderly who have difficulty moving in their daily lives due to senile diseases. Long-term hospitalization of the elderly due to rapid aging may cause a rapid expansion in medical expenses, which may threaten the social security system itself. In order to prevent this, home welfare services should be strengthened, such as reorganizing and expanding the currently operated social welfare facilities according to their purpose, expanding family service dispatch projects, day protection, and short-term protection facilities. Of course, professional manpower has been trained in accordance with the long-term care system for the elderly, which has been in effect since 2008.

3) Development of Leisure Programs

Appropriate leisure programs should be developed to comprehensively satisfy the overall needs of the elderly, such as health care, liberal arts and cultural activities, and leisure use of the middle-class or higher, as well as low-income families. The Senior Welfare Center, which has been implemented on a trial basis since 1996, should adjust its role so that it can play a central role in the implementation of these programs.

It would be desirable to provide health and leisure facilities such as health counseling rooms, sports facilities, baths, joint workshops, aerobics or fork dance rooms, and audio-visual rooms, and develop and operate various programs such as recreation, community service, and health and welfare offices.

It is necessary to make the senior citizen center a "love room" so that the elderly living in the community can gather to rest and share friendship, and to this end, not only support the reconstruction and renovation of facilities, but also expand support for operating and heating costs. By developing various programs through cooperation with community welfare centers, senior citizens' welfare centers, and health and welfare offices, it should be a place to increase the motivation to live beyond the level of a simple meeting place.

Chapter 17 Women and Family Welfare

1. Women's Welfare

1) Human Rights Issue

In the 21st century, it is no exaggeration to say that the development and input speed of female manpower determine half of the national power. The reason for this is that the reform of the consciousness of patriarchal ideology and the redevelopment of the "**female nature**" that patriarchal and radical feminists have ignored are urgently requested at the same time. On the other hand, the state should develop women's new mental and functional abilities so that women can play economic, social, and political roles at a different level than before. To this end, the direction of women's welfare policy is also essential for the "**productive women's welfare**" policy to support women's self-support will and self-support ability development, and to guide women to new jobs to achieve welfare through work. Only the "productive women's welfare" policy will finally provide a realistic basis for the lonely revolutionary topic of Condorcet(Condorcet, Marquis de, 1743.9.17~1794.3.29) more than 200 years ago.

2) Concept of Women's Welfare

(1) Broad-Minded Women's Welfare

As women are equally guaranteed human dignity and the right to live a human life by the state or society, the living conditions such as women's health, property, and happiness mean a satisfactory state. At the same time, it is a concept that includes all independent efforts to actively improve patriarchal gender discrimination and its based laws, social systems, and culture.

(2) Consultative Women's Welfare

As '**social welfare for women**', it refers to the efforts to redistribute resources attempted to ensure a human life for each woman, and the reality of women's welfare must change according to the state and the times.

3) Principle of Women's Welfare

(1) Principle of Gender Equality

Article 36 of the Constitution stipulates that "marriage and family life must be established and maintained on the basis of individual dignity and equality of gender, and the state guarantees this." Women should not be subject to social inequality and oppression just because they are women, and should guarantee equal rights to men in family life, education, employment, and promotion opportunities.

(2) Principle of Minimum Living Security

Article 34 of the Constitution states, "*All citizens have the right to live a human life. The state is obligated to make efforts to promote social security and social welfare. The state should make efforts to improve women's welfare and rights and interests.*" Therefore, women should be guaranteed human dignity and human rights, the minimum conditions necessary to ensure life for health, property, and happiness, as well as measures to ensure physical, economic, social, and cultural life for women.

(3) Principle of Maternal Protection

Article 36 of the Constitution recognizes the state's obligation to protect motherhood by stipulating that "*the state must strive for the protection of motherhood.*" Women are in a special situation, focusing on the functions of pregnancy, childbirth, and child rearing that only women have. Therefore, such motherhood should be protected by the state and society, and should not be treated socially disadvantaged.

4) Current Status of Women's Welfare Services

(1) Women's Welfare Facilities

A. Maternal and Child Protection and Independence Facilities

As of November 2009, there are 41 mother-and-child protection facilities nationwide that provide basic living protection and self-reliance support for low-income families with children under the age of 18, and provide counseling guidance on mental and psychological conflicts, child rearing issues, and vocational training.

In addition, three mother-child facilities are operated to protect low-income mother-child families who have not been admitted to mother-child care facilities and families with weak self-reliance bases after leaving the mother-child care facilities.

B. Temporary Mother and Child Protection Facilities

A temporary mother and child protection facility is operated to protect mothers and children who may interfere with healthy parenting or maternal health due to their spouse's physical and mental abuse. The period of protection of temporary protection facilities for mothers and children is June(which can be extended within March if necessary), and 14 locations are installed and operated nationwide.

C. Single Mother Facility

It operates a single mother facility with the aim of helping unmarried women deliver safely within six months(extendable within six months if necessary) and protecting them until they recover their mental and physical health. As of November 2009, 26 single mother facilities are installed and operated nationwide, and vocational education is provided during the admission period to support self-support and independence after discharge.

D. Single-Mother and Child-Rearing Families(Parent Group Home)

The parenting mother group home(intermediate home for traditional single mothers) for those who need accommodation and protection as single mothers raising infants under the age of 2 provides not only free accommodation, but also vocational, parenting, personality education and counseling services can be extended within three months. As of November 2009, there are 19 facilities.

E. Urgent Shelter

Emergency shelters are facilities for women who need urgent protection due to unbalanced arrangements by facility type and area, and in areas without women's violence-related protection facilities, counseling centers, women's centers, and private organizations are equipped with 64 temporary shelters nationwide.

F. Prostitution Prevention and Victim Protection Facilities

With the enforcement of the Act on the Prevention of Sexual Trafficking and the Protection of Victims, etc. and the Act on the Punishment of Acts such as Intermediation of Sexual Trafficking, there are 39 facilities nationwide.

(2) Women's Welfare Facilities

A. Women's Welfare Counseling Center

There are domestic violence counseling centers, sexual violence counseling centers, prostitution damage counseling centers, and parent/rich normal counseling centers where low-income families, single mothers, runaway women, and prostitution women provide counseling.

A-1 Domestic Violence Counseling Service

In Korea, the Act on the Prevention of Domestic Violence and the Protection of Victims was enacted in 1997 to foster healthy families by preventing domestic violence and protecting victims of domestic violence.

The first feature of the law is that domestic violence crimes are not treated as criminal cases, but as domestic protection cases to help restore family peace and stability through a two-sided approach to protecting victims. Second, since domestic violence is no longer a personal matter of the family, society and the state intervene actively. Third, there are 268 counseling centers nationwide, with various groups of experts, including social workers, participating in the process of handling family protection cases and the process of protective disposition.

B-1 Sexual Violence Counseling Service

The Sexual Violence Damage Counseling Center supports 43 integrated operation counseling centers to prevent healthy family maintenance and dissolution by preventing domestic violence and sexual violence, protecting victims' human rights and returning to a healthy society.

C-1 Women's Emergency Phone 1366

The installation location of women's emergency calls will be set up by women's centers and private organizations to function as an outpost for eradicating violence against women and a central institution for providing one-stop services. Since 2006, emergency phone 1366 has been installed and operated for migrant women, and the provided languages are English, Russian, Chinese, Thai, Vietnamese, and Mongolian, and the service is open 24 hours a day throughout the year.

B. Women's Hall Management

Article 28-2 of the Framework Act on Women's Development allows the state and local governments to provide support necessary for revitalizing women's volunteer activities, and Article 28-2 of the Enforcement Decree of the Act allows the heads of local governments to operate women's resource centers.

As a facility for use, the women's center aims to be installed one by one in each city, county, and district, especially in areas with high population density, densely populated areas for low-income families, and areas without similar facilities. Women's welfare projects carried out by the Women's Center include counseling projects, women-related research projects, women's volunteer centers, and convenience facilities for local residents, and establishing and operating infant care facilities in the center.

C. Medical Support System for Victims of Sexual Violence

In order to improve the medical environment for sexual violence victims, sexual violence emergency kits for collecting evidence of sexual violence are distributed free of charge to medical institutions, women and school violence one-stop centers, and 324 nationwide.

D. Support Center for Self-Support for Women Affected by De-sexual Trade

It operates two self-support centers(one in each Seoul and Gyeonggi Province) that provide vocational rehabilitation training and job provision programs to help establish a practical self-support foundation for women victims of prostitution who are preparing to move away from prostitution.

In particular, counseling, living expenses support, medical support, legal support, and vocational training are provided for the expansion and systematization of self-support projects at the gathering place.

In addition, the Ministry of Gender Equality and Family and the Credit Counseling and Recovery Commission signed a business agreement on March 16, 2005 to actively support the economic independence of prostitution women by operating a credit recovery support project.

E. Home Protection Service

Family protection for the rich and the mother was transferred from the Ministry of Health and Welfare to the Ministry of Gender Equality and Family on June 23, 2005. Since the enactment of the Maternal and Child Welfare Act in 1989, the need for welfare support for rich families has been raised due to changes in economic structure and social perception, and the government revised the expulsion from the Maternal and Child Welfare Act to the Maternal and Child Welfare Act. Parent-rich welfare programs provide low-income parent-rich families(children under the age of 18) with support for middle and high school children's tuition, vocational training, child rearing expenses(under the age of 6), living(start-up) funds, and permanent rental housing.

5) Women's Welfare Problems

(1) Comprehensiveness of the System

A human being will be exposed to various problems and crises at each stage from birth to death, and the welfare system of a society should be able to provide appropriate services to the problems facing members of society at each stage. Their problems and crises include birth and growth, medical, nutrition, and early childhood education, school education in adolescence, medical, nutrition, socialization, employment in adolescence, marriage, settlement, middle-aged growth, unemployment and reemployment, child re-rearing, divorce and remarriage, old age, retirement, etc.

Most women go through a similar life process and are experiencing a crisis situation that does not deviate significantly from it. In order to improve the level of women's welfare, women's welfare services should be provided to correct the contradictions between gender unequal ideology, the labor market, and the welfare system based on them, and these services should cover women's entire life. However, the current maternal and child welfare system only targets women before old age after childhood, especially women who are required to be protected, so they are not properly playing a complementary role throughout their entire lives.

(2) Scope of the Subject

Today, most women are walking the path of employment-career development with men, or at least want to get a job and build their own social career, and most men are also experiencing the process of marriage-child education. In the case of women, it is common to form a parallel line that maintains tension with each other, or to stop the path of employment due to the burden of marriage-childcare(household)-child education. In other words, men can proceed in a straight line of employment-career development while enjoying women's services in the private realm of family, but women cannot. The crisis situation unique to women, as well as this flat diagram alone, is not clearly revealed, but it is generally a crisis that comes from the double burden of these two processes. Therefore, women's welfare services should faithfully include social protection against the problems and crises pointed out above, as well as support for women's unique problems and crises derived from the double burden of employment and marriage.

Currently, Korea's maternal and child welfare services are relatively indifferent to the crisis situation of many ordinary women going through a universal life process, while services for women who are alienated or deviated from them are mainly provided. Of course, women's group support projects, women's guidance projects, or marriage projects are being carried out for general women, but it is difficult to regard them as welfare services to help women in crisis situations that are commonly experienced. Therefore, the parent-child welfare system has been negligent in taking policies for equal opportunities for women and efforts to ensure their minimum life, to maximize their abilities, expand opportunities for social participation, or prevent problems with women who need protection. In other words, as is often pointed out, the current maternal and child welfare project has the characteristics of a post-treatment service centered on protected women rather than a service that is universally proactive for general women. In other words, it provides selective services mainly for women who are protected, but only a very limited category of women among women who are in the category of women who are protected.

(3) Appropriateness of Welfare Benefits

In order to determine the appropriateness of welfare benefits, it is necessary to find out whether the service level is enough to overcome the problems or crises facing an individual and maintain a normal and cultural life. Since the service itself is not given much for general women, the appropriateness cannot be examined, so we focus on services for women who need protection.

In the case of women's counseling projects, the number of counseling facilities is very insufficient to listen to women's problems and provide assistance to solutions, and women's counselors who directly influence the level of service are also insufficient in number. There are usually about three women's counselors per woman's counseling facility, and with these personnel, it is almost impossible to confirm the measures of the counseling results, follow-up management, and professional counseling.

In addition, the government's support for existing women's welfare facilities is not realistic, and thus the level of protection services for accommodation guardians is very poor. The amount of self-reliance settlement of 1 million won upon discharge is also far from enough to provide stable housing. In 1991, 43,000 won per month was paid to those eligible for home protection, 52,000 won per month to those eligible for facility protection, and 10,000 won per month was paid to the elderly aged 70 or older. In addition, very few single mothers, runaway women, and prostitutes are provided with support equivalent to those eligible for life protection, or only minimal services for treatment or rehabilitation. This level of service is very inappropriate and low-level service for women in crisis to overcome the crisis and lead a cultural life.

(4) Redistribution of Welfare Benefits

In general, the social welfare system is expected to alleviate inequality among classes resulting from free competition and market logic to some extent. In particular, women are experiencing inequality due to patriarchal ideology in addition to inequality between classes, so women's welfare services are expected to alleviate these two inequalities.

The fundamental way to achieve this is to change the Social Security Act or the Social Welfare Service Act to resist patriarchal thinking that presupposes the position of women as mothers or spouses and to recognize that women and men are independent and equal." However, this will be difficult to achieve without changing the perception of poverty and patriarchal ideology in society as a whole, so at this stage, women's welfare services should be expanded to ease the burden on women experiencing double inequality.

One of the ways to find out whether the current welfare system is making such perceptions and efforts is to see the proportion of maternal and child welfare services in the government's expenditure. Looking at the absolute level of social welfare as social welfare expenditure to gross national product, it was only 1.21% in 1988 and 1.49% in 1989, which is significantly smaller compared to 20% to 30% in developed countries. The weak level of total social welfare expenditure is only 0.07% of the gross national product and 0.5% of the government budget for public assistance and social welfare services, which consists of full state expenditure. This passive attitude in social welfare expenditure reflects the government's willingness to attribute the primary responsibility for non-welfare to individuals and families and provide only minimal protection, which is very insufficient to improve and compensate for women's double inequality.

(5) Recommendations for Improving Women's Welfare Levels

To sum up the problems of women's welfare, the current women's welfare system does not cover all the crises of women's entire lives, and only provides services to a limited range of women among women. Now consider ways to compensate for these limitations.

A. Expansion of the Women's Welfare System

A women's welfare system should be prepared for women who are alienated from the current welfare system and women who cannot receive appropriate services under the current welfare system. In other words, a realistic service system should be established for many women, such as victims of sexual violence, women suffering from abuse from husbands or cohabitation men, girls who are physically and sexually abused by in-laws, housewives, and elderly women.

B. Expansion of the Scope of Women's Welfare Recipients

First of all, the scope should be expanded from women-centered services to general women, and universalist operations should be carried out in which any woman included in the category of women-centered care should receive services.

The number of women exposed to various serious crises in the life process without receiving any services despite being protected by the law as a single-parent family support law is 34.8%, more than a third of all maternal families. They should also be given appropriate services to overcome economic and emotional crises.

C. Securing the Appropriateness of Women's Welfare Services

Rich welfare services should be provided quantitatively and qualitatively from a women-centered perspective so that ordinary women or protective women can overcome their crisis and enjoy a normal and cultural life. It should be converted into a service to ease the double burden of agricultural and fishing-related economic activities and housework for women in rural areas as well as urban women, and efforts should be made to reflect their economic activities in social insurance benefits such as medical insurance and national pension. In addition, the level of livelihood protection or facility protection for mother and child families should also be realized.

D. Enhancement of Redistribution Effects

The relative non-welfare of women resulting from unequal positions between men and women will continue in the future without intentional efforts to redistribute social resources through the welfare system of welfare. Finance must be secured first in order to provide social welfare services so that women's unfavorable positions in the labor market do not immediately lead to women's non-welfare.

Increasing private participation in order to secure women's welfare finances is one way, but the government must first express its strong will to achieve a welfare society, and priority should be given to groups currently in poor conditions. However, an increase in welfare expenditure does not naturally increase the budget of the women's welfare sector. Currently, the budget for women's welfare services is only 2.5%(as of 1992) of the total social welfare service budget, which is lower than that of children's welfare(35.5%) or elderly welfare(30.2%). Therefore, in order to substantially improve the level of women's welfare, efforts are requested to increase the budget of the women's welfare sector in addition to the expansion of total social welfare expenditure.

2. Family Welfare

1) Understanding of Family Welfare

(1) Concept of Family Welfare

Family welfare can be divided into a broad meaning and a consultative meaning. In a general sense, family welfare refers to all social services that systematically assist family members to develop healthy personalities and perform their functions as members of society by revitalizing harmonious family relationships and strengthening the active values of family life.

However, in a consultative sense, it can be seen as a family welfare project, which means organizational activities to solve individual family problems and strengthen family life due to poverty, disease, unemployment, family relationship collapse, behavioral problems, mental or physical disabilities.

On the other hand, from a broad perspective, family welfare can be said to be a common social intervention effort or activity at the construction level that provides more integrated and preventive services not only for individual family members but also for the entire family. In other words, responding to the needs and problems of the family as a whole means to provide institutional, policy, and technical services using professional knowledge and skills to satisfy the needs of the family with direct interest in solving and preventing family problems, revitalizing human interactive function.

(2) Purpose of Family Welfare

Welfare for the family, that is, family welfare, does not focus on individual family members, but focuses on the whole family as a unit and promotes the protection, security, and reinforcement of the family. From this point of view, the concept of family welfare can be said to be diverse due to the historical changes of the family, and the concept of family welfare can be said to be a reinforcing aspect of life difficulties in temporary or long-term problems.

In this case, the function of the family is, as family scholars claim, the function of sex and affection as a unique function of the family. In other words, it is a function that guarantees race preservation and legal sex, such as childbirth. In other words, it is a function that guarantees race preservation and legal sex, such as childbirth. It is also a group that provides labor through employment while performing the functions of production and consumption, consumes goods produced by labor to maintain the economic system, and has other educational functions, protection, rest, and entertainment.

Therefore, the family believes that social functions can be achieved smoothly when the function of the family is fully performed as a reference group in which the primary social training is conducted while living together for the rest of the life. However, when such family relationships do not communicate smoothly, social problems related to the family arise, and it is believed that family welfare can be called family welfare in social welfare to prevent or treat the occurrence of family problems or strengthen family functions. Family welfare is a function of economic production and consumption, ethnic preservation and legal marital relationship, educational function of raising children, protection and rest for physical and mental stability, and cultural and entertainment functions. This can be seen for related purposes.

(3) Various Forms of Family

A. Single-Parent Family

A single-parent family refers to a family consisting of a single parent who does not have one parent due to the death, divorce, abandonment, separation, and unmarried mother(unmarried father) of one of the parents, or cannot play the role of one parent legally or practically. Along with the spread of individualism, satisfaction with marriage life is a factor in divorce, and the number is expected to increase steadily over time as laws that were disadvantageous to women, such as property division claims, child rearing, and interview negotiations, are revised. The difficulty of a single-parent family arises from the absence of a father or mother to be, which can cause various economic and emotional problems in the family, such as partial or overall inability to perform family functions and resulting dissatisfaction with family needs(Jung, Min-Sook et al., 2009).

B. Dual-Income Family

Double-income families are structurally formed of extended families or nuclear families with married couples having jobs at the same time, and are common in our society due to the increase in working housewives, high education levels, economic benefits, automation of households, and freedom to participate in economic activities.

3. Remarried Family

In general, a remarried family can be defined as "a man or woman who has already married once or more and has formed a family newly with another spouse." Remarried families are sometimes referred to as reunited families, double nuclear families, reconstructed families, and mixed families.

D. International Marriage Family

International marriage families are formed when men and women of different nationalities get married. International marriage families are caused by the improvement of Korea's international status, the increase of migrant workers in underdeveloped countries to improve class and economic situation, the issue of finding a spouse for rural bachelors, revitalization of marriage agencies, and frequent exchanges with foreign countries.

E. a Family of Boys and Girls

A boy and girl family means "*a person who meets the criteria for selecting a person subject to life protection by the government because boys and girls under the age of 18(can be recognized until the age of 20 in unavoidable cases) are required to lead family life.*" The difficulties of boys and girls' families are complex in terms of economic, psychological, and emotional social adaptation, education, family life, and residential environment.

2) Family Welfare as a Social Issue

The types of family problems subject to family welfare can be classified into family discord, problems of the disabled in the family, children and adolescents, economic problems such as support for the elderly, unemployment or poverty, family violence, and family health. In addition to this, there can be various types of family problems.

From this point of view, the tendency of family problems in Korea can be summarized as follows.

First, an economic problem is the problem of family income. In Korea, the family situation is rapidly changing with the last IMF period.

Overall, in our society, the new words "**Or-Yuk-do**," "**Sa-O-Jeong**," and "**Lee-Tae-Baek**" have emerged, resulting in a situation in which family functions can be viewed dysfunctional. In the case of husbands who are in charge of the family economy, they often have to retire without completing their retirement age at work, and for this reason, they consider changing jobs, but it is not so easy for workers who have only been working in one job for years to find a new job. In the end, the difficulties of the family economy caused by the husband's unemployment continue to the family members, which is one of the causes of family dissolution.

Second, there are changes in lifestyle due to nuclear familyization, an increase in weekend couples, a decrease in the number of children, and changes in housing life. Women's role is relatively growing compared to the past as the structure of society has led to an increase in women's rights based on gender equality in the existing patriarchal situation. In the past, women were mainly in charge of protecting families, but today, women are changing into a function of actively participating in society, and changes in lifestyle are coming along with changes in the existing social structure.

Third, the family's control and control functions are weakened. In the past, in our society, the sequence of senior citizens who respect their superiors flowed to the bottom of society, and of course, families, the basic unit of society, were strictly controlled by the order. Today, however, socialization as a family community and the weakening of the function of emotional support are emerging as major problems, so the problem is spreading in the family, adding to the seriousness of the problem. For example, differences between generations, marital discord, lack of parental roles, and lack of dialogue act as obstacles to performing smooth family functions.

Fourth, it is a problem due to the increase in the number of families with deficits. In fact, there are many difficulties in limiting the problem of the defective family to any one fragment. It can be seen that the economic and educational aspects of society are faced with the structural problems of society, and the problems for them are expressed in various ways.

Therefore, the problem of the defective family is likely to emerge as a problem across society in that it is a problem of the primary constituent group of society, so it is not insufficient to say that it is a major cause of social problems. For example, the divorce problem of parents can be seen as the most primary problem that hinders the function of a healthy family.

3) Family Therapy Services to Solve Family Problems

The practice method of family welfare is mainly related to family treatment services. Family problems as a social problem are a social welfare approach, and its practical task related to policy approaches is to strengthen the function of social services, which can be approached mainly at the clinical level, such as counseling and family therapy.

(1) Family Therapy Service

Since family problems are mainly complex in the entire family, it can affect families without problems, so there are many different ways to approach family problems, so the distinction is not clear.

In response to this problem, academia is mainly studying family treatment methods that can cope with various family problems, mainly citing the complexity of family problems.

A. Currently, the representative family therapy technology mainly used in the field of social welfare practice in relation to family welfare practice is Bowen's family therapy theory and has the most comprehensive view of human behavior and social problems. Bowen was born as the eldest son of a large family in Tennessee, USA, and worked as a psychoanalytic. While working at the Meninger Institute from 1946 to 1954, he began to be interested in emotional adhesion between patients and family relationships while participating in patient treatment. According to Bowen, family is a complex aggregate of a series of interrelated systems and subsystems, and is an emotional relationship based on biological nature. He argued that it is important to know the family of origin in order to understand and treat the family, and that the overall functional form of the family ego mass(a family that is emotionally fixed together) should be identified through at least three generations of family history survey.
According to psychoanalytic Bowen, "*If any member of the family suffers*

from mental illness, it may be a problem of the entire family rather than an individual mental problem." In fact, most of the psychiatric patients he met at the treatment site had very unstable emotional relationships with any member of the family(especially his mother), so his treatment method approached the entire family, not the individual patient.

Bowen, in particular, saw the unstable attachment relationship with his mother as the cause of the problem among his family and tried to explain it as a concept of self-differentiation. People with poor self-differentiation do not have smooth interpersonal relationships, and they usually hide in unconsciousness and appear as mental illness if they are stressed out for too long.

Therefore, Bowen's family therapy is not the treatment of an individual who sees a problem, but the entire family is treated, and it is viewed as a prerequisite for treatment that there are other members who have provided a decisive cause for mental illness.

B. Next is structural family therapy developed by Minuchin. Salvador Minuchin began developing structural family therapy in the 1960s at Wiltwyck School in New York through consultations with delinquent adolescents in defective families. During joint research at the Philadelphia Children's Guidance Clinic in the 1970s, Minuchin elaborated the theory and practice of structural family therapy. The cause of problematic behavior is caused by dysfunctional family structures. Therefore, family therapy is to change the family structure so that family problems can be solved. Correcting the dysfunctional structure reflected by symptoms, that is, correcting the structure of the family, is the primary goal of treatment. He argued that on the premise that problems exist in any family, the treatment was developed focusing on the fact that families belonging to individuals with mental illness have a family structure with unclear boundaries of family roles. For example, suppose one of the family members died in an unexpected accident, and in the case of a family with unclear boundaries, the members blame themselves for the accident, suffer, and suffer from guilt. The family falls into chaos and results in unfaithful to their role, leading to frequent discord, fights, and runaway, leading to the breakdown of the family itself.

C. In addition, there is the theory of Satir in Virginia, which argued for empirical family therapy theory. This is a family therapy technique that helps families communicate smoothly. Since the early 1940s, the Virginia Satire has worked therapeutically to counsel people, and even after the age of 70, who worked for more than 50 years, those who constantly fell with high ideals and enthusiasm to develop human spiritual potential have been passionate in raising them. In other words, she devoted her life to making people in the midst of life's pain and despair realize, know, and develop to experience the joy and fulfillment of life through mature human exchanges with those who fell. Satir majored in psychiatry and social work at the University of Chicago in the United States, and with many clinical experiences at the Chicago Psychological Analysis Institute, established the Palo Alto Mental Institute in California to devise the first family therapy training program. Since then, family therapy workshops have been held around the world to intervene in actual treatment, teach family dynamics at the Family Therapy Training Department, and at the same time, people call her Columbus of Family Therapy. Satir empiricist family therapy integrated psychological dynamics, interactions, and original families, and is attempting treatment not just to stay in treatment for pathological things, but to grow at a holistic level. The philosophical background of the Satir model is existentialism, phenomenology, and humanism. After all, the Satir model deals with families, but the ultimate goal is a model in which humans strictly demand responsibility for their lives, so restoring human integrity is the goal of treatment. The main concepts of Satir's family therapy approach consist of a value system, maturation, self-esteem, communication, and family rules, which are key to building healthy family or relationships. Satir eventually integrated all these concepts and did his best to make people human without abandoning her "**hope for human**" or "**belief in growing people**" until 1988, when she ended her life. Satir saw that family problems arise when there is no conversation due to lack of affection between family members and when they do not take care of each other's emotions.

4) Family Welfare Policy

As described above, family welfare policy can be said to be a field of authoritative government activities to solve social problems, but family welfare policy differs somewhat depending on the views of viewers.

(1) Concept of Family Welfare Policy

It would be correct to view it as a macroscopic and institutional method depending on the aspect of practicing family welfare, and this is the most traditional conceptual classification method. And according to the definition of Kamerman & Kahn, the government's activities for families, policy categories for the state to achieve the purpose of family welfare, and policy categories for other purposes were classified into family welfare policy categories. If this is further subdivided, it can be classified as follows.

A. A Policy Area(a field)

① It refers to a policy field that sets certain specific goals for the family.

② Family planning: Increasing fertility rates, improving child health, reducing parenting burdens, and increasing gender equality

③ Various family welfare policies and programs(cash benefit programs, employment policies, housing policies, nutrition and health) policies, development social services, child protection and development-related services, women's policies).

B. A Means of Policy(a instrument)

This is a means of social control to achieve broader social and political objectives by changing family behavior.

C. Perspective or Criterion for Policymaking

① Applying the perspective of family welfare as a criterion for selecting a specific social policy or evaluating its impact.

② It emphasizes that all social policies in the country should be viewed from a family welfare policy perspective rather than as a concept that categorizes specific policies.

(2) Definition of Zimmerman

A. A series of interrelated policy choices to achieve the agreed objectives of family well-being in order to cope with the various problems experienced by families in society.

B. Focus on "**individuals as family members**" rather than individuals, that is, "**family itself.**"

C. It is pointed out that the specific concept category of family welfare policy is a fluid concept category that is temporarily agreed on because society itself changes dynamically.

D. Family welfare is a service that strengthens family life to pursue the happiness of family members and solves the problems of family members.

(3) Several Opinion of Korean Scholars.

A. Choi, Sung-Jae(1992)

In order to guide the function, structure, and role of the family in a desirable direction and to promote the welfare of the entire family and individuals as family members, it was defined as a series of principles on intentional behavior by the state.

B. Cho, Heung-Sik et al.(2002)

- government's deliberate actions in consideration of family welfare
- a family-related policy even if it deals with individuals
- It is a policy as a means to promote their welfare for family members.

Putting together my views of the scholars discussed above, it can be said that the family welfare policy corresponds to the government's organizational efforts to solve my family's problems.

5) Basic Health and Family Law

The main contents of the current legal system include the Family Inheritance Act of the Civil Act, the Single-parent Family Support Act to support single-parent families, and the Family Violence-related Act. Of course, there is a social welfare law, but it is difficult to say that it is intended to maintain and develop families, and the Basic Health and Family Act, which took effect on January 1, 2005, clarifies the rights and obligations of the people and promotes family welfare. The Framework Act on Healthy Families consists of 5 chapters and 36 groups.

The State and local governments have the Center for Healthy Family Support(hereinafter referred to as the "**Center**") in the central, municipal, provincial, and municipalities(http://www.familynet.or.kr)(Article 35 (1) of the same Act) to prevent and treat family problems, develop programs to maintain health families. In order to carry out a healthy family project, the center shall have experts with knowledge and experience in related fields(hereinafter referred to as "**health family history**")(paragraph 2 of the same Act). A place that provides direct services to local residents is the Health and Family Support Center of Si/Gun/Gu, which conducts common essential and optional projects. Common essential projects include family-friendly culture creation, such as family education, family counseling, family volunteer group operation, family care support projects, various family integration services such as family support for marriage immigrants and the disabled, and family support network. In addition, other projects that meet the characteristics and needs of the community are selected and implemented.

The duties of a health family member include: prevention, counseling, and improvement of family problems;development of health family education (including democratic and gender-equal family relationship education) development of family life culture movement.

Chapter 18 School Social Welfare

1. Significance of School Social Welfare Services

1) Objectives of School Social Welfare Programs

The purpose of the school social welfare program is to help young people with dreams and visions achieve appropriate development tasks while respecting the values, common human needs, and the potential of each individual that is often unnecessarily wasted. Its role should be developed flexibly so that schools, families, and young people can face various environments at hand.

Specifically, it is a task that develops students' confidence, prepares them to learn continuously, and improves their adaptability to the upcoming changes. Therefore, it helps students' ability to "**learn**", "**think**", and solve problems away from the focus of emotional and personality problems. Therefore, it can be said that the purpose of the school social welfare project is a complementary combination of the purpose of social work and the purpose of education.

2) Definition of School Social Welfare Services

The definition of school social welfare projects is difficult to clearly define, but it is important to look at them based on the views of existing social welfare scholars.

Historically, in the early 1900s, when the school social welfare project began, the school social welfare project was defined by focusing on the role of visiting teachers linking home and school cooperation, but from the mid-1990s, the definition focused on psychological treatment and social function improvement of unadjusted students began to become common. Since the 1970s, due to the influence of ecology, the definition of school social welfare services focused on providing social welfare services centered on student-school-family-community links has indeed various aspects.

The Social Work Yearbook 1960 defined, "*School social welfare projects are part of the school's activity plan and are to help students with social and emotional problems that cause difficulties in adapting to school life.*"

According to Costin, who developed the theoretical foundation for school social welfare projects, which are defined as professional social projects that help schools become interested in solving problems and intellectual, social, and emotional needs.

Therefore, school social welfare projects can be said to be a specialized field of social projects that help achieve the educational functions and purposes of schools by utilizing various methods of social projects. School social welfare projects utilize various practical methods of social work. Based on the ecological perspective of interaction between individuals and the social environment, school counseling, group counseling, family therapy, community organization projects.

Ultimately, school social welfare projects can be defined as a specialty of social work practice that promotes the purpose of social welfare that realizes distributed social justice for educational rights and ultimately helps schools and students achieve the educational purpose of all education.

3) Role of School Social Workers

School social workers play a professional role as social workers. This is called the traditional role of school social workers. ① Case workers, ② group workers, ③ truant office teachers: If parents do not want to send their children to school for some reason, social workers intervene as truant teachers. Explain to parents that school-age children must be sent to school under the Mandatory Education Act and persuade them to send their children to school. ④ Counselor: Many of the school's social workers are MSW-educated and possess more advanced diagnostic and psychological skills than other professionals(educational counselors), making school social workers considered psychoanalytic and medical professionals. However, the role of school social workers as counselors with high-quality skills remains very important. ⑤ This includes linking parents(connecting teachers and parents). As the school's expectations for school social workers grew, school social workers went beyond traditional roles and attempted a more advanced new approach. This is called a new role of school social workers, and spokespersons, behavioral specialists: social workers are also experts in human behavior and modifications. Therefore, it helps teachers with problematic behavior to correct student behavior. Behavior modification techniques such as encouragement for teachers and praise and compensation for students are used. ⑥ Mental health consultant: You can also advise schools to reinforce aspects of human relationships that are easily overlooked when developing a curriculum, assess students with emotional or behavioral problems, and take appropriate action(such as commissioning a community mental health center). ⑦ Alcohol and drug abuse experts, Complex team members: School social workers team up with psychologists, speech therapists, special teachers, physical education teachers, general teachers to determine specific programs necessary for special educational purposes(Won, Suk-Jo, 2009).

2. Necessity according to the Subject of School Social Welfare Programs

1) Subject of School Social Welfare Programs

In the practice of social welfare, the task of correcting the object and clarifying the understanding of them corresponds to an important variable in determining the type of service and how to practice it. Therefore, the school social welfare project has been regarded as a priority target for students who need protection or school maladjusted as a field of professional social work to ensure the right to education for all students and effectively achieve the purpose of education.

However, school social welfare projects are professional activities that help students lead quality improved school life and improve the environmental system, as well as students who need protection or school maladjusted students. In other words, it is to help all students develop their potential and abilities as much as possible through school social welfare projects and to provide an optimal educational environment to grow into healthy members of society in the future.

Therefore, the scope and content of school social welfare projects vary widely from micro-system to macro-system in selecting subjects. In the United States, where school social welfare projects are actively carried out, the target was initially started as disabled children and guaranteed equal educational opportunities for all students, but recently, it has been expanding to education and educational reform for children and all students.

2) Necessity of School Social Welfare Services

In Korea's constitution and education law, the right to education is the basic right and obligation of the people. Therefore, all citizens have the right to receive minimum compulsory education regardless of their social conditions or circumstances, and the state is responsible for providing fair educational opportunities to all citizens and creating a desirable educational environment. If the basic educational rights stipulated in the Constitution are not guaranteed to all individuals, social workers have a social responsibility to realize social welfare by professionally intervening in the educational environment to guarantee their educational rights. This is to realize social justice through fair allocation of educational opportunities. Therefore, school is a system in which students and teachers interact most actively, and because it is a social system, it is an area where social work can intervene. In other words, since school is a social place that deals with the desire for education in the context of human interaction with the social environment, it can be the subject of social work practice. Therefore, social workers should intervene in the social place of school to help schools perform their natural social functions and roles properly.

If schools continue to provide entrance examination-oriented and punishment-oriented school education, it will not play a beneficial role in developing students' potential, which will become a source of school pathology and school problems such as dropouts, runaway, pregnancy, violence, delinquency, and crime. Therefore, school social welfare projects have a social responsibility to actively intervene in the school environment to help the school environment become the optimal educational environment for all students. The optimal educational environment means school utopia, which should improve the psychosocial function of each student, provide education suitable for the individual abilities and qualities of the student, and eventually provide an educational environment that ensures individual uniqueness and creativity. Therefore, by cultivating students' ability to actively cope with the internal and external world, they can feel a more fulfilling sense of achievement through internal growth of personal character, and cultivate faithful self-understanding and energy to adapt appropriately to modern society.

3. Practical Models of School Social Welfare Programs

School social welfare projects have gradually developed various practical models required by the social and cultural environment of the time as the field of practice becomes more specialized. The practice models include various intervention purposes and techniques, social worker activities, and approaches according to differences in perspectives on the nature of problems faced by students. Accordingly, several practical models of school social welfare are presented as follows.

1) Traditional Clinical Model

Traditional clinical models are based on their theoretical basis in psychoanalysis, self-psychology, and individual social projects. The basic assumption of this model starts with the fact that students or families are dysfunctional and struggling. It is a view that the cause of students' emotional and mental problems lies in the family rather than other social and environmental factors, and is due to the conflict between parents and children.

The traditional clinical model focuses on individual students who have been identified as having social and static problems that hinder adaptation and academic achievement in school, and is interested in the social and emotional characteristics of students and families that cause academic disabilities.

In particular, this model helps students adapt to school and effectively utilize learning opportunities by modifying student behavior or changing the characteristics of students or parents.

Therefore, social workers mainly provide individual social work services to students and their families while also collectively doing so. In addition, they mainly play the role of those who make it possible for students or their families, supporters, and experts.

2) School Change Model

The school change model is based on its theory of deviation and organizational theory. This model is from the perspective that the school system itself causes students to adapt to school and achieve poor academic achievement. In other words, the school as a target group is viewed as a totality, including all people and subgroups involved in the school. For example, everyone, including students, teachers, principals, vice principals, and general staff, can be targeted.

The school change model aims to change the dysfunctional school's norms and conditions, and changes the systems that appear to be the cause of students' poor academic achievement by identifying the norms and conditions of the dysfunctional school. Therefore, this model is called an institutional change model.

Therefore, school social workers help principals, vice principals, and teachers change school conditions that interfere with students' learning and school adaptation, and provide collective guidance to students and families to eliminate dysfunctional roles. They mainly serve as spokespersons, negotiators, advisors, and mediators.

3) Community Model

The community model is mainly based on community organization theory, general organization theory, system theory, and communication theory. This model believes that the cause of students' problems is due to the lack of school understanding of the social conditions of the community, including poverty, and cultural differences in the community. In particular, this model focuses on explaining the role of schools in the community for vulnerable communities with little understanding and trust in schools, and explaining the dynamics of the community and social factors affecting schools to school staff.

The community model aims to help local communities understand and support the role of schools and develop programs for students in these vulnerable areas. In addition, it helps schools to educate students as a whole by correcting conditions that hinder students from exercising their educational and social skills.

Therefore, the activities of school social workers inform the community of the role and necessity of the school and obtain the understanding and support of the community about the school. It also explains the dynamics and social factors of the community to school staff and develops school programs to help disadvantaged students. In particular, it mainly plays the role of mediators, spokespersons, and outreachers, such as correcting the deficiency environment that causes student difficulties.

4) Interaction Model

The interaction model is based on system theory, collective social project practice theory, and communication theory. This model believes that the cause of the problem is difficult for individuals and various systems to communicate and assist each other in social interaction. The interaction model is interested in the interactions between schools, students, and communities, in particular in dysfunctional relationships and the type and quality of interactions occurring between them. It focuses more on coordination than advocacy of the target system.

The interaction model aims to identify obstacles that interfere with functional interaction between schools, students, and communities, change the type of dysfunctional interaction between systems, and help schools, students, and communities work together.

Therefore, school social workers help schools, students, and communities identify and recognize common grounds, and set mutual goals to improve communication and form a mutual cooperation system. In this process, school social workers directly perform activities with individuals, groups, and communities. The role of school social workers is particularly emphasized as an intermediary rather than a spokesperson, and plays a role as an advisor and a possible person.

5) Trilateral Relationship Model

The three-way relationship model was developed by Costin through a three-year pilot training project conducted by Adams at the University of Illinois in the early 1970s at the College of Social Work to bring about changes in student service. This model includes student groups in similar situations in problem situations, and it is believed that the social behavior of student group members lies in dysfunctional interactions with the situation of the school and community.

The three-way relationship model emphasizes the complexity of interactions between students, schools, and communities. In other words, the relationship between schools, communities, and students focuses on the combination of schools and communities and the characteristics of other systems that interact with the characteristics of student groups when students are at various stress points in the life cycle. The integrated purpose of this model is to help student groups make more effective use of learning opportunities while changing the school-community-student relationship system to relieve the stress of the target student group.

4. Measures to Revitalize School Social Welfare Services in Korea

1) Problem-Solving Plan

(1) Establishment of School Social Welfare Service Concepts

School social welfare projects are defined as professional assistance activities in which students and their families provide various welfare services to solve problems by linking social resources such as community welfare institutions with schools as practice sites. Efforts are required to spread this concept of school social welfare projects to the public through continuous efforts of the social welfare community.

(2) Establishment of the Korean Model and Adjustment of the Relationship between Interest Groups

The school social welfare system is a system developed in the United States, and in order to indigenousize it to suit our reality, clinical and institutional reviews must be preceded in consideration of our school system and culture. The school counseling model currently in effect in Korea and the visiting teacher model using community welfare institutions that appeared in the early stages of the introduction of the school social welfare project system in the United States should be compared and reviewed. In our situation, we will be able to find various ways, especially in the placement of school social workers, the placement of counseling teachers, the relationship between schools and local communities, and the composition of operating entities. In addition, it is necessary to adjust the positions of the educational community, social welfare academia, and the working community as an interest group related to school social welfare projects. Efforts to understand mutual professions should take precedence over claims of vested interests. It is necessary to mutually recognize the other party's activity space as a cooperative relationship that focuses on solving problems of adolescents and finds the best way to solve problems.

(3) Improvement of a System

Relevant laws and regulations need to be revised. The organization of the Ministry of Education and Human Resources Development also needs to establish a department in charge of the school social welfare project system. Therefore, policy support is needed, and the current pilot school should be fully expanded.

2) Institutionalization Strategy and Challenges

Efforts to spread the concept of school social welfare projects to the public are needed. It is appropriate to promote the school social welfare system in cooperation with the education community, and the Ministry of Education and Human Resources Development should accept the step-by-step approach, but legislative activities should be strengthened to insert grounds for school social welfare projects in the Elementary and Secondary Education Act. As the effectiveness of the school social welfare project system is proven, policy support and system reorganization are of paramount importance. In addition, it is necessary to form a friendly cooperative relationship with the education community, and the social welfare community should demand the legislation of the school social welfare project system as a policy of political parties through elections. Lastly, first of all, the pilot project operation cost of the Ministry of Education and Human Resources Development is set too low, making it difficult for school social workers to enter. A strategy to gradually expand finances will be needed by preparing a more gradual and step-by-step arrangement plan.

Many educational officials recognize the necessity and justification of the introduction of school social welfare projects, but there are still institutional challenges to be solved related to the budget. The social welfare community should make efforts to suggest specific measures for the implementation of school social welfare projects using a limited budget by the Ministry of Education and Human Resources Development. In addition, efforts should be made to expand the practice scene of school social welfare projects. Social welfare starts with clients. Students also exist in the community, and if the social welfare center and the local education office cooperate to form a school social welfare service pool system, they will be able to provide professional services to schools in the region. In addition, the social welfare community must constantly cultivate expertise and skills to establish qualitative guarantees for school social welfare projects. It is necessary to create a device that can sustain its own efforts to develop expertise that can accurately grasp the changing environment and needs of clients in a timely and accurate manner and develop and provide necessary services.

Chapter 19 Medical and Mental Health Social Welfare

1. Medical Social Welfare

1) Concept of Medical Social Welfare

Medical social welfare is a social welfare practice activity carried out in the health and medical fields to achieve various purposes such as improving social functions of patients and families, preventing, treating, and rehabilitating diseases(Jeong, Min-Sook et al. 2009).

2) Medical Social Welfare Service

(1) Social Welfare Services Act

According to the Social Welfare Service Act of Korea, Article 2(Definition) In this Act, "**social welfare service**" refers to various welfare activities related to protection and guidance or welfare, social welfare counseling, homelessness, free accommodation, community welfare, medical welfare, home welfare, social welfare, mental illness, and Hansen's disease.

(2) Enforcement Regulations of the Medical Service Act

Article 24(2)5 of the Enforcement Decree of the revised Medical Service Ordinance(Presidential Decree No. 6863) on September 20, 1973 stipulates that "at least one general hospital has a social welfare worker in charge of counseling and guidance for patient rehabilitation, and social return."

The term "**social welfare worker**" was replaced by the term "social welfare worker" according to the revision of the Social Welfare Service Act on May 21, 1983, and Article 28(2)6(the number of medical personnel, etc.) stipulates that "general hospitals have at least two employees in charge of rehabilitation, and social rehabilitation."

(3) Organ Transplantation Act

In Article 25 of the Enforcement Decree of the Organ Transplantation Act, "The standards for facilities, equipment, and manpower to be designated as organ transplant medical institutions(hereinafter referred to as "transplant medical institutions") are as shown in attached Table 1."

(4) Act on the Promotion of Mental Health and Support for Welfare Services for People with Mental Disabilities

Article 17 (1) states, "*The Minister of Health and Welfare may qualify a person trained by a training institution prescribed by Ordinance of the Ministry of Health and Welfare as a mental health clinician and mental health nurse.*"

3) Roles and Targets of Medical Social Workers

(1) Role of Medical Social Workers

In the early days, the role of medical social workers started mainly with post-mortem guidance, home visit guidance, and education in psychosocial aspects after discharge, and then vocational training and rehabilitation activities for patients to return to society were added. Currently, the role of medical social workers is changing and expanding in various ways.

Looking at the role of medical social workers in detail, first, as a psychosocial therapist, it plays a supportive role and a therapeutic role to help solve or alleviate immediate problems. Second, as a service coordinator, it provides psychosocial and economic information to the medical team and is in charge of cooperation and coordination for the team's integrated service. Third, human, material, institutional, and legal resources are developed and utilized as a resource mobilization cost. Fourth, it is the role of rehabilitation and correctional personnel.

(2) Subject of Medical Social Welfare

The targets of medical social welfare can be classified into policy targets and technical targets(Lee, Kwang-Jae, 2005).

policy object	- The medical security system refers to a policy and institutional device to protect the people from medical and economic difficulties caused by diseases and injuries. - Since healthcare is viewed as part of poverty policy, and next, health is a basic condition for human survival, the purpose of medical security is seen as "liberation from disease" beyond protection for the poor.
technical object	- It can be said to be a professional activity that provides help to solve psychological, social, and economic problems experienced by patients with diseases or disabilities and their families. - Therefore, doctors, patients, and their families are the subjects that medical social workers usually match.

2. Mental Health and Social Welfare

1) Concept

According to a report by the National Committee for Mental Hygiene, 'mental health means not just a state of mental illness, but a satisfactory relationship and the ability to maintain it.' In this respect, it refers to "*a state of well-being such as happiness, satisfaction, and achieving what one wants,*" or "*a state of not only no mental illness, but also having a mature personality that can maximize one's ability, adapt to the environment, and handle one's life independently and constructively.*"

Mental health social welfare refers to all human-to-environmental interventions so that people with mental disorders can adapt to the environment, which consists of teamwork with various professionals such as psychiatrists, regular health clinicians, mental health nurses, and occupational therapists.

Mental health social welfare is a social welfare approach to help clients and improve national health through early intervention and prevention of problems.

This method is intended to help clients suffering from mental and emotional disorders live a normal social life, and can be defined as dealing with economic and social problems derived from this problem, and supportive problems resulting from symptom recovery.

However, mental health and social work is not limited to patients visiting medical institutions, but also to rehabilitate and return to society, and mental health services for mentally disabled people are being implemented. Since there are many chronic diseases in the field of psychiatry, the importance of mental health and social work that can play an important role in the background of families and communities is increasing in order to meet continuous assistance and successfully return to society.

2) Subject of Mental Health and Social Welfare

The purpose of the Mental Health Act is to promote the mental health of the entire nation, but the priority target is mental illness patients who are "people with mental illness, personality disorder, and other mental disorders." However, the most important targets of mental health, social health and welfare are clients that need continuous protection, such as mentally ill people, families and communities that care for them, as priority targets.

3) Breakdown of Mental Disorders

Currently the most widely used classification criteria for mental disorders are the International Classification of Disease and Health Problems(ICD-10) and the Fourth Edition of the Diagnostic and Mental Disorder Statistics published by the American Psychiatric Association(DSM-IV).

Mental disorders are divided into mental illness and mental retardation. Mental retardation refers to a deficit in intellectual ability that appeared from birth or childhood, and mental illness usually refers to a case where the condition appeared later, although it was healthy in the past. Mental retardation is divided into four stages according to the degree of delay. ① Mild mental retardation: IQ 50-70; mental age is 9-12; educational group; ② moderate mental retardation: IQ 35-50; mental age is 4-8; trainable group; ③ severe mental retardation: IQ 20-35; mental age is 2-3; complete protective group; ④ profund mental retardation ; IQ 20 or less, mental age is less than 2 years old, complete protection proup.

Mental disorders are classified in DSM-IV as follows. ① Anxiety Disorders (including panic disorder, pananxiety disorder, obsessive compulsive disorder, post-traumatic stress disorder) ② Body type disorder (including somatoform disorder, physicalization disorder, conversion disorder, psychogenic pain disorder, health anxiety, body deformity, and differential type disorder) ③ Dissociative disorder (including psychosomatic memory loss, psychosomatic, dullness, multiple personality, teterozygous disorder, atypical dissociative disorder). ④ emotional disorders (past depression). ⑤ Sexual function and sexual intercourse disorder (sexual and gender indentity, sexual function disorder, sexual addiction disorder, sexual intercourse disorder), and ⑥ Eating disorders (eating disorders, neurological insufficiency, neurological hyperactivity), and ⑦ Sleep disorders.

4) Mental Health and Social Welfare Practice Site

The practice of mental health and social projects is centered on mental health centers, mental medical institutions, mental care facilities, social return facilities, and alcohol counseling centers. The delivery system of mental health and social projects consists of the Central Mental Health Deliberation Committee under the Ministry of Health and Welfare, the National Mental Health Organization(medical, technical support), and local mental health project support groups under the city and province. Hereinafter, the Si/Gun/Gu Health Center(Mental Health Center) includes social return facilities (rehabilitation, housing), alcohol counseling centers(counseling, rehabilitation), mental medical institutions(medical protection, rehabilitation), and mental care facilities(medical protection, rehabilitation). A detailed look at these institutions is as follows.

(1) Psychiatric Institution

Psychiatric institutions refer to psychiatrists established in mental hospitals, psychiatrists, and medical institutions at the hospital level or higher under the Medical Service Act, and aim to hospitalize or treat patients with acute mental illness.

As of March 2007, there are Seoul National Hospital, Chuncheon National Hospital, Gongju National Psychiatric Hospital National Nursing Psychiatric Hospital, Naju National Hospital, and Bugok National Hospital. When should the forced hospitalization of the modern version of 'Iron Mask' end? A legislative hearing was held on March 27, 2007 to revise the Mental Health Act, which is controversial over human rights violations.

(2) Mental Care Facility

Mental care facilities are facilities established under the Mental Health Act and refer to facilities that provide training to promote medical care and return to society by admission of mentally ill and chronically mentally ill patients commissioned by mental medical institutions. The purpose is to improve the quality of life and return to society by entering mental care facilities for chronically mentally ill patients who have difficulty protecting their families.

Those subject to admission are those diagnosed as mentally ill by a psychiatrist, and those who want to enter mental care facilities and those who are obligated to protect them will be admitted to mental care facilities, and the number of facilities is limited to 300 or less.

(3) Rehabilitation Facility

A social return facility refers to a facility that conducts training to promote social return without hospitalizing mentally ill patients in mental medical institutions or entering mental care facilities.

Founded in 1986, Taehwa Spring House(http://www.fountainhouse.or.kr/), Korea's first mental rehabilitation program, operates a member-centered program that accepts mentally disabled people as members of society, recognizes their potential, and realistically leads social life in Seoul.

(4) Alcohol Counseling Center

The Alcohol Counseling Center is a facility that provides counseling and training for the prevention, treatment, and rehabilitation of alcoholism to local residents such as alcoholics, prospective addicts, and their families.

As of March 2007, 13 centers are operating in Seoul, including the Seoul Alcohol Counseling Center(Korea Alcohol Culture Research Center), the Seoul Caritas Alcohol Counseling Center(Catholic Caritas Sisterhood Foundation), and the Suwon Alcohol Counseling Center in Gyeonggi Province(www.neuropsychiartry.co.kr). The important projects of the center are as follows.

A. Basic Business

① Community research project
② Development of community resources and establishment of a linkage system with related organizations
③ Prevention, publicity, education, etc. of alcohol dependence
④ Alcohol abuse and dependency discovery and registration business
⑤ Alcoholics, Home Telephone, Visiting Consultations
⑥ Alcohol-dependent rehabilitation program
⑦ Consultation on intra-regional alcohol dependence
⑧ Managing and connecting volunteers
⑨ Operation of steering committee
⑩ Advisory committee operation

B. Subsidiary Business

① Day care program
② Development and implementation of alcohol-dependent treatment and rehabilitation programs
③ Support for self-help groups for alcoholics and families

④ Probation program for drunk drivers and drunk offenders(lecture orders and counseling orders)
⑤ Conducting alcohol-dependent prevention education and programs such as abstinence for students and office workers
⑥ Seminar on alcohol dependence such as temperance
⑦ Publication of a newsletter
⑧ Cyber counseling, etc.

5) Mental Health Social Worker Training(Qualification)

(1) Mental Health Social Worker Qualification

A. Qualifications

① According to the Mental Health Act in 1997, a community-centered approach began as the approach to mentally disabled people shifted from long-term hospitalization to community-centered early detection, early treatment, and rehabilitation.
② Mental health social workers are awarded national certificates awarded by the Ministry of Health and Welfare and are divided into grades 1 and 2.
③ Class 2 mental health social workers must complete a one-year training course after obtaining a level 1 qualification as a social worker. During the second-class training period, you must complete 150 hours of theory, 830 hours of practice, and 20 hours of academic activities.
④ Class 1 mental health social worker must have at least 5 years of practical experience at related institutions after graduating from graduate school related to social welfare and acquiring class 2 for 3 years in mental health practice.
⑤ Mental health social workers practice social welfare in the field of mental health to promote rehabilitation of people with mental conditions, detect and prevent mental diseases early, and improve national mental health.

B. Role

It plays a role as a teacher in charge of providing services necessary for treatment and rehabilitation to clients and families with mental disorders in the community and hospitals.

C. Legal Basis

① In the Mental Health Act, the mental health specialist system was stipulated, and mental health specialists were required to be placed in public health centers, and one mental health specialist per 100 inpatients was assigned to each mental hospital or general hospital psychiatrist.

② As of the end of December 2009, there were 440 mental health social workers in the first grade and 1,777 in the second grade, a total of 2,217 people, and 84 training institutions nationwide.

③ Mental health social workers are working in teams with psychiatrists, mental health clinical psychologists, and mental health nurses. Mental health social workers are interested in the return of mentally disabled people to society within the community.

(2) Function of Mental Health Social Workers

A. Services for Hospitalized Patients

① Clients and families with mental disorders may be curious and anxious about hospital life. Therefore, explain hospital facilities and programs to clients and families.

② It helps solve family problems caused by clients being hospitalized. In other words, efforts are made to solve the life problems of children following their mothers' hospitalization.

③ Families are worried and anxious about whether their clients will die or not due to mental illness, so they try to alleviate family anxiety.

④ If there are economic difficulties, discuss with your family for an economic solution.

⑤ By explaining the hospital's treatment procedures, clients and families should be cooperative in treatment.

⑥ Investigate the client's personal history to identify the client's problems and support problem solving.

⑦ Provide necessary group counseling to hospitalized clients.

⑧ Help solve the problems of the client's family.

⑨ Plan the discharge of the client. If a client lives with his or her family after discharge, it prepares the client and family to reunite and helps them adapt well to the workplace and community.

B. Outpatient Services

① Outpatients are mentally ill people who have some degree of mental disability but are capable of performing their daily functions in the community, who are mentally ill, drug or alcoholics, adolescents with school adaptation problems, families with serious conflicts, and people facing crisis.

② Patients admitted to the psychiatric ward are often forced to be hospitalized, but outpatients are motivated for treatment, so they often want to receive treatment voluntarily.

③ Mental health social workers provide psychotherapy and group counseling for outpatients, connect clients with other resources in the community, and provide counseling and education to the client's family and employers.

C. Part-Time Hospitalization Services

① Partial hospitalization services belong to the middle of hospital and outpatient services, which means receiving treatment for several hours a day and performing daily activities at home or at work.

② There are day hospitals and night hospitals in the form. During the day, a hospital means receiving entertainment therapy, work therapy, group therapy, or individual treatment at a hospital or center during the day, and then returning home in the evening to live with your family. Night hospitals refer to activities at home, work, or school during the day, and at night, they come to the hospital to participate in treatment programs.

③ Partial hospitalization services have the advantage of providing more organized services than outpatient services and being less restricted by hospital admission, and serve as a bridge between inpatients and outpatients so that they can easily return to normal daily life after being discharged from the hospital.

④ Mental health social workers support clients, educate specific coping skills, and provide follow-up services that combine client personal skills research, program orientation, take work, individual counseling, group counseling, family treatment, and discharge plan.

D. Non-Traditional Services

① Mental health services through counseling and education related to mental health are provided at secondary social welfare sites such as industries, correctional institutions, rehabilitation services, schools, and counseling institutions.

② For example, in the industry, employees' crises or emotional problems cause productivity to decrease, so mental health should be maintained and promoted through mental health services in the workplace.

Chapter 20 Correctional Welfare

1. Concept of Correctional Welfare

1) Concept of Correctional Welfare

Correction is a term that has the meaning of Chinese characters to teach and correct, and in the academic field, it is a concept distinct from the current power system performed on criminals. In this sense, the purpose of correction is to prevent recidivism and re-delingency and to help return to society by improving the anti-ethics and antisociality of those who are detained in correctional facilities or discharged from hospital.

The punishment system for criminals developed from a freestyle that deprives criminals of their freedom to a labor type that imposes forced labor and then a punishment type that imposes cruel punishment.

Since the 19th century, the development of rational thinking has led to a recognition that more attention should be paid to removing social and psychological conditions that hinder them from normal social behavior rather than punishing individuals. In other words, they became aware of the social responsibility that caused harmful environments or wrong socialization of delinquency and crime. Therefore, it can be said that corrective social welfare has emerged to control the environment for re-socialization and social treatment through psychotherapy.

The types of corrections in modern society include those conducted in and outside the facilities, and correction in facilities refers to correction and treatment after being accommodated in correctional facilities such as prisons, juvenile centers, and detention centers. In addition, corrections other than facilities include a probation system or a social service order system that corrects and treats by means of guidance, supervision, and sponsorship of vocational reports within society.

2) Concept of Correctional Welfare

Based on the understanding of correction revealed above, it can be seen that the concept of correctional welfare is as follows.

Correctional welfare is the practice of social welfare and can be said to be a specialized field for the edification of criminals. In terms of crime prevention, a comprehensive activity in which professionals in each field cooperate can be called correctional welfare. In addition, correctional welfare is a service that helps rehabilitate criminals and delinquent adolescents who fail to adapt to society. In other words, it refers to welfare treatment and organizational service support activities to prevent recidivism by independently overcoming the anti-ethics and antisociality of prisoners detained in correctional facilities or discharged from hospital for illegal acts. Therefore, it can be said that correctional welfare refers to re-activity that is socially treated by environmental control and psychotherapy for re-socialization to those who have committed or are likely to commit a crime.

2. Basic Principles of Correctional Welfare

The basic principles of correctional welfare call for reflection on the inhumane execution based on humanitarian ideas, and promote respect for humanity and guarantee of human rights, such as prohibition of pain, use of detention, individualization of improvement measures, abolition of death penalty and torture. Next, the cause of crime, scientific analysis and classification of criminals, corrective treatment, and return to society are the basic structures, and scientificization and individualization of treatment are important. In addition, in order to return to society and adapt well, it is necessary to interact with the general society rather than isolate it in an unnatural environment, so it gives freedom and functions for social life to handle matters related to oneself. Therefore, laws related to correctional welfare include the Juvenile Act(1958), the Juvenile Service Act(1958), the Act on Probation, etc.(1988), and the Protection of Minors Act(1961).

3. Practical Sectors of Correctional Welfare

Correctional welfare is largely divided into public and private sectors in terms of supply subjects, and the public sector is organized into courts, prosecutors, police, prisons, juvenile detention centers, and probation offices, and welfare services are provided by courts, organizations, and individuals.

4. Causes of Juvenile Delinquency

Unlike adult crimes, the causes and characteristics of juvenile delinquency are many different, and the probability of change depending on the surrounding conditions and circumstances is very high. Therefore, it has both contradictory aspects of punishment and tolerance. However, compared to adult crimes, juvenile delinquency is more likely to depend on the treatment method, so punishment-oriented punishment is not desirable to be carried out for correction and edification rather than punishment-oriented administration. The reason is that in terms of society, the more society develops, the greater the side effects are, so crime is not much different from the social situation.

1) Definition of Juvenile Delinquency

(1) Concept and Scope of Delinquency

The concept of delinquency refers to all antisocial behaviors when defined in a broad sense, but juvenile delinquency is generally used as a consultation. For example, the former sees the shape of the head, clothing, and behavior that violate the standards prescribed by the authorities as delinquency. In the latter case, the act of adolescents is subject to litigation in the juvenile court.

The legal classification of juvenile delinquents is as follows. First, a criminal juvenile: a juvenile aged 14 to 20 years old who has committed an act that violates the penal code. This is accompanied by criminal responsibility. Second, unlawful Juvenile: A boy aged 12 to 20 years old who has committed an act that violates the penal statutes. However, criminal responsibility does not follow. Third, a juvenile offender: a boy aged 10 to 20 years old who has a nature of disobedience to the legitimate supervision of his guardian, or who is likely to commit a crime in the future due to reasons such as breaking away from his family, criminality, or dating an unscrupulous person. Fourth, a juvenile delinquent: a boy under the age of 20 who harms the virtues of himself or others by drinking, smoking, stabbing, making fun of women, entering the box office, making bad friends, having bad relationships, joining a bad group, fighting, etc. Fifth, juvenile caregivers: Those who are not delinquent boys, but who are abused, overworked, neglected, or who are separated or cannot be raised by their guardians, or who are required to be protected under the Act on the Performance of Police Officers' Duty or the Child Welfare. However, the juvenile delinquent are not distinguished from the behavior itself, and they are reasonably determined depending on whether there is a concern about committing a crime in the future.

(2) Characteristics of Juvenile Delinquency

Today's juvenile delinquency and crime have several characteristics. First, the number of juvenile delinquency and crimes is increasing rapidly. Second, the motivation for delinquency or crime is gradually changing from primary (physiological, physical, and safety needs) to secondary(pleasant, aesthetic, and social needs). In the past, they used to commit delinquency due to poverty and physical threats, but today more and more delinquents and crimes are being committed for entertainment, false greed, success, and enjoyment. Third, delinquency and crime are evenly distributed across different classes of society. In other words, it cannot be said that there are unusually many juvenile delinquents in the poor compared to other social classes. Fourth, juvenile delinquency and the aging of criminals are phenomenon. The age of committing the first misconduct or crime will be lowered to elementary school students. Fifth, a tracking phenomenon is shown. In other words, it is very difficult for adolescents who have committed a single flight to escape the bondage of delinquents.

In recent years, youth guidance and protection have emerged as serious social problems because juvenile delinquency is on the rise in quantity and deteriorating in quality, such as gangsterization, collectiveization, combustion, and urban concentration.

2) Cause of Juvenile Delinquency

Since the causes of juvenile delinquency are complex and related, it is difficult to make a conclusion focusing on either. Adolescent delinquency can be observed in two aspects. In other words, the personal factors of delinquency are heredity, race, physical character, personality, and psychological disorder, and the environmental factors of delinquency are family life, background, life goals, values, attitudes toward adults, lack of career stability, etc. Here, the causes of juvenile delinquency will be examined as personal factors, social structural factors, school life factors, and social class factors.

(1) Personal Factor

This factor is acquired rather than innate and can be seen in terms of physical and emotional factors. The motivation for crime is expressed as a result of behavior within humans, but due to the complexity of interactions occurring between numerous factors and the difficulty of grasping the factors, these are usually largely distinguished from heredity as an internal element and the environment as an external element.

A. Inheritance

Since the Italian psychiatrist Cesare Lombroso, the physical characteristics of criminals have been investigated from various angles and have become important in relation to criminal personality, which is not a theoretical interpretation of the cause itself. Lombrosso insisted on the theory of criminal heredity that natural criminals, that is, criminals, are eliminated as criminals from birth, ignoring the environment as the cause of the crime and emphasizing genetics and talents. Under Darwin's influence, he made the assumption that criminals would resemble primitive people, which was the conclusion he obtained from observing prisoners in Italian prisons. He argued that certain people become born criminals because of inferior physical and mental inheritance. These specific people believed that physiological and neurological characteristics were similar to those found in monkeys and lower animals, and these characteristics were similar to those of primitive humans. He affirmed that these types of people cannot act according to discipline and any expectations in a civilized society like today. Lombrosso found that the physical characteristics of natural criminals were those with small skulls and deformities, those with uneven teeth, those with low foreheads, and those with too small fists, and Ernest A. Hooton(1887-1954) also found that criminals were generally inferior to normal people.

However, Lombroso's concept of natural criminal punishment was blanked for two reasons: First, it was to observe many prisoners and systematically record the physical characteristics described by Lombrosso, and second, it is the fact that these studies did not support Lombrosso's argument. In 1913, Charles Goring(1870–1919), a British prison doctor, pointed out that the characteristics of Lombrosso's natural criminal sentence did not appear frequently enough to support the theory from 3,000 prisoners he studied. Another important argument is in the study of twins. If one of the twins was a criminal, the other twin should also be criminal, but in fact, many cases were different.

B. Emotional Disorder

Looking at the characteristics and psychological trends of delinquent adolescents, they generally tend to be outgoing, active, angry, rebellious, suspicious, impulsive, and destructive. They have less fear of failure, less interest in adapting well to the social environment, are influenced by authority, but are weak in obedience. According to Burt's survey, 48.1% of delinquents were born with emotional anxiety, 11.7% were normal adolescents, and 91% of delinquent boys were emotionally unstable, while 13.0% were normal boys. Healy & Carr & Gluke refer to delinquency as an expression of internal tension or emotional conflict(discontent, loss, frustration, inferiority, and alienation), which can be a passive cause of delinquency and are mostly social products.

(2) Social Structural Factor

It means that it can occur in all cultural heritages such as customs, traditions, institutions, and norms that directly regulate human behavior based on social structural factors based on the natural environment. Therefore, juvenile crime occurs on a biological and psychological basis as a crisis in life. From a social structural point of view, the theory of cultural transmission that criminals learn criminal culture through others around them, the theory of subculture that attempts to merge these two theories, and social control theory that focuses on criminal justice and social stigma. Social structural factors can analyze juvenile delinquency, focusing on family, friendship, school life, and the media.

A. Defects in the Family

One of the important social structural factors of juvenile delinquency is the family of deficits. This is because the family is the most basic social group in which humans are born and have a decisive influence on the formation of the boy's personality from · the beginning. According to a survey by the U.S. Children's Administration, 37.0 percent of the delinquents and 53.0 percent of the women are in deficit. Broken home can be divided into structural and functional families, the former refers to families without both parents or one of them, which are separated by bereavement, separation, abandonment, disappearance, imprisonment and long-term absence.

The family life of delinquent adolescents is very divided and discordant and unstable. In particular, delinquent adolescents have more cases of growing up in damaged families such as abandonment and divorce than normal boys.

When moral standards are not strict and criminal acts are carried out as they are, they follow after their parents' criminal actions. Here, we can see how important the moral standards of the family are, and the Gleuck report that the delinquent's family is entirely(31%) lacking in unity in their research conclusions. In addition, parents and children are emotionally identified and follow the overall moral norms of parents. Conflict between parents and children becomes a problem with the hostility between father and son that occurs when a child compares his or her parents with other people's parents. And parents' excessive desire or expectation for their children puts serious emotional pressure and psychological stress on their children, and this failure and lack of understanding of achievement increases their children's hostility to their parents.

Goode's view on family dissolution is as follows. Incomplete family units such as illegal cohabitation, voluntary departure of spouses such as divorce, separation, and cultural changes, empty-shell families with little communication, temporary or long-term involuntary absence of spouses, sixth. Among these families, families with deficits are particularly related to juvenile delinquency, and Sargent points out the problem of families with deficits as follows. The first is the conflict and discord between parents before separation or divorce. The second is the tension caused by the visit of a separated single parent. Third, it refers to the problem of adaptation to stepparents due to remarriage, fourth, difficulties in harmony with separated single parents, fifth, insufficient supervision as single parents, sixth, increased family responsibility for children, and seventh, inferiority and instability.

When trying to receive compensation for these difficulties outside the family or acquire a new role and status outside the family, adolescents run away from home and further become delinquent adolescents. As such, families with deficits are a decisive factor in juvenile delinquency.

The cause of juvenile delinquency is not only at home, but family pathology also reflects social problems. However, the key to youth problems lies at home. In particular, the role of parents is very important, and once the educational role of parents is properly played, the path to solving youth problems opens.

B. Friendship Groups as Reference Groups

Friendship has the greatest influence on adolescents after the family environment. Kim, Jung-Hwi said that there are not only no healthy and normal friends beside delinquent boys, but also they do not belong to a normal youth group. In addition, a survey found that companionship is the second most important after home in the consciousness of Korean adolescents.

Crimes in adolescence are usually instantaneous and accidental crimes, and there are more collective crimes than adult crimes. In other words, delinquency occurs as a factor that hangs out with people of the same age and forms a group. Therefore, adolescents' problematic behavior should be studied with interest in youth groups. Therefore, the characteristic of collectivization tendency rather than individualization of flight becomes a factor of flight depending on the nature of the companionship group.

As a reference group(a group that individuals use as a standard for determining their beliefs, attitudes, values, and behaviors), their developmental characteristics are more pronounced due to an anomic phenomenon. These factors satisfy the sense of stability and satisfaction in the culture of their own youth companions by deviating from the general society or promoting the development of partial culture. The experiences of failure in the continuation of adolescents' frustrations or in the fulfillment of elevated needs are rewarded with a sense of pleasure or success that can be rewarded for their deviant behavior. In conclusion, it can be said that undesirable companionship groups become hotbeds of delinquency.

C. Anomorphism of School Life

The maladjustment of school life has a great influence on the formation of social attitudes and values, and is characterized by the formation of friendships according to academic performance. However, the school society is in a serious value crisis or dilemma along with rapid changes. Above all, the most prominent phenomenon is the confusion of educational values and distortion of educational goals and directions. Today's industrial society faces a too severe gap between the relational structure of society as an open society and the concept of phrases. In this gap, poor academic performance and maladjustment in school life cause juvenile delinquency, which not only has lower academic performance than the delinquent youth group, but also has a high attitude of indifference or remarkably dislike of school life. The biggest reason for disliking school like this turned out to be that they were not interested. It can be seen that the triangular relationship between the school society and the juvenile delinquent in the industrial society is complex and must be understood in terms of social structure. The excessive expansion of adolescents' realistic and material needs and the gap between means to properly satisfy those needs are factors of delinquency. This materialistic society has the value that results can justify means or processes, making the problem of juvenile delinquency more difficult. In the midst of this, adolescents lose their ability to effectively regulate their behavior, and suffer an anomie phenomenon without integrating goals and norms as a means to achieve them. Therefore, they are only engulfed in impulsive and sensuous behavior, and perform irresponsible behavior while losing control of behavior.

(3) Social Hierarchy Factor

Flights are often caused by low social and economic status. This poverty is induced more by neglect and conflict that is secondary to poverty than by itself. Poverty here does not mean a lack of material resources alone, but also poverty in social values such as educational opportunities, medical benefits, and status upward movement opportunities, and a lack of psychological levels such as individual achievement motivation and self-realization. The economic factor as a cause of delinquency can be said to be due to the fact that our culture is influenced by the materialism of modern industrial society. Looking at the situation by occupation of juvenile crime by the Supreme Prosecutors' Office, 21% of juvenile offenders were accidentally motivated in 1987, followed by 11.2% of entertainment expenses, 33.3% of unemployed workers, and 29.9% of students. In addition, most(88.7%) of juvenile offenders are in the downstream with low living standards, which is due to the lack of opportunities for parents to protect their children with affection such as guidance, supervision, or counseling partners, or even lack of time to think. As such, the delinquents are economically disadvantaged, and compared to the general public, the delinquents have been working since childhood, receiving low wages, and living in poverty without having a steady workplace. As a result, boys naturally leave their homes and are placed in a criminal environment away from their parents or families who educate or influence society.

5. Correctional Welfare Measures for Juvenile Delinquency

Various conditions related to flight have important meanings independently, but it can be seen that these factors induce flight behavior interrelated or dynamically. Therefore, all programs or services to help delinquents return to their homes, schools, and society as soon as possible are important and urgent. Institutions and facilities in charge of flight measures should newly exert their leadership power in terms of function and practice. In response, Professor Jang, In-Hyeop presented as follows.

1) Follow-Up Measures

(1) Juvenile Police System

It is urgent to establish a juvenile police system. It is desirable to avoid legal measures against juvenile delinquents due to the specialization of juvenile police and play a leading role as individual measures using families or welfare institutions. As part of the current overall police activity or temporary relationship, there is no need to deepen the problem, and through sufficient case studies, treatment should be done through organic contact and coordination with home, school, society, and law enforcement agencies.

(2) Juvenile Temporary Shelter(Juvenile Screening Center)

During the probationary period, the shelter investigates the boy's family environment, his abilities and needs, recruits important data based on clinical research, notifies the court and provides appropriate educational, religious, and medical services. In the case of Korea, these facilities are still merged into juvenile facilities, and the function should be strengthened independently as soon as possible.

(3) Juvenile Detention Center

In the event of an unacceptable misconduct in the home or society, it is inevitably sent to a juvenile detention center for protection. Therefore, in order to improve the boys, it is necessary to provide a foundation for them to completely escape from delinquency with sufficient programs such as education, vocational training, entertainment, and religious activities, more than protection done at home or society. In addition, it should be converted to treatment activities by professional personnel by breaking away from legal confinement or acceptance.

(4) Probation System

The probation system is the best-known community correction program along with the parole system. It is a desirable measure to prevent re-flight under the guidance and supervision of probation officers. Probation officers are social workers who have received professional training and are treated through training, guidance, protection, and guardianship by breaking away from punishment based on close ties with family and society.

(5) Legal Protection System

It is an important project to create a path for self-reliance and self-support for adolescents discharged from juvenile detention centers, allowing them to adapt again in society and prevent recidivism. In Korea, the situation in which about 40% of discharged patients are involved in recidivism shows the need for urgent establishment of this system. The current acceptance protection and observation protection should be further embodied, and this project should be developed through the use of experts as well as the support of the country's more practical budget. In particular, a system that can contribute to industrial manpower by preventing recidivism through the expansion of the legal protection system and enhancing the contents of the project should be established.

2) Precautionary Measures

There are a wide range of aspects to be involved in preventing juvenile delinquency. Therefore, it is divided into policies or laws at the individual, group, institution, community, and national level as follows.

(1) Individual Involvement with Individuals

Just as the factors of delinquency are due to the specificity of nature, direct pre-protection treatment measures should be devised for adolescents who have the potential to fly, whether they are the result of the environment or not.

(2) Involvement in a Group

Since most juvenile delinquency occurs in defective groups, preventive measures should be emphasized. Since problematic groups are scattered around the school or around certain special areas, group guidance and entertainment activities for them should be provided by youth social organizations or related specialized institutions.

(3) Domestic Involvement

Since most of the flight factors are family problems, preventive measures through home are very important. It will be possible to contribute to preventing delinquency by strengthening the family, that is, establishing a public assistance system, providing family counseling and family treatment services to troubled families.

(4) School Involvement

School maladjustment is closely related to delinquency. For whole-person education, we should not focus only on school classes, but should be interested in and guidening students to personally. In addition to teachers, school counseling and school social welfare project systems should be utilized, and preventive efforts should be made through coordination of relationships between schools, families, and local communities.

(5) Religious Involvement

Youth can stay away from delinquency by becoming more aware of human values and dignity through religion. Through churches or other religious organizations, they can provide them with an opportunity to have healthy companionship so that they can radiate their inner desires and experience a desirable lifestyle.

(6) Police Involvement

The police have the first responsibility for delinquent adolescents, so they can greatly help prevent them depending on their activities. It will achieve greater results when it plays a leading role in pre-regulation of harmful environments, early detection or protection of delinquent offenders, and organic contact or cooperation with youth organizations in the region, not as a coercive method.

(7) Community Involvement

This can be thought of as three things, and first, in order to eliminate flight areas, groups, flight culture, and flight ethics through community organization, the overall efforts and systems of the community are needed. If it is revealed that the cause and possibility of flight are within the area, residents, local organizations, and regional relations experts should cooperate to resolve and prevent it, and take preventive measures through coordination with local resources. Second, through social behavior, community-related organizations or community organizations should become organizations that purify the social environment that attract adolescents to delinquency. The third is prevention through proximity to a specific region, which is a preventive approach developed by Clittord & Shaw to develop a sense of proximity and mutual responsibility within a specific slum community. As a prerequisite, leadership should be discovered within the community and should not intervene from outside. In addition, the community itself, which has a factor of delinquency, should be able to self-help through the development of internal cohesion as its self-sustaining leader.

(8) Involvement at the National Level

Policy institutionalization should be considered at the national level. First, it can be classified into a preventive policy for delinquency, that is, an indirect general policy, and second, a countermeasure policy for delinquency, that is, a direct policy. First of all, the indirect general policy on delinquency is that prevention or countermeasures of delinquency are not temporary, but can be effective through long-term and institutional functions, so Korea should urgently have a preventive policy for delinquency. As long-term policy directions, economic security systems, education systems or policies, employment systems, health and housing systems, and living security systems and counseling systems for the poor are presented. Korea is still limited to supplementary and partial measures, causing many disruptions in flight prevention. Since economic instability, deprivation of educational opportunities, and loss of employment opportunities are obsessed with frustration and conflict, preventive measures should be taken first by the establishment of national policies or systems. In particular, the policy of turning many adolescents into industrial personnel who have lost opportunities for education or employment may exclude many possible misconduct. Next, direct general policy on flight is an important task to reconsider. In a situation where the judicial protection system for inmates and the professional personnel system to be involved in them are very incomplete, the vicious cycle of delinquency or crime can be prevented. The correctional system should be established so that the nature and behavior of prisoners and probationers can be corrected so that they can resist the temptation of recidivism. Of course, for them, sufficient legal protection benefits must be provided even after discharge.

(9) Involvement through Laws and Regulations

Restrictive measures such as the Juvenile Act, the Child Welfare Act, and the Labor Standards Act can also contribute to preventing delinquency. Banning minors from entering entertainment centers, abstaining from alcohol, smoking cessation, prohibiting the use of hallucinogens, or sanctions on books, magazines, and the media contribute greatly to preventing delinquency.

Taken together, the youth problem is indeed serious in a diversifying society. Looking at it from this point of view, we defined adolescents' delinquency through concept and scope. In addition, by organizing the causes of juvenile delinquency by factor and identifying them, the exact cause of delinquency was attempted. And when I looked at the current status of juvenile delinquency, I learned the severity. In addition, we tried to present measures and preventive measures to lead this. The most fundamental factor in the occurrence of juvenile delinquents today is that there are many adolescents who have not established a sense of self-identity. Therefore, it is necessary to establish and protect a right understanding of the self and a sense of identity through right human education, instill a personal human life in society, and a attitude of life as a human, so that they can grow into the right person.

6. Correctional Welfare Intervention in the Field of Correctional Welfare Practice

Correctional welfare is a new field of study systematically to contribute to the welfare of members of society by eliminating negative consequences caused by crime or delinquency as well as current problems by intervening in the social environment surrounding them. At the correctional activity site, there are correctional institutions and correctional facilities, as well as private or public and national institutions for counseling, training, and education of the subjects of correction. In addition, judicial institutions such as police, prosecutors, courts, etc., various school religious institutions and facilities, community welfare centers, and various welfare institutions and facilities may be included.

The areas of activities that correctional workers can intervene in social treatment are as follows. In relation to probation, during pre-judgment investigations, environmental investigations, environmental improvement activities, and probation, correctional workers may assist probation officials or be entrusted with part of their duties in the process of supervising probation. Adults and adolescents housed in the Legal Protection Corporation's facilities and consignment facilities usually do not have direct guardians, so correctional workers can use their network of rehabilitation resources, and correctional workers can act as volunteers, sponsors, or partners. In addition, it will be necessary to establish a system in which social workers at welfare centers participate in cooperation with the correctional site and community welfare centers in a situation where the house of intermediate treatment is not officially expanded and implemented.

Correctional welfare practice begins through dialogue between correctional welfare workers and clients at the field of practice of correctional welfare, and correctional welfare workers understand the needs or problems of clients and perform their tasks. What correctional workers are required of them in the course of corrective welfare practice is whether they can carry out delinquency and crime-related programs. Therefore, the intervention activities of correctional workers should be conducted based on thorough correctional welfare practice technology, and the focus should be on rehabilitation of delinquent adolescents and criminals, and prevention of delinquency and crime. One of the key tasks of correctional welfare in Korea is to review the role of social workers in the entire stage of correctional and to predict the intervention and role of social workers in the correctional field in Korea.

In criminal proceedings, a lawyer system suitable for strengthening the situation and status of victims should be introduced, and in fact, a lawyer system should be used to prevent mental distress and face-to-face damage due to witness interrogation in investigation.

Chapter 21 Industrial Welfare

1. Understanding of Industrial Welfare

1) Concept of Industrial Welfare

Based on the qualitative part of human life, welfare can be interpreted as a state of peace and well-being. In other words, when it is directly related to human life, such as expected appearance related to human life, health, stability and harmony, and prosperity, organizational efforts to pursue more than that correspond to welfare.

If so, industrial welfare can be explained as such by collectively referring to the state in which workers are doing well in peace on behalf of workers under the human subject name. In other words, the ideal state of happiness in which health, stability, harmony, and prosperity are guaranteed to workers is industrial welfare.

In other words, industrial welfare can be referred to as industrial welfare, which is made in the background of the industrial field. In other words, it is an effort to pursue the welfare of workers and their families by effectively coping with psychological, institutional, and social problems occurring in the field of industry by applying knowledge and technology of professional social welfare.

In this regard, Isobe said, "*Industrial welfare is an activity that promotes the standard of living of workers and employees, including corporate welfare performed by individual companies, workers' welfare performed by labor unions, and public welfare conducted by the state.*" In other words, industrial welfare includes a comprehensive institutional system centered on companies, workers, and the state.

In addition, Woo, Jae-Hyun said, "*It is a comprehensive and unified system of facility service activities conducted for the purpose of improving living welfare, such as stabilizing the lives of workers and their families, and improving living standards.*"

And foreign scholar Barker said, "It is usually the practice of professional social welfare projects conducted to improve the overall quality of life of workers both inside and outside the workplace under the auspices of employment organizations, trade unions, or both." In addition, Cruzman(P. Jurzman) stipulated that "*a program or service conducted using professional social workers to meet the legitimate social welfare needs of labor organizations or industrial organizations to help employees or unions under the auspices of management or labor.*"

Therefore, when the contents stipulated above are summarized, industrial welfare is a concept that encompasses industrial and social projects and has the following characteristics.

First, industrial welfare is carried out under the auspices of management or labor.

Second, industrial welfare is interested in the overall quality of life of workers in and outside the workplace.

Third, industrial welfare is a practical activity of professional social work by professional social workers.

Fourth, industrial welfare helps meet the needs of management and labor, and workers and their families under the combined support of both.

Fifth, industrial welfare is a practice of professional social work conducted using the knowledge and skills of social work to improve the quality of life of workers, and can be said to be a field of social welfare.

2) Targets for Industrial Welfare

In a broad sense, the object of industrial welfare can be said to be all human beings living in relation to industry. However, in consultation, it can be understood as the situation he is in, centering on each worker, and the group and organization to which he belongs.

From a social welfare perspective when approaching human behavior and social environment, it can be seen that humans are refracted in various social environments. If so, in terms of industrial welfare, humans are an important area in an individual's life through the means of labor, and the individual's ego is largely defined according to the labor he engages in. In addition, through human relationships in industrial sites, individuals are supposed to form their values and secure social positions. Therefore, labor and industrial sites can be a key paradigm for social welfare, and from that point of view, humans become individuals in situations. In order to solve this problem, various approaches must be made to solve the main phenomena of social welfare centered on the industrial field, and since individuals belong to various social structures, everyone in the industrial society is targeted.

3) Role of Industrial Social Workers

Industrial social workers are also recognized as emerging jobs in the United States. Industrial social workers are expected to receive a high salary among social workers, and more and more universities are opening related courses. Currently, industrial social workers in the United States mainly work for Employee Assistance Programs(EAPs). Employee assistance program services, a representative industrial social welfare system in the United States, include counseling on alcohol and drug abuse, counseling on emotional problems, family counseling, career counseling and education, credit loan counseling, and post-retirement planning.

Industrial social workers play a role in managing the company's human resource policies, contributing to activities with tax breaks, and consulting the company on collective agreements and other corporate social responsibility-related activities. In addition, it also plays a role in analyzing legislative activities, managing the health and welfare benefit system, and helping develop programs to sign up workers without unions as union members(Won, Suk-Zo 2009).

2. Background and Characteristics of Industrial Welfare

It can be said that the meaning of labor in an industrial society is greater than anything else. This is because the structure of the industrial society cannot exist outside of labor. In particular, in a capitalist society, the mechanism of realizing high productivity through full employment or providing sufficient jobs and coping with social accidents or obstacles that cannot be solved by redistribution of wages is achieved through social welfare.

Looking at today's social phenomenon, it is causing an imbalance between various industries. As a particular industry develops, other industries degenerate, resulting in considerable difficulties in the work of workers. As a result, various problems arise one after another, and serious problems arise in the worker's environment.

Social problems gradually expand due to inequality in income distribution, polarization of industrial structure and labor market, accumulation of stagnant unemployment, wage gap, immature labor-management negotiations, and social security lag, reaching an absolute point.

Therefore, industrial welfare is a social welfare approach to solve various social problems surrounding workers by giving material and mental stability to workers and their families.

There may be various explanations behind the emergence of such industrial welfare, but in short, it is related to the rights and interests of workers.

Historically, it was a time when the industrial revolution progressed, and in the case of foreign countries, it began to develop mainly by the self-help efforts of workers in the 18th century and reached its turning point in the 19th century.

In the case of Korea, the 1970s can be defined as that period, starting with the 1960s. In other words, the transition from agriculturalization to industrialization is an example, during which full-fledged export-led industrialization began to take place through oppressive policies for labor and support for capital, and this period can be seen as the emergence of industrial welfare.

The main phenomenon of this period was that workers were dissatisfied with their working environment and complained to their employees, resulting in welfare needs in issues to generate benefits for work, when workers no longer adapted to the situation of becoming economic tools for producing goods and services.

Industrial welfare consists of job-oriented services and programs that can increase worker confidence, achievement, and usefulness of the workplace. It can be achieved by helping individuals solve problems through worker welfare services that focus on workers' human rights.

In addition, psychological, economic, and time inconvenience can be reduced by providing better services to enable workers to work in a comfortable state. In fact, if industrial welfare services are provided by companies, they eventually contribute to securing high-quality labor and stabilizing the labor force, contributing to improving corporate productivity, allowing companies to approach the pursuit of profits.

3. Theories of Industrial Welfare

When confirming the theory of industrial welfare, it is necessary to examine the theoretical and political, economic, and cultural theories in the environment surrounding workers(family, small group, community, state, etc.) in industrial organizations where access and practice exist. For example, there are not a few things in the theory of industrial organization, but many organizational theories have their own limitations.

When looking at the industrial welfare theory from the perspective of industrial organization, there are various theories and models, such as the theory of looking at the structure and environment of the organization, the theory of looking at the management process, and the culture and system of the organization. In the midst of this, the limitations of summarizing the theory of industrial welfare are encountered. Defining the theory of industrial welfare from an organizational perspective that is still pouring out is considered to reveal the ambiguity and limitations of the theory of industrial welfare.

Max Weber's bureaucratic ideological organization theory still seems to form the basis of many industrial organizations in Korea, such as examining the individual qualities of leaders according to charismatic authority, revealing a highly efficient system for authority, rule system and organizational rationality.

Taylor's scientific management theory also argues for the improvement of work efficiency and management innovation under the scientific management method through time and motion research, standardization of tools, task management, and discriminatory performance-based pay system.

In such bureaucracy and scientific management theory, passive or negative positions are taken for reasons such as being impossible to generate profits for welfare and unreasonable. In addition, Mayo's theory of human relations, which improved workers' welfare through the introduction of counseling systems, improvement of supervisory skills, re-regulation and expansion of workers' roles, and participation in decision-making, and conflict theory that cannot be a fundamental solution.

1) Scientific Management Theory

Taylor, who argued for scientific management theory, emphasized rationality and high efficiency by calculating time and motion in performing the work, and tried to see it as the best virtue and productivity improvement. The work was intended to be divided as much as possible, and only interested in products, and it was considered that people were driven by incentives.

In other words, in order to move members of an organization, it is necessary to leak what members of the organization may be interested in, but in moving this organization, informal human relationships between organizations were ignored and humans were identified and simplified. This theory has a disadvantage that is difficult to apply socially under the concept of social welfare.

2) Theory of Human Relationship

Elton Mayo's theory of human relations is that human relations play an important role in improving work and productivity.

It was considered that the efficiency of labor and production depends not on human ability, time, motion, or money, but on human relationships. Mayo explained the theory of human relations divided into X theory and Y theory, and X theory was explained on the premise that humans are fundamentally lazy, and considered that control is necessary to engage humans in production activities. On the contrary, Y theory saw that humans are fundamentally diligent, have the ability to control themselves, and strive for self-realization.

3) System Theory

System theory is an integrated form of human relations and scientific management theory, and sees corporate structure as a complex composed of various subsystems. In other words, the management system consists of a production sub-system that performs production-related tasks, a maintenance sub-system that employs or trains employees, and an economic sub-system related to the external environment of the organization, and an adaptive sub-system related to planning and research. Therefore, the management system will be adjusted by synthesizing the above four systems and will play a role in managing them. Therefore, conflicts between each system become inevitable.

4. The Ideology and Policy Direction of Industrial Welfare

1) Industrial Welfare Philosophy

(1) Economic Dimension

The flow of welfare is born through government intervention due to the implementation of pensions and unemployment insurance according to the heyday of infinite capitalism. Since then, as the benefits of welfare have become common due to the Great Depression, the scope of coverage of pensions, medical insurance, public assistance, and family allowances has also. As prosperity and living standards continue to improve from the 1960s to the mid-1970s, new programs to guarantee the socioeconomic rights of minorities, the underprivileged, and the urban poor will be promoted, and the so-called golden age of welfare states will come. However, as the Western economy was hit by the 1973 oil crisis, tax resistance increased along with the revival of conservatism, and public assistance, social security, and government welfare expenditures were reduced.

(2) Political Dimension

On the basis of anti-collectiveism, liberal individualism based on freedom, individualism, and inequality opposes the increase of state power for social welfare, suggesting that welfare services can cause individual dependence, moral hazard, and irresponsibility. In response, limited individualism recognizes the state's intervention and role at a practical and technical level, believing that market logic alone cannot solve all social problems in industrial society. Accordingly, Fabianism attempted to practice individual freedom through the reduction of economic inequality based on the ideology of social democracy. To this end, the role of welfare was recognized as realistic legislation, active actions and efforts of the government, and voluntary participation of workers should be made. To the extreme, Marxism interprets welfare negatively as economic inequality is causing inequality in all parts of society, and the development of a welfare state acts as an obstacle to the transition of capitalism to socialism.

(3) Cultural Dimension

According to Mary Douglas's type of cultural theory, policies, institutions, and services include social historicality, culturality, and value bias. According to Douglas's cultural theory, according to behavior regulation and collective orientation, it is divided into fatalistic lifestyles, hierarchical lifestyles, egalitarian lifestyles, and individualistic lifestyles, which will be effective in defining workers' activities and value systems within industrial organizations. If each organization enjoys social relations with cultural bias, it will form the organizational culture of the organization, and accordingly, the organization will innovate and change culture through interaction with other cultures.

It is believed that more research and rational evidence will be needed because stories at the cultural level are personally thought of by looking at cultural and other industrial theories.

2) Industrial Welfare Policy

(1) Concept of Industrial Welfare Policy

Industrial welfare policy can be said to be part of the process or social planning of comprehensively forming countermeasures for public industrial welfare, corporate welfare, and self-reliance to promote workers' welfare at the government level.

As emphasized earlier, Korea's industrial welfare is the development of social welfare projects originally carried out by large companies, but in recent years, welfare activities of labor unions are being activated, and the proportion of social requests is increasing rapidly.

In Korea, economic development in the 1960s and 1970s led to rapid economic expansion, industrial structure advancement, quantitative increase of employment, and structural change. In addition to the net function of material abundance, various problems(wages related to working conditions) were raised as social problems. Since the 1980s, these labor problems centered on workers have emerged as a national concern, and the government has paid more attention to expanding industrial welfare(labor welfare) to solve the industrial labor advisory system. Therefore, from a policy point of view, industrial welfare is as follows.

(2) Classification of Industrial Welfare Policies by Type

A. State and Local Public Organizations: Public Industrial Welfare(Social Security, Social Welfare) Implementation

Public industrial welfare is a sub-concept of industrial welfare policy and refers to a system of systems and services implemented by national and local public organizations to promote the welfare of workers and their families.

B. Corporate Welfare(In-Company Welfare) Implementation

Corporate welfare is generally aimed at stabilizing the lives of workers and their families, improving living culture, and maintaining and promoting health, including corporate welfare conducted by state social security, social welfare, and environmental hygiene as part of labor management.

C. Trade Unions and their Organizations: Self-Reliance(Worker Welfare(Trade Union welfare)

Independent welfare refers to the entire welfare activities conducted by trade unions and other associations.

D. Types of Industrial Welfare Policies

Industrial welfare policies implemented by the state or public organizations are practically part of labor policies, which can be divided into labor insurance, labor insurance-related projects, severance pay deductions, industrial welfare policies of local governments, and industrial welfare policies.

Chapter 22 Multicultural Welfare

1. Concepts of a Multicultural Society

As of 2008, more than 1 million foreigners live in various forms, including migrant workers, international marriage migrants, their children, and North Korean defectors, forming cultural identity based on their culture. For human co-prosperity, a common task in the 21st century, a uniform and compulsory national state or exclusive nationalism should not be tolerated for any reason. Human co-prosperity requires a transition of perception into a multicultural society where diversity can blend beyond ethnicity, race, class, residence, age, and competence, religion, language, gender, and ideology(Lee, Jong-Bok et al., 2008).

2. Subjects of Multicultural Welfare

1) Foreign Worker

Those who first received attention as a category of migrants are workers who have migrated dreaming of a "**Korean Dream**." As of 2007, there are more than 400,000 foreign workers, including industrial trainees, of which about 230,000 are illegal workers.

2) Female Marriage Immigrant

International marriages, which accounted for 1.2% of all marriages in 1990, are increasing significantly, reaching 13.6% of all marriages in 2005.

3) Saeteomin(North Korean defectors)

Saeteomin is a pure Korean word meaning "*a person who lives with hope in a new place,*" and many people are reluctant to the term "**North Korean**

defectors," so the Ministry of Unification has decided to change the term "**North Korean defectors**" to the term "**Sateomin**" since 2005. Although there are some fluctuations due to changes in North Korea's economic and social control levels, the number of Saeteomins increased steadily from nine in 1991 to 1,387 in 2005, and entered the era of 10,000 Saeteomins in 2007 (www.unikorea.go.kr). Difficulties and cultural conflicts experienced by rapid changes in new settlements can be summarized as job selection, employment, communication problems, job performance process, Korean work culture, and Koreans' perception of Saeteomin.

The government has implemented various support policies for North Korean defectors, such as creating the Act on the Protection and Settlement Support for North Korean defectors and establishing Hanawon, an initial adaptation support office. Currently, the direction of the Saeteomin support policy in Korean society and efforts by church-centered private organizations are not pluralistic approaches to help Saeteomin form their own community culture, so cultural coexistence with North Korea, communication with others, and cultural integration(Lee, Jong-Bok et al., 2008).

3. Current Status of Multicultural Welfare

1) Ministry of Justice: Immigration and Stay Management

Female marriage migrants are foreigners until they acquire Korean nationality, so if they divorce before acquiring Korean nationality, they can return to their home country or become illegal immigrants. Since 2005, the Ministry of Justice has prepared and implemented primary support measures (2005.8) focusing on solving the problem of anxiety in stay and secondary support measures(2005.11) focusing on life support.

2) Ministry of Employment and Labor: Job, Employment and Training

The Ministry of Employment and Labor is preparing and implementing policies related to job, employment, and training to create a stable living environment for female marriage migrant families, and plans to strengthen counseling and job placement services for job seekers. It is also preparing female marriage migrants to enter the public service sector.

3) Ministry of Health and Welfare: Health, Welfare and Medical Services

Multicultural families experience inconvenience or collapse of their families due to language communication problems and cultural differences in their lives, and are alienated from various information, resources, and employment. In order to guarantee the basic livelihood of the people, the National Basic Livelihood Security Act was revised(2005.12), and female marriage migrants were included in the support list of the Emergency Welfare Support Act. In addition, unacquired migrants raising underage children with an actual income of less than 120% of the minimum cost of living were included in the list of self-supporting workers, and mental health counseling services were provided by producing foreign language notices for those who did not subscribe to health insurance. In addition, in order to protect female marriage migrants affected by domestic violence, simultaneous interpretation counseling services are provided through women's emergency calls(1366), and shelters exclusively for foreign women(Incheon and Cheonan) are operated. In addition, it provides separate support for interpretation fees when participating in victim treatment and recovery programs.

4) Ministry of Culture, Sports and Tourism: Culture Policy

There is no tradition of multiculturalism, and there is prejudice and discrimination against female marriage immigrants due to the climate of emphasis on pure blood. In order to provide basic knowledge and life information necessary for Korean life and to improve understanding of cultural differences, cultural guidebooks are distributed, social culture and arts education, art healing demonstration projects and culture and arts education programs.

5) Education, Science and Technology Department: Education for Children from multicultural families

In April 2007, the number of children of international marriage families enrolled in elementary, middle, and high schools reached 13,445(Education and Welfare Policy Division, 2007). Most foreign workers' families have low incomes and poor living and learning environments, so their children have lower basic learning abilities than their peers, and some schools have difficulties avoiding admission to foreign children or rejecting integrated education with domestic students. In particular, in the case of illegal children, there are many cases where they are unable to attend school due to their unstable status, although the Ministry of Education and Human Resources Development has allowed them to enter school only by submitting a lease contract and a neighbor's residence guarantee. Accordingly, the Ministry of Education, Science and Technology has opened after-school programs for children from multicultural families, designated dedicated teachers to guide and consult with children from multicultural families, and activated one-on-one relationships with seniors or peers to support their adaptation to school. In addition, since 2007, a teacher training center has been established to enhance teachers' interest in children from multicultural families and strengthen their ability to guide them. This policy of the Ministry of Education, Science and Technology is being activated as a multicultural family support program centered on local governments through the Regional Human Resource Development(RHRD) project.

6) Private Support Organization

Most of the private support organizations were small groups, and in some cases large groups, and it was difficult to specifically help them on the Internet, but most of their activities were related to Korean language education except medical institutions. Volunteers were mainly the center of activities, and the progress of the project was made through a small number of experts and related people and through religious or general volunteers.

Chapter 23 Volunteer Service

1. Significance of Volunteer Activities

1) Concept of Volunteering

Voluntarism is derived from the Latin word Voluntas, which means free will, and volunteers are called volunteers. Volunteer activities refer to independent activities that occur as the exercise of free will or voluntary spirit based on the common society against human loss and family & community disorganization (Lee, Young-Chul et al., 380).

Volunteer, a Chinese character, means 'helping others because you want to'. Volunteering is an activity in which one's time, talent, and heart are distributed to neighbors in need without any reward or reward, and the entire world, not a specific person, should become a volunteer. These activities are social activities that improve the quality of life of oneself and neighbors while developing local communities and making neighbors and society happy.

The American Social Work Dictionary defines volunteers as individuals who perform various services given to corporations engaged in preventing or improving the effects of various social problems occurring in individuals, groups, and communities.

The British Volunteer Center defines volunteer activities as activities performed by free choice, not directly compensated for themselves or other people other than their direct family members, and not required by the state or institution.

In the case of Japan, the Osaka Volunteer Association broadly stipulates that they are people who voluntarily support activities to solve social problems, and emphasizes spontaneity rather than non-acuteness.

In the case of Australia, it is defined as a person who regularly contributes his time and energy free of charge to private institutions, public institutions, social actions, and self-help groups related to social welfare issues.

In Korean traditional society, there was a beautiful custom of voluntarily participating and helping neighbors in times of hardship and unhappiness. The system for collaboration(meaning diverse according to the practice and purpose of mutual aid: mixed, academic, elderly, Eastern, mixed, set-off, same-aged, poor, etc.), Dure(dure is a village unit organization, adult men's work community: hollow, cooking, neighborhood rice planting, incense, etc. such as the basic form of community sharing). When asked, "*What is volunteer work in Korea?*" ninety-nine out of a hundred will equally answer, "Helping others(good deeds)." On the other hand, in the United States, when asked the same question, "*what someone has to do*" or "*the responsibility of a citizen,*" or even some seven-year-old boy gives an ingenious answer, "*the same thing as delivering pizza on time.*" From this, it can be easily seen that it has a meaning other than simply "*helping others,*" that is, a sense of responsibility.

Although the concept of modern volunteer work is defined differently in terms of monetary compensation, activity, and voluntary, there is a growing awareness that it is possible to receive minimal funding if necessary, as well as individuals, private institutions, and self-help groups.

In another expression, volunteering is 'care'. Taking care of the poor, the sick, the unjust, the marginalized, the fallen, the tradition and culture we cherish, the environment, nature, our children, adolescents, the elderly, the disabled, caring for the country, and caring for humanity. A person who simply refers to all these care as an "altruism spirit" knows only one thing and two do not.

Those who perceive volunteer work as an "*act of helping others*" are likely to be immersed in the superiority that "*the giver*" is better than the "*receiver*" and the stereotype that "*volunteering takes place at the expense of my interests.*" If you think you have to sacrifice your interests, it is not only difficult to start volunteering with determination, but it can also hurt the recipient's heart because of the superiority that you are "*better*" than the other person. Therefore, rather than being interested in solving the problem, it is operated only by convenience to comfort one's conscience, and the effect is halved.

Volunteering is not provided by a superior side, but is a balancing device in which the provider and the recipient are equal regardless of social status, wealth, gender, age, etc.

If we take volunteering as fatefully granted, like any other daily life, as civil responsibility, the price of freedom, or as a human responsibility, or simply as a small task for my family and my community, and realize that my potential is developed and self-realization.

2) Legal Basis

As volunteer activities and their perceptions spread throughout society and volunteer work became urgent, the government sought various ways to promote volunteer work in a national and institutional manner since 1994. After a long attempt, the Framework Act on Volunteer Activities was submitted as a government legislation on August 5, 2005, and finally passed the National Assembly and began to take effect on February 5, 2006. This marks the first step in Korea as an act in which volunteer activities are recognized by the state. The Framework Act on Volunteer Activities consists of a total of 20 groups. The explanation of the main items is as follows.

2. Necessity of Volunteering

The necessity of volunteering can be considered by dividing it into social, personal, political, and ecological aspects.

First, there have always been people in human society who need help(especially when it is not their fault: children, the elderly, the sick, the disabled, etc.). The power of the government to help them - sometimes even the will - has never been enough. The reason for this can be seen as structural, including lack of budget, lack of personnel, and the discovery of belated problems.

Second, humans have several psychological needs, and there is a desire to be recognized by others and realize themselves beyond food, clothing, safety, and friendship. These needs are met through volunteer work or charity.

Third, the conditions of life enjoyed by humans today are perfectly deteriorated due to the serious destruction of the social ecosystem and the natural ecosystem. Severe job search difficulties and traffic difficulties, poor housing and education and working conditions, high crime rates and corruption, high dissatisfaction and distrust, and pollution of mountains, rivers, seas, water, and air are approaching as a total threat to life or Earth. The power of the government alone is not enough to improve this reality, and the power of the private sector alone has limitations. Therefore, in order to solve this problem, a partnership between the public, and companies is established, and voluntary efforts(volunteer work) of each citizen are required to regenerate the ecosystem, which is a common goal.

Fourth, in the United States, where 60% of the employees of private organizations are unpaid, the impact of volunteers is so great that they are called "partners." Most private organizations aiming at social and human reform rely on volunteer activities. Private organizations(YMCA, YWCA, Life Phone, Love Phone, Economic Justice Practice Citizens' Union, Environmental Movement Union, World Vision, Boy Scouts, Welfare Center, etc.) use volunteers to engage in the following activities.

① Thanks to the diverse talents and enthusiasm of volunteers, they engage in purpose activities and try to diversify their programs.

② It promotes the discovery, resolution, and improvement of community problems by volunteers helping and supporting the execution of target projects.

③ Volunteers and paid employees(experts) can work as a team to meet the needs of interpersonal services more broadly.

④ Civil organizations can benefit more local residents through the development and implementation of quality programs with a small budget for volunteers' activities

3. Characteristics of Volunteer Activities

In order to more clearly understand the spirit and essence of volunteer activities, it is necessary to derive common characteristics from various volunteer activities. The characteristics of these volunteer activities can be summarized as follows.

1) Altruism

Volunteer work is not calculated in advance to obtain any reward or reward, but comes from the altruistic spirit of respecting others and living with neighbors. However, even if it is desirable to start with altruistic motives in volunteering, it is impossible to hope for absolute altruism, and even if it started without altruism in the early days of the activity, the spirit of loving neighbors and helping others should be inherent.

2) Independence

Independence refers to self-selection and decision-making without being forced by fate, other individuals, groups, or organizations, and volunteer activities have been able to last in various forms for a long time without financial gain or reward. Therefore, the first thing to consider to revitalize volunteer activities is how to organize and connect volunteers' voluntary motivation to volunteer activities, and whether laws or institutional devices will support their activities without infringing on their spontaneity.

3) Insensitivity

Volunteer activities should not be for the purpose of financial compensation or consideration. However, in recent years, volunteer work itself has a top priority goal, even if it receives economic rewards at night. And if these economic rewards are only a medium for maintaining volunteer activities well, minimum actual support such as transportation and meal expenses can be allowed.

4) Self-Realization

Through volunteer activities, you not only find the possibility and potential of yourself that you have never felt before and have a sense of satisfaction and achievement, but also have the experience of recognizing yourself as a social being through relationships with new people. Of course, not all volunteers are aware of this motivation and start their activities, and this motivation does not always exist, but this self-realization is an important factor influencing the sustainability and satisfaction of volunteer activities.

5) Organizationality

In order to cope with complex and diverse social problems in modern society, it is necessary to organize and systematize volunteer activities. In other words, the needs for volunteer activities are identified, volunteers are recruited and trained to meet their needs, placed in appropriate places, and volunteer managers are managed and supervised to ensure that volunteers perform their maximum functions.

6) Ministry of Education

Volunteer activities are hands-on learning, welfare education, and democratic citizenship education at the same time. Therefore, it is important how much volunteer work has helped others, but how much educational effect volunteer work has gained in the preparation or practice process is also important.

7) Processability

Volunteer activities should not end with one-time or temporary impulsive activities. Even if volunteer activities are initiated by voluntary motivation, they should not end unilaterally and should continue for a certain period of time.

Volunteering is not just an activity of help, but an activity that promotes change through help. And volunteer activities are not personal activities that can be done alone. It is a systematic activity carried out by several people, including volunteers, and coordinators. Therefore, procedures and processes are fundamentally important activities. Change is not made as an impromptu or temporary event, but through a planned series of processes.

8) Ministry of Health and Welfare

Volunteer activities should be related not only to individual self-realization but also to the improvement of the welfare of local residents or people with needs. Volunteer activities are both experiences based on mutual help and community consciousness, provide opportunities for mutual development, and contribute to ensuring that people in need maintain human dignity and live a human life.

9) Publicity(Solidarity)

Volunteer activities do not mean as one's own interests or temporary feelings, but rather as a goal of improving the human welfare of each member of the community or each person in hardship with a sense of responsibility to live a blessed life with neighbors. Therefore, volunteer activities must have welfare or publicity. Even if you have sufficient spontaneity, it cannot be called a volunteer activity if you do not have welfare or publicity.

10) Daily Life

Volunteering should be done naturally like daily life, not a special event. When you are active in a specific place, it is difficult to find yourself as a volunteer if you leave the site only as a volunteer. For example, when you drive to a facility far away on purpose, you act like an embodiment of love, but ignore the difficulties of the disabled in your neighborhood, or be indifferent to the overflow of garbage in front of your house.

11) Pioneering

Volunteer activities supplement the limitations of social welfare services by exercising individuality, creativity, and experimental efforts.

4. Volunteer Service Areas and Volunteer Organizations

As for the classification of volunteer activities in Korea, when the Korean Social Welfare Council developed the Volunteer Program Encyclopedia in 1996, Korea's volunteer activities are classified into a total of 11 areas.

① Volunteer for children and adolescents
② Volunteering for the elderly
③ Volunteer work for the disabled
④ Volunteer for women
⑤ Community-based volunteer work
⑥ Volunteer in the healthcare field
⑦ Environmental volunteer
⑧ Transportation volunteer
⑨ Cultural and artistic volunteers
⑩ Volunteers in sports
⑪ Volunteer in the field of international cooperation

Part VI Prospects and Challenges for Social Welfare

1. Introduction

Social welfare is a study aimed at humans, and it can be said that it is a professional job only when basic attitudes and ethics respecting humans are established based on the acquisition of knowledge and skills.

Human beings, whether rich or poor, disabled or non-disabled, are all equal and valuable beings and must be recognized for their individuality and dignity.

The beginning of social welfare activities in Korea originated from the activities of mutual aid and communities. In the West, it was developed by religious organizations. From an early age, Korea has made it a habit to help each other when there are difficulties. This can be found in our own traditional customs such as labor and local medicine. In the West, the first place to start social welfare activities was the UK, and Christian charity became the center of social welfare activities.

Today, social welfare should move away from the passive welfare level of relief for the absolute poor in the past and move toward the optimal level of welfare for all citizens. From this point of view, through the following several proposals, the direction in which social welfare in Korea should move forward is presented in relation to the service sector from a social security perspective as follows.

2. Prospects and Challenges for Korean Social Welfare

1) Income Security System

The characteristic of Korea's income security system is, first, that Korea has the basic framework of the income security system, but the linkage between the system and the system is insufficient in the process of legislating each system individually. The National Basic Livelihood Security System as a public assistance system, the public pension system as a social insurance system, the industrial accident insurance system, and the employment insurance system are tasks to be shared and solved together as an income security system. Second, there is no social consensus necessary for the subjects. The level of demand for the subject is high, but it cannot be paid as required for the equity of the recipient and the responsible person. However, even if there is a budget limit, the minimum guarantee should be maintained. Third, it is a limit to securing stable financial resources. In the case of the National Basic Livelihood Security System, which relies on general tax sources, the scope of application is limited, and the National Pension Service also has a problem of long-term financial instability in a high-end and low-burden structure. Therefore, it is difficult to improve the system dramatically without preparing a new financing plan. In addition, there is still a limit to the existence of a blind spot for income security so that the entire nation can be guaranteed a minimum life.

Welfare demand is expected to increase rapidly due to the aging of the population and the increase in family dissolution due to divorce, and it is urgent to establish a systematic income security system that can flexibly respond to future changes.

2) Employment Security Policy

The employment security policy aims to help people with working ability to become independent without relying on income security policies by resolving various disadvantages. Therefore, solving the poverty problem through employment security policy can reduce the burden of income security policy and reduce problems such as weakening motivation to work, weakening savings motivation, and excessive program operating costs.

The contents of the employment security policy promoted by the government can be categorized into employment security policy, job creation policy, employment possibility improvement policy, and social protection policy. It is desirable that the government first accepts employment security policies in the face of mass unemployment(IMF). However, although the government said it would focus on job creation, public work projects focused on stabilizing the lives of the unemployed and questioning the effectiveness of job creation are weak.

A security device should be prepared to sufficiently review the long-term and short-term effects of individual systems at the national level and to create employment while maintaining a close system of work cooperation between the state and private sectors.

3) Health Care Policy

The goal of healthcare is to provide high levels of health care at appropriate costs and to pay for them according to their capabilities, so when considering reform, they should always consider three goals: quality of health care, control of health care, and equity in cost.

Regarding the quality of medical services, it is most important to increase patient satisfaction. In terms of demand, it is necessary to significantly reduce the burden on oneself to reduce the financial burden and to meet comprehensive needs through linkage with other social welfare services so that services can be conveniently received. To this end, measures should be devised to enhance the authority of policyholders as consumers. In other words, consumers' choices should be strengthened, but organizational managers should be able to be selected from a single management organization rather than an insurer organization based on market principles.

For example, by having subscribers elect the chairman of the National Health Insurance Service, it will be able to effectively reflect the opinions of subscribers and strengthen the status of the corporation in negotiations with the government or other interest groups. In terms of supply, new medical technologies should be continuously introduced, and the morale of doctors and other medical providers should be increased. To this end, autonomy based on their expertise must be guaranteed as much as possible in medical practice.

In order to suppress medical expenses, the primary care function of the home nursing system and health care services must be strengthened, and the current fee system for each action must be converted to a total budget system. Since the overall introduction of the total budget system has various problems, it should be introduced in stages, and sufficient information on medical institutions' medical practices and management status must be secured.

Regarding the equity of the medical security system, it is very important to accurately grasp the income of local subscribers. This is because the problem of equity with office workers can be solved only when insurance premiums based on accurate income are imposed. In addition, the integration of medical insurance and medical protection should be considered because the discriminatory treatment and stigma effect on those subject to medical protection are serious. If state subsidies for local unions are intended to support premiums for low-income families, premiums may be paid with the funds required for medical benefits of beneficiaries of the National Basic Livelihood Security. If this is possible, there is no reason to operate medical insurance and medical benefits separately. The problem is that these three healthcare goals are in tradeoff with each other, and the interests of each group are intertwined behind them.

The public may have to pay more taxes and premiums. However, if the quality of medical services increases and the self-burden decreases, more insurance premiums may be willing to be paid. Meanwhile, medical providers oppose the total budget system.

Moreover, it would be possible to agree if autonomy in medical practice could be obtained in return. Therefore, if the total amount of medical expenses can be controlled, the Examination and Evaluation Institute can be entrusted to a doctor's organization to examine individual treatments on its own.

Therefore, the most urgent task of the Korean medical security system is to reach a social consensus on the appropriate level of national medical expenses that our society can bear and to achieve a great compromise between groups to protect them.

3. Social Welfare Service Policy

1) Direction of Child Welfare Policy

(1) Changing Awareness of Child Welfare

Until now, Korea's child welfare projects have been recognized as passive protection projects, such as accommodating and protecting underprivileged children and providing food, clothing, and shelter.

Although there are many deficiencies in child welfare projects in the wake of the second revision of the Child Welfare Act in 2000.

Child welfare should be recognized in a new dimension as improving the welfare of all children, including not only satisfying the actual welfare needs for underprivileged children but also promoting the healthy growth and development of general children.

To this end, child welfare programs necessary for the maintenance of a sound family should be developed and implemented.

(2) Home-Centered Service Provision

The core of child welfare policy should be derived from an integrated concept that combines children and families. This is because families are the best place to be inseparable from children in child welfare security. In 1909, President Roosevelt said, "Family life is the best and best product produced by civilization," based on the direction of child welfare in the 20th century.

Therefore, the state and society should mobilize all efforts and resources to prevent a situation in which children are separated from their families for any reason.

Even after children are separated from their families, child welfare policies should be established and consistently promoted to create welfare conditions closest to their families. To this end, it is necessary to actively promote domestic adoption projects, home consignment protection projects, and recently operated group home projects, which have not made much progress since 1977. In addition, the underprivileged children's partnership project should encourage voluntary and continuous participation of the public so that it can go beyond economic and emotional support for children and further maximize the experience of family life.

(3) Development of Child Welfare Service Models

A child welfare service model suitable for our situation should be developed considering the economic, social, cultural, and historical background of our society. For example, Korea's blood-related values can be said to be obstacles to domestic adoption and family consignment protection projects.

It can be seen empirically from the case of dissolution that the model that accepted the Western adoption procedure as it is to enhance domestic adoption cannot already be effectively settled in our society. Accordingly, Lee Myung-Hong(1994) proposed a combination of the adoption system and the training system of our tradition. In this way, efforts to develop a new model that mixes advanced countries' models and our traditional models should continue.

(4) Activation of Child Counseling Programs

Programs that can actively intervene in children's mental problems such as parent-child relationship problems, anxiety, depression, peer relationship problems, and relationship problems with others such as teachers should be activated in childhood.

This is because children's mental health problems can continue to have a great influence on the child's development process.

In particular, due to the interpersonal relationship experienced in childhood, trauma greatly affects the interpersonal relationship pattern in adulthood in the future, so appropriate intervention is required early.

However, the current child welfare policy mainly consists of limited policy content for children who need to be protected.

Therefore, in the future, there should be efforts to develop professional social service policies that can detect and solve these problems along with increasing social interest in children who are concerned about mental health problems.

In childhood, oppression, frustration, or a desire to fail to achieve one's purpose are factors that cause schizophrenia.

4. Direction of Youth Welfare Policy

Currently, the Ministry of Health and Welfare and the Ministry of Culture, Sports and Tourism are mainly in charge of and implementing youth-related welfare policies in Korea.

Youth-related policies by the Ministry of Health and Welfare are included in child welfare, and the Ministry of Culture, Tourism and Sports establishes and promotes long- and short-term plans related to youth development and guidance, expansion of youth facilities, youth counseling, and support for underprivileged youth. In this situation, the comprehensive management of the practice of 'youth welfare' is neglected.

In order to institutionalize various youth welfare programs, regulations on "**youth welfare**" and "**youth welfare facilities**" should be specified in the Framework Act on Youth and youth welfare projects should be included in the Social Welfare Services Act.;

At the local government level, it is necessary to maintain an administrative system that can continuously and systematically support youth protection activities and support activities at the local youth level, such as local youth offices. In addition, a system that can organically connect and integrate various resources used in youth-related projects should be organized at the community level.

In conclusion, the factors affecting youth welfare are various factors derived from various systems such as individual-family-community, so prevention and resolution measures should also be a complex and integrated approach for various systems.

In Korea, since institutions for the supply of youth welfare services have not yet been sufficiently developed, integrated problem-solving efforts through cooperation between service agencies have not yet been actively sought.

Therefore, it is necessary to become the center of one institution to prepare various integrated services and to elicit cooperation from individuals, families, schools, and communities for its implementation.

5. Acceptance of Welfare Models in Developed Countries in Korea

In the case of Japan, a nearby neighboring country, welfare facilities, a complex of children and the elderly, are being operated to bridge the gap between generations and establish a new welfare model.

Currently, it is well received for its exemplary facility operation, but the initial start was not smooth. When it was established in 1987, the idea of operating welfare facilities for the elderly and childcare centers together was not accepted, making it difficult to obtain permission. After the establishment, some parents expressed reluctance to allow children to use the same space as the elderly. Therefore, in the early days, mobile walls were installed to divide the living space of the elderly and children, but contrary to concerns, there was no mishap, and it has now become the most popular welfare facility in the vicinity.

Only a handful of welfare facilities in this form are still available in Japan. However, such new attempts have also affected other welfare facilities, and many daycare centers and elderly facilities across Japan are now engaged in active exchanges, such as sisterhood relationships and holding events together.

This is a welfare facility like a large family, where different generations gather together, from infants who have just passed the stone to the 90-year-old elderly. A system that combines daycare centers for childcare and welfare facilities for the elderly for nursing and care. Of the total four-story buildings, a nursery is provided on the first floor, and nursing spaces for the elderly are provided on the second and third floors. The fourth floor is a free space where children and the elderly can drink and interact with each other.

Formally, children and the elderly live separately, but in reality, there are no special restrictions. Children study on the first floor, go up to the second floor and take a nap with the elderly, and help grandmothers and grandfathers change their clothes. When spring comes, sports days and swimming competitions are held together, and on Christmas, teams are formed to play.

Hayashi, the director in charge of this place, said, "*The combination of elderly facilities and daycare centers will become a new model for welfare facilities in Japan in the future.*" It is believed that Korea should also be an active research model on welfare facilities as a case study on the model of neighboring Japan. This is because Jin will become a national task aimed at a welfare state in the 21st century. Therefore, the acceptance of the welfare model should be reorganized according to the Korean situation.

In Korea, the Yanggu National Forest Management Office has recently attracted attention by operating a "Forest Notchwon Center" for the elderly living alone in the region. According to the Yanggu National Forest Service on September 22, 2010, the Yanggu Love Sharing Welfare Association recently signed a business agreement for the operation of a "**Forest Notchwon Center**" for senior citizens living alone. Forest Notchwon is a nature learning program to allow elderly people living alone to experience forests in connection with the recent popularity of forest kindergartens for children. Accordingly, the Yanggu National Forest Service will help the elderly living alone breathe the fresh air in the forest, enjoy forest bathing and ecological experiences, and prevent senile diseases. 319 elderly people living alone participated in the forest kindergarten, which has been held since the 15th(Yonhap News on September 22, 2010).

6. Research Projects in Korean Social Welfare Studies

In order to establish the identity of Korean social welfare studies, it is necessary to refine the spirit of practice that increases accessibility and intimacy to our cases while prioritizing the suitability of theory and knowledge. Looking at the characteristics of Korean social welfare at the individual-centered micro-welfare level, it means "**weak professionalism**" in social work practice and "**weakness of national welfare**" at the macro-welfare level(Kim, Sang-Gyun et al., 84).

Bibliography

Ko, Myung-Seok(2008). **Introduction to Social Welfare**. Seoul: Dongmunsa.

Kong, Kai-Shun et al.(2009). **Theories of Child Welfare**. Seoul: Hakjisa.

Kwon, Oh-Kyun et al.(2009). **Introduction to Social Welfare**. Gyeonggi: Community.

Kwon, Jin-Sook et al.(2009). **Theory of Mental Health and Social Welfare** Gyeonggi: Yangseowon.

Kwon, Jin-Sook et al.(2010). **Actual State of Case Management** Gyeonggi: Community.

Kim, Ki-Tae et al.(2009). **Understanding of Social Welfare**. Seoul: Parkyung Publsihing.

Kim, Dong-Bae et al.(2009). **Understanding of Volunteering**. Seoul: Hakjisa.

Kim, Myung-Hee et al.(2009). **Introduction to Social Welfare**. Seoul: Dongmunsa.

Kim, Sang-Gyun et al.(2009). **Introduction to Social Welfare**. Gyeonggi: Nanam Publishing.

Kim, Young-Hwa et al.(2009). **Modern Society and Women's Welfare**. Kyungki: Amnesty International.

Nam, Ki-Min(2008). **Social Welfare Policy Theory**. Seoul: Hakjisa.

Nam, Il-Jae et al.(2009). **Introduction to Social Welfare**. Gyeonggi: Hakhyeonsa Temple.

Ryu, Jong-Hoon(2007). **Introduction to Social Welfare Studies**. Seoul: Bumlonsa.

Moon, Soo-Yeol et al.(2010). **Understanding of Social Welfare** Seoul: Changjisa.

Park, Kyung-Il et al.(2010). **Lectures on Social Welfare Studies**. Gyeonggi: Yangseowon.

Park, Sang-Ha et al.(2009). **Introduction to Social Welfare**. Gyeonggi: Yangseowon.

Park, Seok-Don et al.(2009). **Social Welfare for the Aged**. Gyeonggi: Yangseowon.

Park, Seok-Don et al.(2010). **Introduction to Social Welfare**. Gyeonggi: Yangseowon.

Park, Cha-Sang et al.(2010). **Introduction to Social Welfare Studies**. Gyeonggi: Hakhyeonsa.

Bae, Ki-Hyo et al.(2009). **Introduction to Social Welfare**. Seoul: Changjisa.

Son, Byung-Duk et al.(2009). **Family Welfare Theory**. Seoul: Hakjisa.

Seo, Bo-Joon et al.(2018). **Introduction to Social Welfare**. Gyeonggi: Community.

Oh, Jung-Soo et al.(2009). **Community Welfare Theory** Seoul: Hakjisae.

Ok, Pil-Hun(2012). **A Study on the Characteristic of the Corrective Welfare in Restorative Justice**. Ph.D. thesis at the Graduate School of Southwest University.

Won, Suk-Zo(2009). **Introduction to Social Welfare**.. Gyeonggi: Yangseowon.

Yoon, Chul-Soo et al.(2011). **Introduction to Social Welfare**. Seoul: Hakjisa.

Lee, Gyeong-Nam et al.(2009). **Introduction to Social Welfare**. Gyeonggi: Community.

Lee, Young-Chul et al.(2007). **Social Welfare Department**. Gyeonggi: Yangseowon.

Lee, Jung-Hwan et al.(2007). **Industrial Welfare Theory**. Gyeonggi: Education, Science Publishing.

Lee, Jong-Bok et al.(2008). **Introduction to Social Welfare**. Gyeonggi: Hakhyeonsa.

Lee, Chang-Hee et al.(2010). **Social Welfare Investigation Theory**. Seoul: Changjisa.

Lim, Woo-Suk et al.(2012). **Introduction to Social Welfare**. Gyeonggi: Community.

Jeong, Min-Sook et al.(2009). **Introduction to Social Welfare**. Gyeonggi: Community.

Jeong, Il-Kyo et al.(2009). **Theory of Welfare for the Disabled**. Gyeonggi: Yangseowon.

Cho, Chu-Yong et al.(2008). **Introduction to Social Welfare**. Seoul: Changjisa.

Chae, Gu-Muk(2009). **Social Welfare Survey Methodology**. Gyeonggi: Yangseowon.

Choi, Ok-Chae(2010). **Soocial Welfare Practice**. Gyeonggi: Yangseowon.

Choi, Il-Seop(2018). **Introduction to Social Welfare**. Gyeonggi: Community.

Choi, Il-Seop et al.(2008). **Understanding of Modern Social Welfare**. Gyeonggi: Community.

Han, Dong-Il et al.(2009). **Social Welfare Administration Theory**. Gyeonggi: Community.

Hong, Geum-Ja et al.(2009). **The Theory of Correctional Welfare**. Gyeonggi: Hakhyeonsa.

Hong, Bong-Sun et al.(2009). **School Social Welfare Theory**. Gyeonggi: Community.

Friedlander, W. A., & Apte, R, Z.(1980). **Introduction to Social Welfare**. Prentice-Hall.

Wilensky, H. L., & Lebeaux, C. N.(1965). **Industrial Society & Social Welfare**. New York: The Free Press.

Ok, Pil-hun has been a professor at Vision College of Jeonju for 18 years since 2005. He served as the head of the police administration department at Vision College of Jeonju, the head of the child welfare department at Vision College of Jeonju, and the head of the V-3E coupling project in Jeollabuk-do. In the community, he serves as the chairman of the Honam branch of the Korean Christian University Graduate School Council and serves as a member of the Jeonbuk CBS Choir.

[Academic background]

- Occasional Research Degree, Department of Juvenile Law, Graduate School of Law, Birmingham University, United Kingdom.
- M. Phil's course Supervision in crime department at the Keele University, United Kingdom.
- Graduated from Chonbuk National University College of Law(**Ph.D in Law**)
- Graduated from Wonkwang University's Department of Police Administration (**Ph.D in Police Studies**)
- Graduated from the Department of Social Welfare at Southwest University (**Ph.D in Social Welfare**)
- Graduated from Chonju University(**Ph.D. in Theology**).
- Graduated from WooSeok University's Department of Special Early Childhood Education(**Ph.D in Special Education**)

[Ph.D. Dissertation]

- **A study on the actual conditions and countermeasures of economic crime** (Doctor's thesis at Chonbuk National University, 2006.8)
- **A Study on the Actual State and Developmental Countermeasure of Jeju Municipal Police**(Wonkwang University Ph.D. thesis, 2009.2)
- **A Study on the Characteristic of the Corrective Welfare in Restorative Justice**(Doctor's thesis at Seonam University, 2012.2)
- **Welfare Mission for Abused Children Based on Missio Dei**(Doctor's thesis at Chonju University, 2019.2)
- **A Study on Policies of Settlement for Psychomotor Qualification System** (Doctor's thesis at Woosuk University, 2021.8)

[Main Books]

- **Introduction to Law**(Jinyoung Publishing, 2008)
- **Investigation Ⅰ・Ⅱ**(BNM Books, 2008)
- **Understanding and Precedents of Criminal Law**(Jinyoung Publishing, 2009)
- **Understanding and Precedents of the Criminal Procedure Law**(Jinyoung Publishing, 2009)
- **Criminology and Criminal Policy**(Jinyoung Publishing, 2009)
- **Family Welfare Theory**(Community, 2015)
- **Social Welfare Introduction [1st Edition]**(Community, 2015)
- **Social Welfare Laws**(Community, 2017)
- **Social Welfare Practice and Skills Theory**(Community, 2017)
- **Understanding of Child Abuse in Criminal Theology**(Community, 2017)
- **Social Welfare Introduction [2nd Edition]**(Community, 2018)
- **The Truth of the Gospel in the Bible**(Hakyesa, 2018)
- **Family Welfare Theory**(Knowledge Community, 2019)
- **Social Welfare Laws and Practice**(Knowledge Community, 2019)
- **Wellare Mission for Abused Children based on Missio Dei**(Community, 2019)
- **Introduction to Social Welfare Studies**(Knowledge Community, 2020)

- **Law & Life**(Parkyung Publishing, 2020)
- **Child Rights and Welfare**(Community, 2021)
- **Criminology and Criminal Policy [3nd Edition]**(Jinyoung Publishing, 2022)